DIMENSIONS OF PSYCHOTHERAPY SUPERVISION

Maps and Means

By the same author

Please Help Me with This Family:
Using Consultants as Resources in Family Therapy
(co-editor with Maurizio Andolfi)

A NORTON PROFESSIONAL BOOK

DIMENSIONS OF PSYCHOTHERAPY SUPERVISION

Maps and Means

RUSSELL HABER, Ph.D., ABPP

*Coordinator of Training, Counseling and Human Development Center,
University of South Carolina
Director, South Carolina Institute for Systemic/Experiential Therapy*

W.W. Norton & Company
New York   London

Printed in the United States of America

First Edition

Manufacturing by Haddon Craftsmen

For information about permission to reproduce selections
from this book, write to
Permissions, W. W. Norton & Company, Inc., 500 Fifth Avenue,
New York, NY 10110.

Library of Congress Cataloging-in-Publication Data

Haber, Russell.
    Dimensions of psychotherapy supervision : maps and means / Russell
Haber.
        p.   cm.
    "A Norton professional book."
    Includes bibliographical references and index.
    ISBN 0-393-70217-0
    1. Psychotherapists—Supervision of.   2. Psychotherapy—Study and
teaching.   I. Title.
RC459.H33   1996
616.89′14—dc20   96-16411   CIP

W. W. Norton & Company, Inc., 500 Fifth Avenue, New York, N.Y. 10110
                    http://web.wwnorton.com
W. W. Norton & Company, Ltd., 10 Coptic Street, London WC1A 1PU

1   2   3   4   5   6   7   8   9   0

To Karen and Nathan,
who mutually balance love, life, work, and joy in our family.
Thanks for your perseverance!!!

Foreword

Clinical supervision is one of the central activities of our profession; yet many supervisors do not have a clear perspective of the essential issues, processes, and methods. While articles and books have been written about various aspects of supervision, few describe a model that is simultaneously comprehensive, humane, imaginative, and immediately applicable to supervisory work.

Russell Haber has elucidated an integrative model of supervision that touches one's mind, heart, and intuition, thus opening the door to a new understanding of the entire process of supervision. The proposed model is broad in scope, integrating the relational, contextual, theoretical, and technical dimensions of supervision in a thought-provoking, creative, and inspiring manner. Those of us involved in the supervision of mental health practitioners will welcome the richness and freshness of these ideas and illustrative clinical examples. As a senior supervisor, I found myself intrigued by the theoretical complexity yet methodological simplicity of applying his ideas in ongoing supervisory practice.

The book's challenge to supervisors comes from the emphasis on the need for multilevel intervention. Supervision is a complex process because it involves transactions between and variations in four components: supervisor, supervisee, client, and the institutional setting in which the supervision of therapy occurs. Throughout the process of supervision, supervisors struggle with the recurring dilemma: "What might I think, feel, or do in my relationship with this particular supervisee at this specific point in time as the therapeutic process unfolds with this unique family within this supervisory setting?" Haber's strongest contribution is helping supervisors to readily grasp the complexity of this phenomenon while providing clarity of focus in clinical supervisory intervention.

In the first section of the book, Haber uses the metaphors of the "professional's house" and the "client house" to artfully explore overlapping current and historical factors affecting the supervisory/therapeutic system. By identifying the supervisee's position in the client's world and the professional realm, the supervisor can quickly highlight the advantages and limitations of the therapeutic process as well as the potential for supervisory intervention.

Supervisors will be helped by Haber's conceptualization of the range of therapist competencies along four dimensions, which include the ability to master ideology (using the "head") and methodology (using the "hands") and to expand the emotional range of supervisees (using the "heart") and intuition (using the "nose"). In the area of ethics, a clear framework is also delineated for critically evaluating ethical decisions, particularly when ethical principles are in conflict.

The second section of the book applies Haber's multimodel approach to the supervisory modalities of case management, video supervision, experiential work with metaphors and metaphorical objects, consultation, and apprentice supervision. A debt of gratitude is owed to Haber for providing specific, practical, invaluable information on how to maximize the usefulness of these modalities. The careful delineation of how, when, and where to use them highlights the author's extraordinary conceptual depth and clinical creativity. For example, supervisors who want to transform case management supervision into an imaginative experience will delight in Haber's description of the "empty chair" and "role play" techniques, as well as ways in which metaphorical objects can be used to clarify therapeutic impasses for supervisees.

The book illuminates the difficult journey of supervisors. Those who read it carefully, adapting its wisdom and insights to their own settings, capabilities and talents will experience a sense of renewal, excitement, and expanded options.

Marion Lindblad-Goldberg, Ph.D.
Philadelphia Child Guidance Center

Contents

Foreword by Marion Lindblad-Goldberg   vii
Acknowledgments   xi

1.   My Professional Journey   1

SECTION ONE   ROAD MAPS FOR SUPERVISION

2.   The Supervisory Relationship   19
3.   Diversity in the Supervisory Relationship   46
4.   Supervisory Dimensions   77
5.   Ethical Supervision   104

SECTION TWO   VEHICLES FOR SUPERVISION

6.   Multimodal Approach to Supervision   135
7.   Case Management Supervision   140
8.   Live Supervision   163
9.   Consultation as a Supervisory Intervention   183

10.   Apprentice Cotherapy: Working Side by Side with a Supervisor   202
      by Shirley Kirby

References   217
Index   227

Acknowledgments

The work of a supervisor does more than prepare professionals for clinical work. It keeps us professionally alive! For that gift, I am especially appreciative of supervisors and supervisees who have enriched and extended my life by sharing the essence of their craft. Intense ideas based in relationship do not die; they leave indelible footprints in the membranes of our experience. This book is a testament to the permeation and integration of relational exchanges from my grandparents, parents, siblings, and children on my professional and personal genograms. Without them, the endeavor of this book would have been unthinkable.

My family of origin, especially my mother, father, and brother, live inside my head and heart. Their passion, questions, courage, and lessons have given me a point of departure in my work, as well as in my life.

Chris and Darelyn also live brightly in my head and heart and have helped me bridge the world between adult and adolescent.

Many supervisees and clients through the years have enriched my work through sharing their growth process with me. Thanks especially to those supervisees and clients who have prompted the clinical anecdotes that illustrate the many dimensions of supervision. Thanks also to Pat Edwards and the rest of the gang at the Greenville Alcohol and Drug Abuse Commission for assisting me in the supervision of therapist relationships afflicted with addictions.

Elizabeth Ridgely and Shirley Kirby provided support, encouragement, and ideas throughout the preparation of this book. Libby's perspective of gender sensitive supervision (in Chapter 3) and Shirley's vantage point as a former supervisee (Chapter 10) highlight the added dimension of their voices.

Finally, I humbly and gratefully acknowledge other colleagues, Ann Weitzman-Swain, Shannon Dammann, and Marsha Purvis, who have each enlivened and enlightened the manuscript. In addition, Roger Bowersock, Carolyn Sutton, and Deborah Scott have supported me in the preparation of the manuscript. My editors at Norton, Susan Munro and Regina Dahlgren Ardini, have made this manuscript infinitely more readible, eloquent, and substantively coherent. Thanks y'all.

DIMENSIONS OF PSYCHOTHERAPY SUPERVISION

Maps and Means

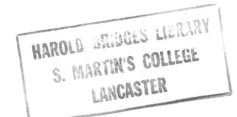

1

My Professional Journey

THIS BOOK PRESENTS A MODEL that integrates the relational, contextual, theoretical, and technical dimensions of supervision. As in the practice of supervision, my theoretical and experiential bias as a writer interacts with the reader's (supervisee's) position to form a unique integration. My goal as a supervisor or writer is not to produce human replicas of my work, but to provide a context that increases options and expertise. Another parallel to the supervision process is the adherence to the goal of exploring supervisory dimensions with both depth and breadth. The approach is broad enough to offer supervisors plenty of road maps and vehicles for further development of supervisory expertise and deep enough to touch chords of professional congruence, creativity, and coherence.

Consistent with establishing a supervisory relationship, building a contextual foundation for my approach begins with my professional journey. My supervisees see how I swim, hear a discussion of my ideology and methodology regarding teaching strokes, and become familiar with the rules of the pool. This "show and tell" approach not only demystifies the swimming process, but also reveals my swimming abilities and biases. This process builds trust with people (like me) who have a basic mistrust of lifeguards who have proficient whistles but never get wet. It also begins the implicit and explicit thoughts and questions about the range of possibilities, goals, and commitments in the learning process. Therefore, I will begin this book personally, by discussing my evolution from a fledgling swimmer to swimming instructor.

This idiosyncratic beginning seems fitting because I did not learn supervision in a course, but through my own supervision and training experiences and, most poignantly, through my trials, successes, and errors. In this sense, supervision can be compared with parenting. Parents often, for better or for worse, wittingly or unwittingly, parent the way they were parented. Despite parenting manuals and developmental theories, parents' early childhood experiences profoundly affect role-identity, values, coping skills, and a general philosophy of life. Similarly, our early supervisory experiences not only organize the way that we conduct therapy but also influence the "parental" upbringing of our trainees. Grandparents, on the other hand, frequently perceive and experience life with their grandchildren with much more patience and wisdom than when they were parents. Through a lifetime of trial and error, grandparents have the time and hindsight to rearrange priorities and become more available to family members with a diminished degree of *knee-jerk*, emotional reactivity. In a like manner, as supervisors age and become professional grandparents, they can develop a more flexible and less anxious presence in the supervision process. They know when and how to assist, support, or challenge the maturing professional.

As I become increasingly aware and appreciative of the commitment and talents of my supervisors, I am more conscious about the opportunity and responsibility of passing the baton of clinical knowledge to my supervisees. The bittersweet remnants of my supervisory experiences induce me to ponder questions such as:

What happens in supervision that fosters an impact? Do supervisees feel personally and professionally respected and understood? Can I "speak" their language? Do I support them enough to tolerate the pains of being stretched? Do they feel that I am accessible to their professional concerns and emergencies? Can I help them avoid hurting their clients? Will they feel more confident with their interviewing and intervention skills? Can my attention to their intuition keep them safe and creative in their role as therapists? Can I help them respond to their untold and unseen clients in the future? Will they know when and how to change directions in a therapeutic impasse? Will they become responsible, talented, and ethical professionals? Will they learn how to get along with their colleagues and avoid burn-out? Will they know how to elicit help with problems and realize the limits of their ability? Can I help them become personally more able to deal with a wide range of clientele and clinical problems? Which supervisory interventions will leave a lasting impression? What type of supervisors will they become?

In an effort to respond to these questions, I have detailed a supervisory methodology that considers the internal processes of the therapist (ideology, intuition, use of self, and technical skills) and the external positions in the therapeutic milieu. My teachers have helped me coordinate the *intra* and *inter*, the *inside* and *between*, to maintain a dialectical balance. Thus, this "parenting" manual would have been infinitely more difficult and limited, if not impossible, without my professional family who have supported and provoked me in my learning process. Their "voices" will echo through these pages.

My Professional Genogram

Grandparents

As illustrated at the top of my professional genogram (figure 1.1), my grandparents began my evolution; they imparted a genetic code before I even knew my parents. I met my first grandparent, Mel Foulds, Ph.D., during a Gestalt Marathon Group when I was an undergraduate, non-introspective, pre-law major. The Gestalt Marathon opened my eyes to an internal world full of powerful images and feelings that were heretofore only subliminally noticed. During this initial encounter, Mel said that he liked my voice and my perceptions, and felt that I could become a good therapist. Up to this point, I had been resigned to go to law school without ever considering the pursuit of the profession of psychology. However, the creative, healing power of the group and Mel's encouragement influenced me to study the field of psychotherapy. Later, he advised me to enroll in the rehabilitation counseling program. He offered to mentor me and promptly gave me a two-page bibliography coded with two and three stars for the "must read" books. I devoured the books on the list, which mostly included authors such as Maslow, Rogers, Perls, Lowen, Schutz, Pesso, Jourard, Berne, and many other writers of humanistic and transpersonal psychology. Mel's mentoring continued throughout my master's degree program, which included countless hours of "sitting in" on his cases, cotherapy, and subsequent observance and discussion of my work. Mel modeled and taught me to intuitively bridge the mind-body duality by setting up experiential activities that would enable clients to encounter and assimilate distant and disowned aspects of themselves. Mel's integrated version of Gestalt therapy, bioenergetics, psychomotor therapy, and psychosynthesis revealed his belief to lead the client by following the wisdom of the body and to trust the creativity of intuition. Mel gave me a blueprint of therapy that included a

Figure 1.1: *My professional genogram*

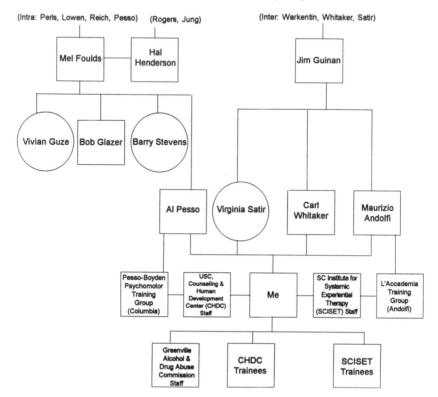

respectful and creative encounter with the self of the client and the self of the therapist.

Mel also led me to my second grandparent, Jim Guinan, Ph.D. Through the past 23 years, Jim has had many roles in my life. Initially, he was my therapist (at Mel's suggestion), later he became a second mentor and supervisor, thereafter he became, and remains, a colleague and dear friend. The capacity for us to have a quadruple (double a dual) relationship was connected to Jim's humanistic, ethical clarity of his professional and personal roles in hierarchical and collaborative relationships. He has a fascination with the absurd, humorous, and unpredictable. Yet, he can become very vulnerable and tender moments later. He taught me how to wear different hats with the same people or within the same family. His seemingly effortless ability to change hats was organized by his interpersonal approach to change. He was influenced by Whitaker, Warkentin, Sullivan,

Satir, and Haley as well as by several intrapsychic therapists. Through Jim's work, I learned that the client is the system, and that I am an integral part of the system. I learned how to play with young children, tease people older than me, move around the room to join and intervene with different parts of the system, use metaphors and stories, and work indirectly.

I also had a great-uncle, Hal Henderson, Ph.D., who was the guiding light in my master's program. His attention, warmth, positive regard, trust, and flexibility helped me develop my needs for direction and autonomy (specifically, he allowed me to take five independent courses). He personified Rogers' conditions of a healing relationship. Besides experientially and academically teaching me the life-enhancing power of a client-centered approach, Hal introduced me to the symbolic world of C. G. Jung. He encouraged me to keep a dream diary and always encouraged me to learn more about myself. What I learned from Hal, as well as Mel and Jim, was the phenomenological feeling of being valued for who I was and challenged to become more of who I could be. I have tried to extend this spirit to my supervisees through supporting them in their experiences and challenging them to stretch their skills to their potential.

These men also taught me to place one foot in the "inside" world and one foot in the "between" world. My task has been to use this foundation as a way to develop a house that can accommodate the idiosyncrasies, development, and internal constructs of the individual while respecting the influence, constructs, and developmental needs of the social system. This dialectic was aptly described in Koestler's (1978) treatise about the mythology of the two faces of Janus. He described the downward-looking face as a separate entity who defined itself *apart from* its context, while the upward-looking face looked to be *a part of* a system greater than itself. Although this duality seems logical enough, the vastly different needs and world view of each polarity made it difficult for me to maintain a vision of both poles in the same field. The conceptual incompatibility of the intrapsychic and interpersonal dimensions led to a great deal of confusion with the appropriate balance in the units of intervention (Haber, 1979). Although I am still working to develop greater breadth and depth with this dialectic, I have found parents, siblings, and children who have collectively shown road maps and vehicles to more quickly and aptly shuttle between the intrapsychic and the interpersonal (in press, a).

Parents

The difference between a professional genogram and personal genogram is that the professional can *choose* the types and combinations of parents that could logistically and economically be managed. My grandparents were lucky geographical accidents rather than consciously selected for their personal, clinical, and supervisory qualities. However, I was much more purposeful and conscious in choosing my parents. In order to afford training with selected parents, I concurrently facilitated training experiences. Thus, I could both learn and teach. Actually, the teaching also helped my learning because it forced me to conceptualize and practice what I learned. The reciprocal nature of learning and training has induced me to look for opportunities to safely put my supervisees in supervisory, consultative, and training positions. As is commonly said, *the best way to learn a subject is to teach it.*

Initially, I expanded my work with intrapsychic modalities. I studied Gestalt therapy with Barry Stevens and bioenergetics with Vivian Guze and Bob Glazer, Ph.D. Gestalt therapy was my home base. When I became confused during a session, my introjected version of Fritz Perls would remind me to pay attention to the *here and now* and move from *thinking* to *experiencing*. Similarly, bioenergetic training provided a map that assessed and navigated the character structure and energy of the body. Vivian Guze had a very soft approach to working very deeply. Conversely, Bob Glazer had a more energetic approach to working somatically. Both had a very clear analytic approach, based on Lowen's adaptation of Wilhelm Reich's work. They provided a clear demonstration about the benefits of regressive therapy in the service of ameliorating early deficits. Their style of teaching routinely included lectures, exercises, personal work, and subsequent supervised sessions. Thus, the boundaries around personal, professional skills, and intellectual development programmatically overlapped. I placed these neo-Foulds' influences on the genogram as siblings to my parents because my contact with them was significant but did not endure a long-term relationship. On the other hand, those designated as *parents* have substantially influenced my approach to therapy, training, and supervision for well over ten years.

The first parent, who continued an analytic, experiential, somatically based approach, is Al Pesso, cofounder of Pesso-Boyden Psychomotor Therapy (PBPT). Al codeveloped a methodology that worked with the internalized family. His approach psychodramatizes the internalized narrative and muscular contractions that inhibit energy, action, interaction, and meaning. The psychomotor *structure* works with the client's *story* and follows the motoric experience of body energy, physical action, interactional contact, and internalized meaning. This process encourages greater satisfaction and physical, emotional, and spiritual wellness by developing antidotes and new maps to ameliorate wounds and unmet needs. In addition to Al's sophisticated dictionary of "body language," this work taught me the power and creativity of dramatically externalizing narratives (Haber, in press a). The approach also works to differentiate the *voices* of the internalized family. Like bioenergetics and Gestalt therapy, PBPT combines teaching, personal work, and supervision in the training context. Al powerfully modeled the usefulness of the "check-in," which allowed people to center themselves in the training group through sharing their emotions, symbols, developments in their life, and goals for the training experience. I have found a focused, abbreviated version of the check-in (it could be as short as two minutes per person) to be a very settling way to structure a group supervisory experience.

Virginia Satir, the "mother" of family therapy, had professional children around the globe. Despite the size of her family, she remembered an incredible amount of personal and professional information about many of them. For example, she remembered specific facts and nuances of reconstructions that she did with my spouse and me prior to our marriage, some ten years earlier. Through the years, she continued her concern for my personal/familial growth through her gentle and adroit guidance through family life cycle events around adoption and stepfamily issues. Virginia involved herself in the personal lives of many of her trainees. Her process of training the "self of the therapist" immeasurably aided my capacity for compassion, knowledge, and transformative interventions with clients and trainees. Virginia was my first significant female mentor. Her theory, presentation, and personal presence portrayed a clear, powerful, compassionate, humorous, and creative feminine voice. When Virginia spoke with me, I felt as if the world stopped and that we were the only two people on the planet. She "walked her talk" as she epitomized attention to congruence, awareness, clear communications, and self-esteem.

Virginia was a genius, the smartest person that I ever met. Besides her intellectual capacity and creativity, Virginia had the ability to integrate selected aspects from diverse approaches. She once told me that she responded affirmatively to all of the items on a questionnaire that solicited the techniques that the "Masters" used because each had something to offer at different times. Her integrative qualities brought me to Virginia. I wanted to learn to integrate human potential movement approaches (humanistic psychology) with systems therapy. For me, she was the first, and perhaps still the clearest, to integrate the intrapsychic with the systemic. Her definition of system, historically, went from the cellular to the cosmic. She facilitated my journey of working in a house with the *between* and the *inside*. I do not think that her work as the Director of Esalen has been sufficiently acknowledged for shaping her work with families. She was so much more than a "communications" systemic therapist. Her deft work with body energies, touch, sculptures, psychosynthesis, process communities, and active visualization demonstrated her integration of self and system.

Virginia introduced me to one of her younger professional sisters, Laura Dodson, Ph.D., in 1979. Laura is a certified Jungian analyst and substantially trained in many different theoretical modalities. She is the type of person who can work with any method due to her relational, intellectual, and intuitive capabilities. Her combination of systemic and Jungian approaches has been a great model for learning the tasks of integration while respecting integrity and uniqueness. The fourth chapter, on supervisory dimensions, has been guided by her ability to elucidate Jungian concepts in a way that empowers the process of therapy and supervision.

Carl Whitaker, M.D., felt like both a grandfather and father. His ideas and "right-brain" approach had been with me since my work with Jim Guinan, but I did not personally begin working with him until 1980. Carl's gift was his "abnormal sense of integrity." His access to his internal world of images and self-talk enabled him to approach clinical dilemmas indirectly and inferentially. He credited his personal and creative approach to learning his craft from children in play therapy, his colleagues, and his clients, rather than being traditionally taught. Although he had a storehouse of ideas, his therapy existed in "process." More than any of my other parents, Carl's phrases, metaphors, and stories (such as: "I had a crazy idea," or "Marriage is frequently bilateral psychotherapy," or "Men are hopeless") live within me as an internal consultant in my daily practice.

Although Carl was extremely personal and disclosing, he was crystal clear about the boundaries around his roles. He preferred to work inferentially. Thus, when discussing my cases, he never inquired about my family or historical issues, but would discuss how his childhood organized him. He taught by breaking only enough ground to plant a seed rather than undertake a major excavation. During many live and telephone consultations, I learned a great deal about my role in the system through Carl's deft questions ("When did you adopt the children? Do you think their father will get angry with you?"). He taught me to differentiate and integrate the person and the role of therapy (Haber, 1994a, b).

Carl, typically paradoxical, was both distant and intensely intimate. On the one hand, Carl was only a phone call away, as he had compassionately helped me through a moment of professional angst. On the other hand, he reinforced the boundary between the personal and the professional by avoiding therapeutic responses to our training group. Most often, he spoke with me inferentially by telling me stories and allowing me to find my own feet. He modeled an abnormal sense of integrity as he was always close to the human and vulnerable parts of himself. Carl's depth and breadth of role-flexibility enabled him to be a consummate mentor.

Maurizio Andolfi, M.D., has been my latest and most influential parent. Age-wise he is only old enough to be an older brother. However, I am thankful to have recruited a parent that was closer to my age than Virginia and Carl. In spite of their age, sex, and personality differences, there are more similarities than differences between Satir, Whitaker, and Andolfi. Each employed his or her own version of a highly metaphorical, transgenerational, experiential therapy with an emphasis on the *self* of the therapist. I did not feel triangled theoretically or personally among these three great teachers. Despite their similarities, mutual appreciation, and respect of one another, they each looked quite different as trainers or therapists. Virginia worked like a mother (very close, warm, and personal); Carl, like a grandfather (wise, disclosing through stories, and "meta"); and Maurizio, like a father (energetic, directive, and playful).

Maurizio taught me a great deal about supervision and training. Besides his creative approaches to live supervision and consultation, he taught me ways to navigate the boundaries between the interface of the personal and the professional. My experiential work with him on my "professional handicaps" poignantly illustrated the connection between my personal character and the role that I assumed in certain clinical situations (Haber, 1990a). In addition, his work with toys and metaphorical objects has been extremely useful in both therapy and supervision. Finally, his zeal in challenging rigid familial or therapeutic systems, his use of provocation balanced with support, and balance between engagement and separation all fit my characterological ways of working with families. His work, as did Whitaker's, increased my personal sense of professional freedom.

I participated in Maurizio's first international practicum in 1981 (Haber, 1981, 1983) and have attended triannual training experiences to date. This core group of international, collegial brothers and sisters have taught me a great deal about cultural diversity and transcultural commonality. I will always be grateful to Maurizio for establishing this intimate, fun-loving international network of highly creative siblings. I also respect his developmental commitment to decentralize himself while encouraging us to learn from one another. In this way, Maurizio has coengineered the adult development of his professional children. Although Maurizio is still a mentor, co-birthing and co-editing *Please Help Me with This Family: Using Consultants as Resources in Family Therapy* (Andolfi & Haber, 1994) provided a rite of passage as we collegially worked to shape our book. His attention to developmental issues is endemic to his clinical and training model.

Maurizio's work is a creative blend of psychoanalytic (Karen Horney), structural, strategic, and experiential therapies. I agree with his belief that it is important to learn structure, then process. Sal Minuchin has been an important voice in Maurizio's head and has helped organize my thinking.

In addition, I resonated with Maurizio's attention to both the presenting problem and the existential, experiential aspects of the system. Thus, Jay Haley has been another clear voice as to the purposefulness of therapy and supervision. Although, I have not trained with Minuchin or Haley for an extended period of time, their books and workshops have been important markers for my work as a therapist and supervisor. I have employed their pragmatic, clinical orientation, and hierarchical approach to developing expertise with my supervisees.

Siblings

As Whitaker colorfully put it, we need "cuddle groups" to help us better survive the daily encounter of emotional forces that pervade our offices. Grandparents and parents can provide wisdom and direction, but siblings provide a forum for integration, reality checks, support, new ideas and applications, and good-natured banter.

As I have a cadre of parents, I also have a large contingency of siblings. They come from four different aspects of my professional world:

1. The Counseling and Human Development Center consists of a multi-disciplinary staff and training program — psychology, social work, and psychiatry. I have been there for sixteen years with Judy Small, Ph.D., Roger Bowersock, Ph.D., Ruthann Fox-Hines, Ph.D., Leon Spencer, Ed.D., Malcolm Anderson, M.A., Richard Lashley, M.D., and Sue Nelson, M.S.W. We regularly consult with one another on our difficult cases. We have each trained in both similar and different areas; therefore, our training program has places of commonality and divergence. Through our trainees, we have broadened each other's perspective about therapy and supervision. In addition, I have co-led a supervision of supervision group with Sue Nelson for the past four years.

2. My connection with the "Andolfi" (actually we do not have a name) group has persisted for fourteen years. We have watched each other mature as senior professionals (funny how the aging process works). Libby Ridgely, MSW, who contributed the section on gendered supervision in chapter 3 of this book, has clarified the feminine voice for me many times. Her Canadian sense of the absurd has never let me forget the day when I proved my masculine incompetence by turning on the dryer without putting the clothes in. Susy Jutoran, Lic., who has spent a week with us during each of the last four years, has been a professional sister who accompanies me in my various professional contexts. Besides providing excellent consultation, supervision, and training, I have enjoyed having a female perspective from someone who converses in the same professional language, although with an Argentine accent. Lars Brok, M.D., and Rick Pluut, Ph.D., have been

kind enough to invite me to the Netherlands several times and have fre-
quented Columbia, South Carolina, through the years. They bring a refreshing view of the absurdity and play of life. Both have done excellent
consultations for me that have poignantly touched the heart of the system.
Yoel Elizur, who has worked with the Kibbutz Clinic in Israel, naturally
generates an ecosystemic perspective of any context. Mary Hotvedt, Ph.D.,
the resident sex expert, helps me broaden my outlook on cases with sexual
deviance. Each of these dear siblings, and many others in the group, have
learned the same language from Andolfi, but have found different accents,
applications, and emphases of the language.

3. I have been in a training group with Al Pesso in Columbia for most of
the past fourteen years. The group provides an incredible richness of talent
and trust. My enthusiasm for psychomotor therapy through these years
would not have persisted without this cuddle group. Through the years,
we have found ways to work together, even though we speak different
professional languages. Although none of us is a pure psychomotor therapist, this has been an extremely useful "country" to live in six days a year.

4. My final sibling group has been in my private practice. Two members, Marsha Purvis, Ph.D., and Shirley Kirby, Ph.D., have been supervisees and now are colleagues. Cotherapy has become the most prevalent
medium of our present professional collaborations. These cotherapy relationships have reinforced the distinct channel of each gender's voice in
therapeutic systems. Judy Small, Ph.D., is a multiple sibling. We work
together at the private practice and the university and have mutually studied
with Satir, Pesso, and Whitaker. She has reinforced all my different parts
and has provided countless consultations in the car driving from one context to another. Finally, my favorite sibling is the one to whom I dedicated this book—my spouse, Karen Cooper-Haber, Ph.D. We have been
working together since the beginning of our relationship, 19 years ago. We
have consistently carried cotherapy cases (Haber & Cooper-Haber, 1987)
and episodically consult for one another. She continues to teach me the
subtlety and power of working with the ecology of the adolescent as well as
the ability to bring the therapist's feelings into the therapy room. Her instincts, ideas, and interventions in clinical work have become second nature
for me.

Children

The siblings that I have developed have helped me to be a better father with
my children. They have helped by sharing their stories with their children
and by providing a generational boundary that protects the children from
parental enmeshment, dependence, or overidentification. Thus, children

can learn as children and develop the intimacy of their own sibling relationships. In this sense, group supervision offers more types of feedback than the isolated system of individual supervision.

I have had sustained training and supervisory relationships primarily in three sites: the University of South Carolina, South Carolina Institute for Systemic and Experiential Therapy (SCISET), and the Greenville Commission of Alcohol and Drug Abuse. Each context has required different responsibilities and roles with supervisees and trainees. In addition, the three sites have enabled me to teach different disciplines: psychology, social work, and counseling at the university; marriage and family therapy at SCISET; and alcohol and drug counseling at the Greenville Commission. Each context has taught me about different specializations and clinical populations. Perhaps I should not let this secret out of the bag, but supervisors learn a great deal from the work of their supervisees. Most every time I supervise a session, I hear a phrase, see a nuance, or learn an approach that I can carry into my role as therapist. For this reason, I frequently encourage my supervisees to find an appropriate context in which to provide supervision and consultation.

In addition to learning new ideas from my supervisees; the supervisory experience forces me to clarify my position about the process of therapy and supervision. I am able to see what I am cocreating and can make necessary adjustments. It is infinitely easier to become conceptually clearer when I am behind the mirror, as opposed to responding to the clinical demands. Very often my supervisees illuminate my own struggles. By working with them, I vicariously work with myself. For instance, if I encourage a supervisee to be discontinuous, I have less tolerance of my rigid, predictable behavior during the next hour. Children inspire me to be more coherent with my values and approach to therapy.

Much like actual parenting, some children can be rebellious, withdrawn, and complex. Others can be delightful, cooperative, eager, and entertaining in the supervision process. In different ways, the easy and difficult children stimulate me to learn more about my approach. When they are really ready to leave home, I revel in their confidence and ability as competent professionals. Although I have too many children to recognize in this context, my work with them echoes through these pages.

THE INTERNALIZED PROFESSIONAL FAMILY: INTROJECTS OR ASSIMILATES?

My grandparents, uncles, aunts, parents, and children are an internalized cast of characters in my head. Sometimes they pop into my head as internal consultants; other times they influence me without my awareness. Sometimes I consciously call them to the fore when I am in a difficult situation. What would Carl do with a couple who are brutalizing one another in front of their children? How would Libby handle this gender war? Which voice fits for me right now? These hallucinated voices, images, and memories may not be actual or accurate representations of my professional family; however, they give me the freedom and permission to approach my work differently. Thus, the hallucinations work best when they assimilate into my voice and fit the context of the clinical problem and relationship. On too many occasions, especially in my earlier professional days, I awkwardly and indiscriminately applied interventions that did not fit me or the professional context. My hallucinations were introjects (unassimilated foreign ideas). Now, most influences from my professional genogram fit within my theoretical, personal, and methodological frameworks to help make up my uniqueness. These translated voices usually work together as an integrated team, rather than a group of individualized players going in different directions.

Clearly the voices I hear do not mean that everything is the same, or that eclecticism is beautiful. The demands of a situation, and my own possibilities and limitations, still operate selectively. . . . Within the possibilities open to us, the best in us always learns from the best of others. (Minuchin, 1989, p. 80)

YOUR PROFESSIONAL GENOGRAM

The purposes of exploring my professional journey are threefold: first, to provide the reader with my historical perspective as a backdrop to the remaining contents of this book on supervisory dimensions; second, to give credit to my professional family; and third, to encourage the reader to consider the past, present, and potential influence of a professional genogram. Making this process more conscious has helped me know more parts of myself.

Readers may consider exploring their own professional genogram as well as those of their supervisees. It can be treated as a clinical genogram by looking for patterns, unfinished business, healthy and problematic triangles, etc. Additionally, the genogram can be dramatized through sculpture, role-play, or dialogues among selected members of the professional family. The supervisee could also consider where to put his or her present supervisor in the genogram. The inclusion of the supervisor in the genogram further clarifies the supervisory relationship.

ABOUT THIS BOOK

The book is divided into two sections: Road Maps for Supervision and Vehicles for Supervision. The first section delineates relevant dimensions of the supervisory experience while the second illustrates methods of navigating through the supervisory experience. A book about supervision inherently faces therapeutic issues. Although this is not a book about therapy, therapeutic cases depict choices, decisions, and focus for the supervisor. Due to the parallel processes of supervision and therapy, I interchange terms (supervisee, therapist, trainee or supervisor, consultant, or trainer) that describe the same protagonist.

The next chapter, "The Supervisory Relationship: Generational Position in the Professional and Family Houses," explores the contexts and interactions of the three players: supervisor, supervisee, and client. Their juxtaposition is affected by both the present contextual fit and historical experiences. By identifying the supervisee's position in the clients' world and the professional realm, the supervisor can quickly identify the advantages and limitations of the therapeutic process as well as the potential for the supervisory intervention. Thus, supervision must accommodate to the influences of the client system and work context as well as the supervisee's specific choices for intervention.

Just as no two clients or families are alike, each supervisee, underneath the professional veneer, presents a unique constellation of personal qualities that enter into the role of the professional. The third chapter addresses the fundamental reality of the diversity of supervisees. Supervisory interventions must accommodate the confidence, knowledge, and skill of the supervisee. Likewise, supervision must acknowledge the interactional consequences of cultural, characterological, and gender influences in the supervisor-supervisee-clients triadic system. Sensitivity to these issues fosters relevant and flexible supervisory relationships that respect and unravel diversity dilemmas. In order to present a female voice in the book, I have asked a colleague, Elizabeth Ridgely, MSW, to write the section on gendered supervision.

Chapter 4, "Supervisory Dimensions," distinguishes four functions necessary for the development of a skillful practitioner. Therapists need to cultivate the ability to relate clinical experience to theoretical postulates (using one's head), to aptly apply methods and techniques to further clinical progress (using one's hands), to use the self as an instrument in the therapeutic endeavor (using one's heart), and to access intuitive and creative ideas to promote different possibilities (using one's nose). Although supervisees have preferences and aptitudes for these different, albeit interrelated, functions, the selective identification of head, hands, heart, and nose issues enables the supervisor and supervisee to map, analyze, and envision the need for supervisory interventions.

The final chapter in section I, "Ethical Supervision," deals with a topic that permeates each and every chapter. Like the contextual issues in chapter 2 and diversity issues in chapter 3, the ethics of clinical and supervisory relationships must be considered in each and every supervisory intervention. This chapter clinically applies a supervisory model for ethical inquiry and further explores the role of values in therapy and supervision, the dynamic consideration of the welfare of each individual in the system, and ethical issues applied to the supervisory relationship.

The chapter on a "Multimodal Approach to Supervision" introduces section II, Vehicles for Supervision. Although the chapter contrasts the value of different supervisory approaches, it underscores the importance of the supervisory relationship as critical to the successful use of supervision techniques.

"Case Management Supervision" focuses on indirect methods of supervision. Through an indirect (without clients) approach to supervision, the supervisor can expeditiously comprehend the breadth of the supervisee's caseload and focus on a few compelling cases. The chapter highlights the use of case discussion, videotape review, metaphors and metaphorical objects, and experiential approaches in the supervision process. Each of these approaches highlights selective areas previously described as the head, hands, heart, and nose.

The trilogy of chapters on direct supervisory approaches begins with the description of "Live Supervision" in chapter 8. Direct (in the immediate presence of clients) supervision enables the supervisor to perceive, experience, and intervene during the actual session. The immediacy of live supervision involves the supervisor in the process and outcome of the session, as opposed to keeping the supervisor as a "Monday morning quarterback" who comments on the process after the fact. The chapter details advantages and disadvantages of introducing ideas through the therapist, clients, or supervisor, as well as using the boundary of the mirror to mark different structural alignments. The chapter espouses a creative, yet judicious and parsimonious, approach to the intrusion of a live supervision intervention.

"Consultation in the Supervisory Moment" details and illustrates a supervisory approach that is used less than case discussion, videotape, or live supervision. Consultation is an extremely effective procedure for dealing with therapeutic impasse, ethical dilemmas, increasing leverage to expand the therapeutic system, as well supervision for helping to organize and evaluate therapy. It provides an opportunity for the supervisee to watch the supervisor work with his or her clients. Thus, the supervisor, as consultant, typically models a different approach to the clinical dilemma and enables the supervisee to draw from the voice of the consultation throughout the therapy.

The final chapter, written by Shirley Kirby, Ph.D., is about the use of apprentice cotherapy. It is poignant that a former supervisee and present colleague wrote this chapter because the goal of supervision is to move the supervisee from apprentice to colleague. Cotherapy is an effective procedure in the beginning, end, and throughout the supervisory process. It allows the supervisor and supervisee to work side by side and provides a safe structure for the supervisee to assume incremental responsibility for the direction of the therapeutic process. In addition, it enables a context for the supervisee to witness the moment-to-moment actions of the supervisor. The importance of this type of modeling process is frequently underestimated by supervisors.

My goal in writing this book is to present a comprehensive overlay to the process of supervision that transcends theories and specific disciplines. Through descriptions of the maps and means of supervision, interspersed with illustrative clinical examples, I have attempted to balance *describing* the process of supervision with *showing* the trials and tribulations.

Section One

ROAD MAPS FOR SUPERVISION

2

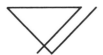

The Supervisory Relationship

WHO COMPRISES THE SUPERVISORY RELATIONSHIP? A fly on the wall might only see two people conversing in a room, perhaps over some folders or while watching a videotape. This typical fly on the wall would be impervious to all of the invisible people in the room. However, if it *could* detect unseen emotional influences of the two protagonists, it would perceive a much more crowded room. Most obviously, the clients in the folders or videotapes would be emotionally present. More subtly, the inhabitants of the "houses" of the therapist, client, and supervisor could be present. Thus, the superfly would see two beings influenced by a myriad of ghostly influences. In order to sort out the supervisory relationship, the nature of the *professional* and the *clients'* house needs to be ascertained and understood.

THE PROFESSIONAL HOUSE

The professional house contains the ecosystems of both the supervisor and the supervisee. Supervision almost always consists of a relationship embedded with dual relationships. That is, the domicile of supervisor and supervisee overlap as opposed to residing in isolated professional houses. Besides providing professional training, the supervisor often incurs legal responsibility for the supervisee's clinical cases and furnishes administrative and/or professional evaluations or recommendations. Due to the hierarchical nature of clinical, training, legal, and administrative decision making, it is imperative that the supervisory roles be carried out in a fair and ethical manner for all parties—especially, the clients. Therefore, it is necessary to explicate the roles, parameters, and responsibilities of the supervisory relationship by insuring that other roles in the professional and personal houses do not interfere with the delivery of effective supervision. The floor plan of the professional house in figure 2.1 can help elucidate previously unseen influences.

The Bottom Floor

The bottom floor contains the self of the professional—whether therapist, supervisee, or supervisor. The self of the therapist includes all of the internal experiences, personal characteristics, and relational affiliations of the professional. The self lives within the confines of professional roles. Since we professionals are not machines, we personally react to the professional situations that we encounter. Our uniqueness—personal history, personal style, strengths and weaknesses, gender and cultural perspective, emotional responses, physical and characterological capabilities and limitations— comprises our singular version of humanness. These qualities can add to or delimit the power of the therapeutic and supervisory relationships.

If the therapist is privy to his or her internal world, then this self-knowledge may illuminate relational knowledge of what it is like to be in

Figure 2.1: *The professional house*

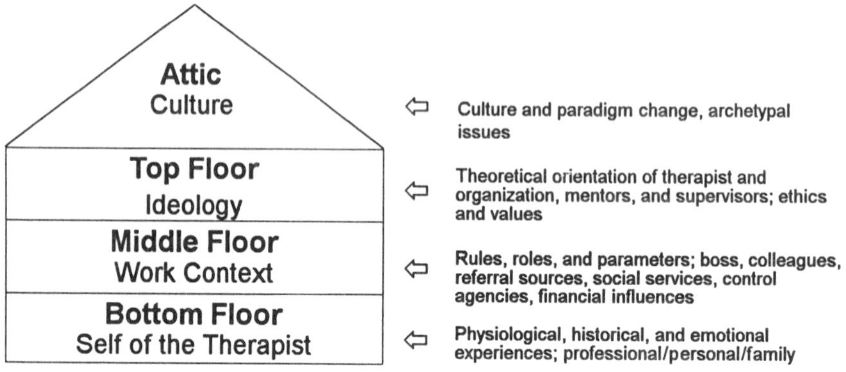

the family. With this perspective, the self becomes a reference point to the collective. Knowing our personal reactions can help us better join, understand, and differentiate the forces that influence the professional context.

As we have seen in too many families and social organizations, the role receives more credence and reinforcement than the self. The self is frequently left to manage on its own and consequently is more primitive, unconscious, unconventional, and mysterious than the professional role. The self uses the language of dreams, metaphors, feelings, symbols, intuition, and physiological responses to represent its reality. We can learn to ignore this language, like a dream in the middle of the night, but we are still influenced by the experience of these symbols. We can also learn to ignore our role within the structure of our professional responsibility, and consequently struggle with our narcissism by being too self-absorbed at the expense of the clients' needs. Optimally, the self and the role of the professional can coexist in an acknowledged, functional, creative, and respectful union. Thus, the storehouse of the *self's* professional and personal experiences and relationships offers valuable consultative recommendations to the professional *role*. The *self* generates information and images; the *role* decides whether and how to use the information (Haber, 1994a).

The personal and professional characteristics of the supervisor and therapist invariably affect the supervisory and the treatment process. Often the relational dance between the supervisor and supervisee is unknown or minimized. When boundaries are inexplicably crossed in the communication process, the relationship can result in one stepping on another's toes. Once these crossed boundaries result in damaged toes, fear, defensiveness, and loss of trust emerge in the supervisory process. For this reason, chapter 3 explores a number of relational parameters that affect the quality of the supervisory dance. Sometimes more attention needs to be directed to the *process*, as opposed to the goals, of supervision. In other words, the relationship and chemistry of the dancers could be more important and influential than the technical aspects of the dance.

The Middle Floor

The middle floor relates to the role configuration and environment of the work context. In the supervisee's context, the administrative and clinical lines of responsibility are especially important. Thus, the tenor of the dance of an arranged, involuntary, or professionally obligatory relationship would be sufficiently different from a mutually selected, voluntary supervision match.

The dance could also require a significant energy expenditure and responsibility in an agency setting or be more delimited in a private practice setting. Therefore, clearly expressed expectations of the supervisory relationship will clarify the roles and responsibilities of the dancers. The supervisory relationship does not create a personal hierarchy (one person is not better or more important than the other), but a professional hierarchy that distinguishes professional roles and obligations. Kaslow (1986) succinctly put this issue in perspective, "In any role that inherently entails responsibility, there must be concomitant authority" (p. 2).

The supervisor must carefully consider the culture of the workplace. In order to provide competent supervision, the supervisor should survey the treatment context by asking questions such as the following: How often can the clients be seen? Does the supervisee have psychiatric back-up? Can this case be followed through to termination or will referral be necessary? Thus, the supervisor needs to consider the unique policies and procedures of the supervisee's work context. For instance, it does not make sense to tell a supervisee who works in a school system to work with client subsystems, such as nonstudents, who are not eligible for services. However, it may be necessary for the supervisor to challenge the bureaucratic constraints that inhibit creative clinical services. In such a case, the supervisor needs to determine strategies that can help change the work setting. It would be unwise to encourage a supervisee to single-handedly take on a rigid bureaucracy, but the supervisee may explore other alternatives to help deal with bureaucratic problems.

The images of colleagues, referral sources, and other health-care providers are also recognizable in the middle floor. Since they influence the supervisee and the clients, the supervisor needs to consider their involvement in the treatment process. The supervisor also has to reflect on his or her position in the work context. For example, I have less direct influence with cases that I supervise in my private practice than I have with cases that I supervise at the university. Furthermore, when I provide monthly supervision at an alcohol and drug abuse commission, my comments, suggestions, and questions carry the quality of an outside consultant rather than a fellow dweller in that professional house. Thus, the supervisor must go far beyond the triangle of clients-supervisor-supervisee when considering how the goals of the supervisory system (supervisor and supervisee) and the therapeutic system (therapist and clients) can mutually be met.

The Top Floor

The top floor represents the ideology of the supervisee and the treatment agency. It also includes the ethics and values of the professional associations and licensing boards. Furthermore, the supervisee's unique ideologies, values, and ethics organize the therapy. For instance, during supervision of couple therapy, a male supervisee chose, on two occasions, not to respond or inquire about a woman's remark about being sexually harassed. Since this issue seemed relevant to both the presenting problem and the process of the therapy, I suggested that the therapist ask the client to describe her harassment in greater detail. My rationale was that the issues of trust, blurred boundaries, and disrespect were important to the couple because the woman's unfortunate experiences could be projected into the couple's or the therapeutic relationship. Thus, a fuller explanation of this dynamic could offer guidelines about the type of support needed in the therapeutic or couple system.

However, the supervisee chose not to pursue my suggestion during the session. In the post-session interview, he related his concern that further discussion about the details of the sexual harassment could cause further exposure of the woman's sexuality, and that such exposure would be further abuse. He also stated that his previous supervisor recommended a more passive approach to working with women who have been sexually abused. This information clarified my supervisee's reluctance to respond to my supervisory suggestion. He was triangled between the former supervisor in his head and me. We discussed this triangle and looked for a respectful and permission-seeking way to work with the woman's stories of abuse should they come up in a following session.

During the next session, the woman brought up feelings about an earlier harassment by a coach and the therapist was able to work with her in a way that was both respectful and healing. By identifying the competing voice in his head, I was better able to understand and accommodate for the impact of his values and ideological position.

This possibility of a competitive triangle would be similar with a supervisee whose theoretical perspective differed from mine. Typically, I do not believe that an ultimatum, "either-or," position is a necessary or useful approach in this situation. Similarly, I do not think it wise to negate my approach because it differs from the supervisee's. Rather, I examine the possibility of the mentor in the supervisee's head working with my perspective. Thus, if it is possible, we would establish a "both-and" position. As a supervisor in a "meta" position, I have a good vantage point to make process interventions that are relevant and collaborative even if I do not define the process with the same terms. However, if I cannot use the language from my supervisee's model, I would ask him or her to define it. Additionally, I would ask questions to see how the supervisee's mentor would describe or handle the therapeutic process. "How would Patterson define this stage of the therapy? What would he do? What would his goals be?" These questions would explore the triangle between my supervisee, his or her ideology, and my approach in order to explore ways to work together as a team.

To establish a competitive or disrespectful relationship with the supervisee's mentor would be to create a noncollaborative, dysfunctional triangle. In such a triangle, the supervisee could feel stuck in a loyalty bind, adopt an antagonistic or resistant position with the supervisor, or passively withdraw from a long-term resource. In either scenario, the supervisee would probably be confused with his clients. Thus, the alternative of collaboration on the top floor can help establish an integrated theoretical and clinical position.

The Attic

The attic has more mystical and symbolic influences than the other three floors. Our culture is so immersed in popular consciousness that it is difficult to understand its influence. Thus, the relics in the attic can be very cryptic. The attic contains the archetypal issues and paradigmatic changes evidenced in the arts, media, politics, and popular culture. This information transcends person, workplace, and ideological issues. For instance, the changing roles of men and women have been well established as clear forces that confront our framework and interventions. The consciousness of gender issues, as evidenced by the barrage of media programming, pervades the development and identity of individuals, partners, and families. In addition, the United States culture is undergoing a massive political change that seems to reflect a paradigm change. The culture seems to be shifting from the focus on the "wounded child" (as seen in the proliferation of "adult child" groups) to a philosophy of nonintervention. This is evidenced in the shift from comprehensive mental health benefits to a minimalist, managed care approach. The supervisor needs to consider how this shift affects the expectations of the work setting and the clients.

It is now evident that there is more than meets the eye when a professional comes into our office for supervision. The supervisee appears with a cast of characters that may not be noticed at first, but will likely emerge at a later time. Consideration of these *ghosts* will demystify their presence and give space for them to be explored in the supervision room whenever necessary. Similarly, there is more than meets the eye when clients come into our office. We work with their ecosystem whether we are conscious of it or not (Haber, 1990b). The following section explores the rooms and floors of the clients' house so that the supervisor can then better understand *where* and *how* the therapist enters this house.

THE CLIENTS' HOUSE

Maurizio Andolfi often uses a metaphor that describes the three genera-tional floors in the household: the children live on the bottom floor, parents on the middle floor, and grandparents on the top floor. In addition, the attic contains the artifacts of the ancestors (see figure 2.2). This section will explore the nature of each floor. The generational and gender issues on each floor reflect the diversity of therapeutic assumptions and choices. The following section responds to the role of the supervisor in the assessment and intervention of the supervisee's generation position.

Each floor has different views, goals, customs, language, jobs or activi-ties, physical capabilities, relationships, perceptions, and priorities concern-ing the past, present, and future. Each floor connects in its own way with the outside community. Each floor has rooms or spaces for the males and females that reflect differences based on gender rather than generation (Gol-dner, 1988). For instance, despite the proclivity of dual career families, females have often remained more attentive to the activities and aesthetics within the home, whereas males are usually less preoccupied with the home and more concerned with outside matters. Each floor needs more or less attention at different points of the family life cycle. Finally, each floor is linked by a biological-psychological-sociological staircase. Even if only one member of one floor requests help, the other household members are only a floor or two away from being present in the room. Perhaps the individual(s) on the floor who requests help has been selected by the rest of the group to solicit new information and resources (Andolfi, Angelo, Menghi, & Nicolo-Corigliano, 1983).

Figure 2.2: *The clients' house*

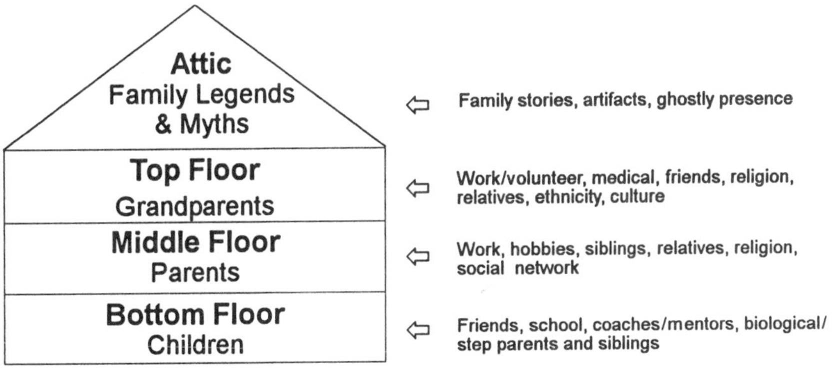

The Bottom Floor

The bottom floor, representing the children, requires nurturance, protection, support, and limits (Haber, 1984; Pesso, 1973) for development from total dependence to greater autonomy. Children are the natural glue of the family since they represent the biopsychosocial mixture from the maternal, paternal, and extended family. This cocktail requires that the child integrate diverse aspects of self while differentiating his or her uniqueness and integrity, thus manifesting the creative potential of the future species. Difficulties can arise when the child has difficulty with integrating or differentiating certain aspects of the self because the children are caught in a political struggle within the household. Children may be induced to take sides, withdraw from parts of the household, referee the family squabbles, assume the role of peacemaker, detour conflict through self-defeating actions, or apply some other rigid approach to maintaining the family stasis. The task of integration and differentiation becomes more difficult as the geometric progression of parents and grandparents increases. Many children have learned the art of packing a suitcase one day and then being transported to a different place, with different rules and customs, on the next day. Children often learn that certain values that they bring from one parent's house do not apply or belong in the house of the other parents. Therefore, therapists should pay careful attention to the children's task of packing and unpacking suitcases in highly mobile families.

Children, particularly when they are younger, speak the language of inference (Whitaker, 1989). They present their concerns through the symbolic language of play, metaphor, story, and symptom rather than direct disclosures of their problem. Therefore, if therapists visit the bottom floor, they need to know how to exist in the playrooms. They need to be familiar with toys, metaphors, and stories, and learn to speak and sometimes translate the language of the bottom floor. The therapist needs to reassure the child that the therapist can handle the job of balancing the family while providing an opportunity for the family to grow. The child (especially the symptomatic child) can function as a tremendous consultant and cotherapist for the therapist (Andolfi, 1994; Ridgely, 1994a).

Once the therapist becomes accustomed to the language and activity of children, the therapist can become more privy to the children's world, inside or outside of the family home. School, athletic teams, religious groups, and clubs are pivotal social laboratories where children learn new skills and other social coping strategies, where they are able to see how other systems work, to examine the transferability of skills learned from their households to community contexts, and to learn from other children, rather than just their parents. It is an adult-centric view that children learn better from adults than other children. Therefore, therapists need to understand how the child fares in the social milieu of school and peer groups and to recruit these resources to the therapy when necessary (Haber, 1987).

The Middle Floor

The middle floor, representing the parents, is a particularly busy and productive floor. Even though there is less activity in the middle floor than in the bottom floor, the parents provide the architecture, building, financing, and transportation for the home. They have multiple responsibilities — running the home, working, contributing to the community, raising the children, and providing assistance to their parents on the top floor. The middle floor creates a sandwich topped and bottomed with responsibilities and loyalties. The parents have the dual experience of raising children and being an adult child simultaneously. This process helps them understand their parents (Williamson, 1992) and gives them the opportunity to become adult friends with them. Thus, they have the opportunity to forgive their parents for improperly meeting their developmental needs and can choose more appropriate parenting styles with their children. Williamson believes this developmental process, which occurs in one's thirties and forties, offers an opportunity for parents to become more differentiated and intimate with the family members on each of the three floors.

The parents represent the primary non-blood relationship in the household. Despite the dreams and expectations of the wonders of marriage, the heavy dose of today's stresses and demands contribute to the severance of this relationship almost half of the time. If there is divorce, chronic illness, or other psychological or physical vacancies in the middle floor, the therapist must recognize the necessary adjustments in the nontraditional house. For example, it would not be unusual for children or grandparents to assume parental responsibilities and spend more time in the middle floor managing the household than is typical.

The therapist must realize that there is more to the middle floor than just the bedroom, although the relationship in the bedroom is a key issue in many marriages. The therapist must learn to relate to the space of each adult in the middle floor. The sexual politics become evident in the middle and top floors; therefore, the therapist needs to speak the language of both sexes. The poignant issues about money management, division of labor, communication patterns, affiliation needs, and use of leisure time need to be understood and negotiated from each gender perspective. Besides creatively resolving conflict in the middle floor, the therapist must help each spouse attend to individual growth. The crucial project of individual growth will foster a differentiated presence in the family. This will help each spouse better handle loneliness without the juvenile fantasy that the spouse or other household members will meet all of his or her missing needs.

The therapist must also help the adults on the middle floor deal with their relationships outside the household. Particularly important is their ability to develop friendships (Haber, 1994c) and community resources (spiritual, professional, and otherwise). Additionally, the parents spend a significant percentage of their week at work. Thus, their relationship to the world of work will directly impact the household. As those on the middle floor mature, their bodies often become less resilient. Thus, attention has to be paid to the flexibility and limits of resources. As their parents age, the issue of mortality is no longer just a philosophical notion. The midlife crisis in the middle years is an opportunity to make the necessary developmental and household adjustments to prepare for their ascension to the top floor.

The Top Floor

The grandparent floor is a complex floor because it comprises two family systems with different family values, expectations, and practices. Often the two families come from very different ethnic cultures. However, even when the two sets of grandparents come from the same locale, each family has its unique culture, rules, mores, idiosyncrasies, emotionality, history, and family legacies. The marriage on the middle floor is a physical manifestation of two different cultures. The onset of children, who embody this biopsychosocial integration, links the wisdom and life experience of the top floor with the potentiality of the bottom floor. Thus, parenting becomes a process where the parents on the middle floor try to merge the best of each family system from the top floor. In this way, they can avoid the marital dilemma concisely and poignantly described by Whitaker: "It's really just two scapegoats sent out by two families to reproduce each other. . . . The battle is which one will it be" (1982a, p. 368).

Frequently, the grandparents get along better with the grandchildren than with the parents. The grandparents have the wisdom of time to mellow their intensity and often can be much more intimate and helpful with their grandchildren than they were with their children. They do not have the pressure of trying to make it in the world while handling the expense and anxiety of raising a family. Their perspective of time makes it much easier to handle school failure than the parents who take each test as a marker of how their children will fare in the world. The grandparents know the ebb and flow of success and failure. The grandparents shed light on the present by connecting the family with the past (Keith, 1994). Perhaps they remember similar generational struggles when their children were on the bottom floor. Since they knew the parents on the middle floor as infants, they can help the grandchildren see the "child" parts of the parents, rather than seeing only the authority figure. The view of the parent as a child creates a natural alliance and empathy in the parent-child relationship. Instead of the linear image of an authoritarian parent squashing an adolescent rebellion, the grandparents can hold the picture of different generations of *children*, from a different time and space, mutually involved in the project of self-actualization.

In addition to presenting the parents' childhood parts, the grandparents can illustrate the generations that preceded their own lives. Their stories about their parents and grandparents bring a five-generational (along with themselves, children, and grandchildren) perspective of the family. Thus, they can continue the tradition of passing the family legacies and myths from generation to generation.

Since the grandparents are chronologically closer to death than the other generations, they connect the family to the life beyond the parameters of the house. This view of life realigns the priorities of the other two floors. Somehow the proximity to death offers a renewed interest in life for the family members.

Quite often one set of grandparents exerts much more obvious influence over the family than the other grandparents. It is as if there are stairs only to one-half of the top floor. This unbalance results in one of the parents being an "orphan" (Ridgely, 1994b). Having stairs to only one side of the top floor can be mistakenly interpreted as the missing side's being relatively unimportant. Yet the missing parents always loom in the picture. Usually their "ghostly" presence creates a more confusing effect than would their actual presence. It is important to resurrect the staircase to the unseen top floor so that the parent on the middle floor does not have to remain an orphan. This is particularly important because of the propensity of children on the bottom floor to fill in for the vacancy on the top floor.

If the parents become divorced, the structure of the house becomes infinitely more complex. This affects the top floor as well. This is unfortunate because the grandparents can provide the stability in times of flux when it is not being provided in a divided middle floor. The grandparents, by their proximate position, can link the children to the attic even when the family is undergoing massive upheaval. Perhaps the stories in the attic contain lessons for handling great stress.

The Attic

The attic represents a part of the house that is not visited very often. However, for the curious, the attic contains a treasure trove of artifacts, pictures, legends, myths, and stories. The attic may also contain blueprints for the house that have long been misplaced. These blueprints can shed light on the type of foundation laid for the structure long ago. Additionally, the blueprints may hold clues to the remodeling tasks necessary for the house to run more effectively. Perhaps the house used asbestos as insulation because that made sense at the time the house was built, but no longer makes sense with the scientific knowledge of today. Therefore, certain aspects of the attic are not the most healthy fit for today's house. Virginia Satir (1988) explained the problem of antiquated rules and patterns with her classic story about a curious young girl who questioned her mother, and then her grandmother, about why they cut the edges off the pot roast. Mother and grandmother explained that this was the way that they were taught. So the girl brought her curiosity to her great-grandmother, who laughed and explained that she cut the edges off the pot roast because she had a very small oven and had to put the pot roast into two different pots. Great-grandmother added that thankfully she no longer has to engage in this time-consuming process because she now has a larger oven. This story is a clear example of the importance of exploring the attic when one sees inexplicable rules or patterns on other floors of the house.

Although the structure of most family houses contains bedrooms, a kitchen, a bathroom, and perhaps recreational rooms, they have diverse structural designs and very different interior designs. Some houses do not have any closed doors, others have areas that are off limits to the different generations. Some fit the children's activities while others meet the needs of the grandparents. Some have at least one parent home most of the day, whereas others have parents who are barely home at all. There is no single, inherently "correct" architectural design for the family home, but endless possibilities for best using the resources and variables that comprise the group considered as the "relevant" family. When there are sufficient and unresolvable problems among residents on the floors, between the floors, or with the community, the family may look for professional resources to resolve the impasse. The questions *where* and *how* to belong and be in the clients' house should guide the supervisor's assessment of the therapist's choices and impact. In times of impasse and confusion, the supervisor can help the therapist reflect on the choice of position in the house as well as consider alternate places and approaches.

THE GENERATIONAL POSITION
OF THE THERAPIST

Usually, the marital/parental, middle floor makes the request for therapy — for one of them, the marriage, or for the child(ren). Once this request has been made, the therapist has many methodological decisions about the way to approach the problem and the system. Should the therapist initially join the floor of the children, parents, or grandparents? Should the therapist explore the attic? Should the therapist temporarily align with one parent or one of the children? Should the therapist request the grandparents to come into the therapy? Should the therapist join the seriousness of the parents, the playfulness and irreverence of the children, or the respectful distance of the grandparents? Should the therapist agree to see a member of the household individually in therapy? Should the therapist push for the family to bring in the noncustodial parent and grandparents? The answers to such questions will invariably expose the therapist's accommodation to the different floors.

No matter what system the therapist sees (families, individuals, couples, other subsystems, or social networks), the definition of the problem, goal, and type of intervention will indicate the therapist's position in the clients' house. The agile therapist will feel free to roam the stairs and corridors so that he or she can work from the perspective of distinct rooms on the different floors. The therapist's ability and proclivity to navigate the corridors and staircase can be constricted by the therapist's emotional and chronological position in his or her family of origin. For example, a therapist who was a child from a single-parent family could have a learned tendency to operate from the middle floor, thus becoming a coparent when working with a single-parent client family.

Similarly, the gender roles and patterns learned in a therapist's culture or family of origin will be unwittingly transmitted by therapeutic alignments, communication patterns, or conceptualization of the problem. For instance, a therapist whose father was frequently out of control might shy away from issues in a family therapy that could provoke the father's strong feelings. In such a case, the therapist would unwittingly reiterate a family rule to compensate for the father's abuse of power or emotional frailty. Additionally, the therapist's past and present position in the life cycle in his or her procreated family could also significantly influence the therapeutic process (Simon, 1989). For instance, I have immediately favored an 11-year-old boy because he reminded me of my son. Likewise, a therapist might overempathize with a beleaguered parent of an adolescent if he or she is raising a teenager. Therefore, the focus of changing the rigid proclivities of the therapist may be more instructional, at times, than attending to theories, strategies, and techniques (Haber, 1990b).

If a therapist regularly prefers one floor over the other two, then the therapist's position in the family house will be evident to the different generations. The children may assume that the therapist is always in the marital bedroom or the parlor on the parental floor. This perception of adult bias by children is typical since the therapist usually belongs chronologically to the parental generation and is being paid by the parents to assume responsibility for helping the family. The agile and creative therapist, however, is one who can move up and down the stairs to the different floors. When this occurs, the generation gap becomes less obvious as the family members learn to perceive, understand, and communicate with each other's reality. In this scenario, the family could truly become mutually resourceful.

Although I am espousing a position of therapeutic flexibility, the therapist should not strive to become a multigenerational and gender chameleon. Rather, the therapist should consider how best to exist in the different rooms in the house. For instance, I can act as if I am a teenage girl by being worried about having a brain and losing boys, wondering how to say no to sex, caring for my mother's losses, being concerned about weight and appearance, and favoring the *now* of the pop culture over *future* responsibilities — but I wonder if I actually pull it off. At best, I think I can spend 10 to 15 minutes in a female teenager's room without knowing what to do, how to do it, and generally, how to be in that world. Recently, I have become more comfortable in a female teenager's room. I am more apt to be myself while she teaches me what is important and valued in her world. As a therapist, I do not have to be in the room as a parent, but more like an anthropologist with the goal of understanding her world view. This perspective helps me translate and bridge the world views from the floor of the parents and the teenagers and extends to the other generational and gendered rooms in the rest of the house.

Although I have more biopsychosocial similarities with an adult male, I still may have an awkward experience dealing with a man's pathology, life cycle, and cultural issues that are different from my own. Although the furniture in the room may look familiar, I still may misunderstand the subtlety and meaning of the different objects in the room. Therefore, I would need to get permission to spend time in his room to understand the meaning of his bed, desk, pictures, clothes, medicine, and his abilities to relate to guests from the other rooms in the house. Being in his room would give me experiential and relational information about what it is like for me to be with him. Perhaps my experience would be similar to the experience of other household members. Or, perhaps I can uncover aspects of him that are unknown to the rest of the family. In either case, the information generated from my experience in the room can be integrated, as appropriate, into the rest of the household.

If a therapist cannot work in certain rooms, then consultants can help the therapist become more culturally sensitive to the different generations and genders in the household (Haber 1987, 1990b, 1994c). For instance, in a couple's therapy, the wife, a homemaker, was complaining about being extremely stressed by her list of chores. When asked about the list, she embarrassingly reported a few items on the list and commented that neither the therapist nor her husband could understand her problem. The therapist, a working male married to another professional, did not really empathize with the homemaker's problem. The supervisor directed the therapist to inquire about how the wife's homemaker friends would respond to her problem of feeling overwhelmed. Through the image of her friends, she became much more creative in approaching resolutions to her stress and the therapist became more attuned to her predicament. Therapists should consider their experience in the room, perceived position in the family genogram, limitations and opportunities in each room, and the differences in world views. Supervisors can teach, support, and provoke therapists' ability to function in different environments.

THE ROLE OF SUPERVISOR IN THE HOUSE

Since therapists encounter a wide diversity of different houses, rooms, furniture, decorations, art work, metaphorical objects, toys, beds, etc., it is impossible to have proficiency and expertise in all situations. Although there are benefits to developing expertise with special problems and populations, a myopic view of specialization severely handicaps the therapist's ability to work in different milieus. Optimally, the therapist needs to develop a proficient methodology, theory, and personal ability to work in a variety of environments inhabited by culturally diverse people. A therapist who is a generalist needs to expedite personal and relational development by activating the personal and social immune system in order to amplify, partner with, utilize, and redirect the clients' resources. However, despite the best intentions to overcome symptomatic and developmental impasses, it is quite common for the therapist and family to become bogged down in stereotypical roles in the different rooms and floors. The therapist's position could become as predictable and limited as the clients' roles before entering therapy.

> The more rigid the family system, the more difficult it is for the therapist to avoid being trapped in the pre-existing family rules. When this happens he/she may make contradictory requests to the supervisor, such as, "Help me to foster the differentiation of the family members (explicit request), while keeping it dependent on me (implicit request)." . . . The therapist represents an element of continuity for the family and offers them a relationship which can be developed and deepened; for that very reason he/she runs the risk of becoming enmeshed in the family rules. The supervisor, on the other hand,

carries out his/her function of reinforcing the therapist's unpredictability by maintaining an invisible presence. (Andolfi & Menghi,
1982, pp. 184–185)

The supervisor can reinforce spontaneity and creativity by helping the
therapist join and work in the rooms and floors that are foreign, emotionally provocative, difficult, overwhelming, or simply uncomfortable. Part of
the job of the supervisor, then, is promoting the therapist's individuation in
the service of being more free and adept in helping the family. The two
houses illustrated above can become a shorthand language of identifying
where the therapist focuses and *how* the therapist intervenes. Many factors,
as indicated by the illustrations of the professional and client houses, and
outlined in table 2.1, can limit the *whereabouts* and *impact* of the therapist.

As the therapist encounters the emotional, relational, and intellectual
effects of the variables listed in table 2.1, the supervisor can be a vital
resource to help the therapist develop and differentiate in both houses.
Therefore, supervision can be defined as a professional relationship that
monitors, assists, redirects, and amplifies the therapist's clinical work, first
and foremost, and promotes the conceptual, intuitive, personal, and methodological skills necessary for professional development.

"Super-vision," the multidirectional ability to observe the therapist-client
interactions in the houses, provides the time and space to reflect on a broad
picture of the therapeutic system without the immediate pressure to react.
The supervisor can unobtrusively perceive the rules, roles, emotionality,
rigidity, ghosts, and resources of the house from the sidelines rather than
from the playing field. From this meta-perspective the supervisor feels less
pressure to conform to the demands of the family. In contrast, the family
frequently has a clear idea about how the therapist should operate in the
house. Unfortunately, the request for the therapist to be a certain way may
be a "more of the same" approach to change—the solution reinforces and,
thus, becomes the problem. The sensitive therapist must balance being a
more productive force in the house with belonging to the therapeutic system. Therefore, the therapist has to both gain entry into the family house
and challenge dysfunctional rules, communication patterns, prescribed
roles, problem-saturated stories, and contextual relationships.

The supervisor, who does not have this same pressure, can encourage
the therapist to behave differently from the family's prescription. Thus, the
supervisor can exist as a countercultural agent in the household: "Talk
about how you experience mother's anger or father's passivity." "Help the
parents confront the sibling rivalry rather than doing it yourself." At other
times, the therapist may be too distant from certain rooms. In these cases,
the supervisor will need to encourage and guide the therapist to be closer

TABLE 2.1

Therapist's Relational Position in the Houses

Professional's House
  Top Floor
  - Therapist's translation of theories, methodologies, professional ethics and values.
  Middle Floor
  - Rules, roles, relationships, and parameters of the work context.
  - Therapist's support systems at work.
  - Therapist's relationship with the supervisor.
  Bottom Floor
  - Professional development stage of the therapist.
  - Personal life cycle stage and emotional maturity of the therapist.
  - Therapist's personal characteristics (ethnicity, physical appearance, sense of humor, tenacity, intellectual ability, communication style, warmth, congruence)
  - Past and present personal and professional relational experiences.
Clients' House
  - Clients' typology, degree of symptomatology, and life cycle issues.
  - Emotional demands by the different floors and rooms of the clients' house.
  - Connection with clients' support systems.
Professional's and Clients' House
  - Transmission of cultural values such as gender power, work ethic, family roles, life cycle expectations.
  - Similarities and differences between the professional's and clients' houses.

---

and more involved: "Move closer to the woman when she begins talking about the orphanage." "Ask each family member to identify something in the room that reminds them of the deceased family member." "Discuss why you are so protective with the clients." Obviously, when the supervisor guides the therapist to a different position in the house, this will affect the tenor of the house. This combination of therapy for the therapeutic relationship and professional growth for the therapist results in greater differentiation and relational flexibility in both the clients' and professional's houses.

Supervision should not be thought of as a project dedicated to the therapy or the personal growth of the therapist (although personal growth may be an invaluable byproduct of professional growth). The beginning and end point of the supervisory session should focus on increasing clinical and professional competence; otherwise, the supervisor would inadvertently be teaching the therapist to blur boundaries by confusing the goals and the contract of a professional relationship (Haley, 1988). After all, the goal of supervision rests with the progression of clinical and professional competence, not the personal growth of a patient. Therefore, Haley's support of a bill of rights by clinical students should be judiciously considered:

> No teacher may inquire into the personal life of a therapy student, no matter how benevolently, unless, (1) he/she can justify how this information is relevant to the immediate therapy task in a case, and (2) he/she can state specifically how this inquiry will change the therapist's behavior in the way desired. (Haley, 1976, pp. 176–177)

Since the therapist's choice of where and how to work in the client house may reflect personal values (Aponte, 1985), personal characteristics (Kantor & Kupferman, 1985), gender bias (Goldner, 1985), cultural prejudice and naiveté (Falicov, 1988), or unfinished family of origin issues (Kramer, 1985), the project of supervision needs to deal with the personal aspects that constrict the therapist's clinical effectiveness. However, the supervisor needs to keep the above bill of rights in mind in order to maintain clarity as to the boundary of clinical and professional development versus personal growth. Therefore, the golden rule of beginning and ending with the supervisee as professional encourages the supervisory system to respect the integrity of this professional relationship. If this boundary becomes blurred, it may result in the supervisee's becoming excessively dependent, confused, and unclear about the professional role. The supervisor would need to clearly structure the objectives of the supervisory experience so that the supervisee makes the transition of assuming the responsibility of a professional role. In cases where a therapist has difficulty with clinical responsibility and competence, the supervisor is responsible for appropriately monitoring the clinical cases. In addition, the supervisor would need to consider whether a referral for personal therapy would directly help the supervisee and his or her clientele. The supervisory responses to therapist impairment must protect the welfare of the clients. The bottom line of supervision must echo the Hippocratic oath, "Above all else, do no harm."

The confusion and difficulty of developing a professional identity are not pathological problems, but reflect a predictable developmental process for the novice therapist. The supervisor needs to help a beginning therapist through the transition of overidentifying with his/her clients to developing appropriate professional distance and boundaries. The fourth chapter in this book will detail an array of supervisory dimensions, based on the Jungian typology, that will guide the supervisor in structuring different competencies for the different functions of clinical skill development. For example, a supervisee who felt overwhelmed by her emotional responses to her clients regularly brought her personal concerns to supervision. Consequently, the supervision involved a great deal of soul-searching and emoting. A parallel process of blurred boundaries existed in both the therapeutic and supervisory systems. The supervisor questioned the usefulness of this approach because the supervisee continued to feel overwhelmed by her clients' problems. He redirected the focus by attending to the theoretical development of the supervisee. This attention resulted in the therapist's developing more clarity and confidence with her clients and professional identity.

The supervisor, then, is a necessary vehicle to help the trainee develop an effective, clear, diverse, and creative professional identity. As reflected in the Latin roots of the word supervisor (*super*, over + *videre*, to see), the vantage point of being outside the clients' house can promote the supervisor's meta-perspective. Since the therapist's body and mind are located in both houses, supervision can simultaneously work with the therapist's expertise and congruence in both houses. This can be accomplished by redirecting, supporting, and challenging the therapist's professional position and use of self. These mind/body supervisory interventions can enhance the therapist's adaptability, flexibility, creativity, and intensity in the different floors and rooms of the family house. After all, the natural limitation of the therapist's body is that it can only exist in one place at any given point in time. Therefore, the perspective of the supervisor can broaden or reinforce the therapist's direction of attention. The following informational questions (where, what, who, when, why, and how) give examples of the inquiry of the therapist's experience and rationale of the position in the house as well as the possible impact of alternatives.

- **Where** are you in the house? With the kids, parents, grandparents, or in the attic? Who invited you into the house and where did they want you to focus your skills? How often are you on this floor or in these rooms? What would happen if you moved to another place in the house? How would the particular family members react to such a move? What could the move accomplish? What may be lost in the move? Where are you in the gender and generational politics of this house?

- **What** is your role in the position in the house? Are you a problematic or favored child, distant cousin, friend, plumber, coach, older brother, judicious grandparent, or substitute parent? How do the clients reinforce your role? What would happen if you chose a different role? What would you need to do in order to expand your role in the house? What do you like and dislike about your role?

- **Who** are you in this family? Who are you closest to or most distant from? Who do you enjoy the most, who seems the most antagonistic to you, the most receptive, the most needy, the scariest? Who do you want to support the most in the family and who do you want to challenge? Do you have unusual or repetitious feelings in certain rooms of the house? Do you have any crazy fantasies of being different in the house?

- **When** do you more or less occupy the role during the session? Are you different in the beginning or end of the session? When in the therapy did you notice shifting to a different role? Did your shift fit the developmental tempo in the family? When do you think that the family will no longer require a substitute parent? How will you know when this happens?

- **Why** are you occupying this position? Is your motivation based upon a role or value that you learned from your family of origin? Do you feel pressured by your agency or referral source to play such a role? Are you afraid that you will lose the family? Do they remind you of clients you had in the past? What is the theoretical rationale for your position in the family? Why do you think that you are making an exception with this family?

- **How** do you feel in this role? Do you feel energetic, creative, defeated, fearful, sad, pressured, etc.? If these feelings were your supervisor, what would they be telling you to do? How do you think you would feel if you moved your chair closest to the most distant member in the family? How would you feel sharing your depression or fear in the session? How would you feel with a family of origin member in the room? How could this work out better for you? How can I (the supervisor) help?

The answers to these questions can help uncover unacknowledged motivation and unrealized choices of how the therapist coconstructs the therapeutic story. Furthermore, these questions demonstrate how the supervisor's attention can help redirect the therapist. Such questions and supervisory interventions challenge the therapist to work from different perspectives in both the professional and client house. Thus, through the therapist, the supervisor's ideas and meta-perspective can infiltrate the house. Therefore, the supervisor needs to reflectively pay attention to his or her experience of the clients' house and the therapist's position in the house. Similar where, what, who, when, why, and how questions by the supervisor would also clarify past, present, and potential roles and motivations in the household. These questions recognize that the supervisor, like the therapist, actively co-constructs the relationship within the house. The supervisor's relationship with the therapist becomes complicated because three households are involved: the supervisor's professional house, the supervisee's professional house, and the supervisee's position in the clients' house. Each of these houses influences the where, what, who, when, why, and how experiences of the supervisor.

Supervision, unlike consultation, takes place in an enduring relationship. Observation of a therapist's work over time usually betrays certain operational patterns. These patterns portray both strengths and limitations. Sometimes therapists give too much attention to certain floors and rooms, shy away from other places, or work from a particular stance as opposed to a wide range of therapeutic relationships. These ingrained patterns can guide operational goals for the supervisee to develop greater breadth and depth in his or her work in the clients' house.

For instance, one of my supervisees frequently operates from a maternal perspective. She asked for a supervisory consultation with a long-term individual client, a depressed, unmotivated college student. The recent crisis was that the student could not focus on her schoolwork and did not know how to change her apathy toward school. In addition, she expressed feeling unsupported by and disdainful of her needy mother and distant father. As the therapist turned over the session for my consultative inquiry, I was aware of the client's sad eyes and my feelings of being an unwanted barrier between the client's sadness and her therapist. Therefore, I suggested that the therapist begin the session and that I remain on the sidelines until later. Both the client and therapist seemed relieved to be able to begin without my interference.

The more that the client spoke hopelessly about her parents, the more that the therapist tried to reassure, nurture, and process her feelings. The therapist became the *good mother* as she offset the perceived lack of attention and understanding from the client's description of a self-indulgent, narcissistic mother. They both seemed oblivious to my presence in the room as they participated in this dance. It seemed that the more the client expressed her feelings, the less hopeful she became about her ability to control her destiny. She just became more infantile. After about a half-hour, their attention gazed toward me as if to ask me to enter the relationship. Being on the sideline allowed me to observe the client's and the therapist's positions in the house and to plan a different entrance into the system. Being male, I felt drawn, and had easy access, to the father's side of the house. I was attracted by the client's metaphor that her father only saw her as a tax break. She previously stated that his only reason for paying for her education was so he could claim her as a dependent on his taxes. I initially positioned myself as an accountant trying to figure out how much money father was saving by paying her tuition at school and getting a tax break. (It turned out that father's tax break resulted in a net loss of about five thousand dollars.) This strange entrance, from feelings to money, amused the client and made her somewhat curious about the motivation of her father, a very shrewd executive, to lose so much money on his tax break. The interview continued to explore father's cut-off with his homeland after immigration and the resulting emotional distance with his spouse and children. Was she to be the next one to "fire" father after she finished her education? Her academic impasse became construed as a way to avoid defining herself. After all, she felt completely undefined by her parents. The paradox was that the lack of ability to define herself as a student would result in school failure and ultimately a return to the quagmire of her family home, since she had no other plans. The session ended with a gentle confrontation of her *choice*.

The session helped the therapist to see a different approach to working with her client. The advantage of a supervisory consultation is that a therapist can "loan" the client for an hour and observe the supervisor's different, discontinuous way of working with the same client. Following the session, the therapist decided to broaden her role with her client through involvement within the father's room, rather than mostly acting as a substitute mother. She decided to pursue the idea of bringing father into the session, or at least on the intercom. Finding a new position in the house allowed the therapist more options to explore with the client. The client moved from a position of self-destructively rebelling against the father (by not being able to focus on school) to seeing the father as unable to communicate his feelings. This new view enabled the client to be less angry with father and somehow resulted in her becoming much more focused with her schoolwork.

The consultation could have further explored the mother's room in the house, the aspects of mother that were not actualized. Through the interior of mother's room, a consultant could have explored how mother learned from her family to limit her expectations and further inquire into the impact of mother's deep frustration on the client. Instead of a ball and chain, mother's life story could be seen as an impetus for the client to make changes in her view of herself in relationship to others, including family members. The ultimate goal of exploring father's or mother's room more fully would be the same: to extricate this youngest, adult child from feeling emotionally responsible for her parents' welfare so that she could have her own life while still being connected to the family home. Likewise, the goal of the therapy shifted from mostly giving the client emotional support to searching for how the client can find her own legs. This seemed to fit the present stage of therapy because of the previous work that the therapist had done with this client.

PARALLEL PROCESSES IN THE TWO HOUSES

The metaphor of the different rooms and floors of the two houses provides a map for understanding the related concepts of parallel processes (Searles,

1965) and isomorphism (Liddle, 1988). These concepts illustrate that feelings, behaviors, and organization in one room maybe replicated in other rooms, floors, or houses. Systems theory (Von Bertanlaffy, 1968) states that interrelated parts in a system are mutually influential. Parallel process takes this one step further by proposing that corresponding parts have tendencies to *match* one another. For example, Minuchin (1974) observed that the dynamics of sibling relationships often resemble the relationship in the parental subsystem. Thus, a conflictual sibling relationship could resemble disharmony in the marriage. Parallel processes can also occur through time. Transgenerational therapists (Roberto, 1992) pointed out that historic, generational patterns can unwittingly replicate when feelings from earlier generations become repressed and projected onto later generations. In this regard, the uncanny, transgenerational cycle of abuse pathetically illustrates parallel process.

In a fascinating study, Doehrman (1976) investigated eight supervisor-trainee-client triads over a period of 32 weeks to determine whether the level of interrelationship in this triad supported the functionality of parallel processes. She found, in fact, that positive or negative aspects in the supervisory relationship correlated with similar aspects in the therapeutic relationship.She also found that working through transference problems in the supervisory relationship and countertransference problems in the therapeutic relationship fostered a healthier therapeutic relationship. Therefore, she strongly advocated that supervisors and trainees work through their relational and personal impasses in the service of ultimately helping the therapeutic relationship.

Friedlander, Siegel, and Brenock (1989) also studied the relationship of the interactional processes of supervision to the interactional events in therapy. They found strong relationships between verbal communication patterns in the concurrent supervisory and therapy sessions. In addition, they found that there were strong correlation between the participants' ratings of the supervision and therapy sessions. They concluded that supervisors must carefully consider their relationship with the supervisee since they are the link between the supervisory system and therapeutic system.

Williams (1995) described how the parallel process could systemically ripple from the *bottom up* or *top down*. If a client is suicidal, the resultant worry, concern, and anxiety generated from the problem will certainly affect the therapist and supervisor. On the other hand, if the supervisor is very distant and apathetic with the therapist, then this attitude could extend into the therapy room. Therefore, it is important for the supervisor to carefully consider not only his or her impact upon the therapist but also his or her reaction to the clients or therapist. Since supervisors themselves are the only independent variable in the equation of the professional and clients' houses that they can control, repositioning the *self* of the supervisor could disrupt dysfunctional patterns in the supervisory or therapeutic systems. They could use the ripple effect of parallel process to advance the potential for change in the professional and clients' houses.

> The replication of certain processes across system boundaries can be detrimental to the therapeutic and supervisory systems. Using the isomorphism perspective, the supervisor can transform this replication into an intervention, redirecting a therapist's behavior and thereby influencing interactions at various levels of the system. . . . Supervisors are not passive observers of pattern replication, but intervenors and intentional shapers of the misdirected sequences they perceive, participate in, and co-create. (Liddle, 1988, p. 155)

A previous example (p. 39), in which a supervisor helped an overwhelmed therapist focus on theoretical understanding of her clients as opposed to working with her emotional and personal reactions to her clinical cases, is a good example of using the parallel process to look for a more *perpendicular* solution. That is, the supervisor's persistence in helping the therapist clarify her theoretical rationale rather than her emotionality helped facilitate the supervisee's development of a clearer boundary in her role as a therapist. The perpendicular intervention modeled permission for this beginning therapist to avoid confronting feelings in times of confusion. Thus, the supervisor's intervention stopped the parallel process by intervening from a different angle. The result of the perpendicular intervention was a significant improvement in the therapist's ability to contain and handle the emotional process of her clients without overidentification.

Interestingly, the supervisor in this case had parallel concerns about her emotional responses to various professional situations, including the supervisory relationship with her emotional supervisee. Although she had developed a close relationship with her supervisee, she was concerned about her supervisee's diffuse boundaries and lack of confidence. Thus, the lack of confidence and overwhelming emotionality represented a parallel issue between client and supervisee, and supervisee and supervisor. When she brought this issue to a supervision-of-supervision group, she became tearful and seemed emotionally exhausted. My initial reaction was to go over and hug her and offer my support. As I fast-forwarded my imaginary video replay of this possible intervention, it looked very patronizing and demeaning of the professional maturity of this highly competent clinician. Furthermore, it looked like too predictable of a response that did not offer "news of a difference" (Bateson, 1972). Therefore, I rejected the idea of offering *direct* physical and emotional support and decided to look for a way to offer her *indirect* support by modifying her position with her supervisee. Sometimes it can be more supportive to give a nudge than provide a shoulder. Instead of dealing with her personal concerns, I asked her to engage in a role-play with her supervisee, with me as a support system for her. She agreed to let me know when she felt confused and overwhelmed with the role-play supervisee. With some supervisory input, she aptly translated her emotional concerns into supervisory techniques to facilitate the professional growth of her role-play supervisee.

In a subsequent live supervision of supervision session, the supervisor helped the supervisee *externalize* (White & Epston, 1990) her worries through working with the placement of metaphorical figures representing the relationship between her client, client's family, and herself (Williams, 1995). This metaphorical approach to externalizing the problem helped the supervisee think differently about her approach to the problems of her client. Thus, the supervision-of-supervision relationship began a top down externalization process that went through the supervisory relationship to the therapeutic relationships. The supervisor trainee reported, in a group evaluation session, that allowing space for her vulnerability without acting on it was an important step in her development as a supervisor. She learned to respond differentially to the emotional process of her supervisee and her clients rather than only choosing a caretaking option. She felt more respectful of the supervisee's capacity to handle and grow from tolerable vulnerability. Incidentally, she also reported that, after the live session, the supervisee began bringing tapes of clients to the supervisory sessions. The supervisor felt positively about the general quality of her supervisee's skill development.

Should There Be a Hierarchy in Supervision?

The danger of a perpendicular, top down intervention by the supervisor correlates with the controversial issue of power and hierarchy in supervisory and therapeutic relationships (Haber, 1994a). The arbitrary decision to approach the parallel process perpendicularly instigates change. The danger of top down change is that it may misdirect and restrict the subsystem's ability to change at a self-directed pace and manner. The person in a hierarchical position has to modulate self-determinism with the responsibility to facilitate and monitor the supervisee's and clients' development. In the previous example, the role-playing and metaphorical interventions attempted to foster the development of the therapist and supervisor through externalizing the problem and shifting attention away from personal emotional issues. However, this developmental maneuver could be construed as a patriarchal determination of the supervisory and therapeutic direction for two women. If either of them saw the interventions from this perspective, then there would be considerable resistance from the bottom up.

In a reaction to Simon's (1993) suggestion that hierarchy be recast as a necessary developmental phenomenon rather than a power and control stratagem, Goldner (1993) discussed the necessity of contemplating the values of our interventions. "Psychotherapists (or supervisors) cannot help beaming their version of the 'truth' to their clients, no matter how committed they are to a stance of neutrality" (p. 160). However, rather than inventing a politically correct school of family therapy, Goldner advises the therapist to take an ethically reflexive position: "What we need, perhaps, is a way of observing our own thinking and our preferred practices so that we don't mistake our own truths for the truth" (p. 161). In the concluding commentary of Simon's article, Atkinson (1993) proposed that the therapist could mitigate the damaging effects of therapeutic control by becoming more congruent and differentiated with his or her emotional reactions. "I have found that the more I get clear, honest, and direct about my own process (my thoughts, feelings, reactions, beliefs, values, assumptions), the more my clients (or supervisees) are able to clarify their own process" (p. 170).

Therefore, hierarchy is less of a problem than disrespect, egocentrism, and rigidity. The goal and responsibility of the supervisory relationship are to enhance the professional expertise of the supervisee. This necessitates being sensitive to the transition from being more dependent on supervisory feedback to becoming more autonomous. The supervisor needs to know how and when to flatten the hierarchy. This, in turn, will help the supervisee appropriately trust the clients' direction rather than remain the "know it all" professional. Clients must learn this lesson in their own families. The transition of relinquishing hierarchical responsibilities is best summed up by Ridgely (1995): "The more I share power, the more aware I become of the power I have."

CONCLUSION

The supervisor must reflexively consider his or her personal investment and relational impact of the intervention. Without a compatible supervisory relationship, the process will interfere with the progress. The more the supervisor understands and respects the interplay of the rooms and floors of the professional house (particularly the bottom floor), the easier it will be to relate to the complexity of the house. Such a supervisor would realize and appreciate the unique personal and contextual differences of the houses. Despite such concern, perpendicular interventions will inevitably produce problematic angles with different people. "Better is always different. Different is not always better" (Pluut, 1989). However, the resulting feedback could initiate the search for the difference that makes a *better* difference.

The next chapter will focus on the relational variables between supervisor and therapist. Attention to these differences may minimize supervisory, relational impasses and model the ability to develop healthy, congruent, and satisfying relationships.

If you will, take some time to use the house metaphor with one of your supervisees or clients. Note the place and the manner of your position in the clients' house. How does your and/or your supervisee's situation in the professional house influence the choice of how to be and where to belong in the clients' house? Imagine shifting your and/or your supervisee's approach and style and location to different rooms or floors in the clients' house. What would you have to do with your supervisee or yourself in order to manifest such a change? What impact would that have with the clients?

3

Diversity in the
Supervisory Relationship

VIRGINIA SATIR (1988) developed the exercise "With Whom Am I Having the Pleasure?" to demonstrate the inevitability and clarification of projections in a relationship. In this exercise, workshop participants select a partner and sequentially process the following:

- How they came together
- First impressions of the other's physical appearance
- Resemblance to other people
- Uncensored prejudices and stereotypes about the partner
- Differences between the self and the other
- Fantasy of the partner's experience (How do you feel?)
- Fantasy of partner's perception of the interaction (How do you see me?)
- Memories of past experiences that were triggered by associations with the other person
- Level of physical comfort, and the level of acceptance of the present relationship

The ensuing discussion usually moves people from a relationship influenced by past associations, *there and then*, to one that appreciates the uniqueness of each individual, *here and now*. The exercise promotes a conversation about our prejudices and associations. For instance, a tonal, physical, or characterological nuance may be all that is necessary to induce an individual to project past relational feelings onto an unsuspecting and innocent associate.

Latent awareness discovered in this exercise clearly illustrates the unnoticed associational baggage that exists in relationships. This camouflaged baggage can encumber or facilitate the compatibility and cooperation in a relationship. This occurs even when the baggage does not fit in the reality of the present relationship. Awareness and articulation of our biases and inclinations offer the possibility of a *reality check* and the opportunity to resolve the negative effects of our inclinations. A benevolent process of working through our associations will aid the evolution of relational congruence, acceptance, trust, cohesion, and growth. These factors, most notably described by Carl Rogers (1951) as necessary conditions for a therapeutic relationship, are also vital ingredients in the supervisory process.

RESPONSE-ABILITY AND RESPONSIBILITY

It would be irresponsible to literally and indiscriminately translate the intent and steps of this workshop exercise into the rubric of the supervisory or therapeutic relationship. The loose, perhaps brutal, honesty of haphazardly sharing fantasies with supervisees could damage the trust and safety of the supervisory encounter. For instance, a male supervisor in a supervision-of-supervision group experienced an immediate sexual attraction to his supervisee. He debated whether or not to share this information with his supervisee. In order to explore this question, he engaged in an "empty chair" dialogue where he played both the female supervisee and the part of him that was sexually attracted to her. In the role of the female supervisee, he expressed discomfort with the supervisor's revelation of sexual attractiveness. He realized, in that role, that the revelation instilled mistrust and placed responsibility for keeping the supervisor role-appropriate on the supervisee. This unwarranted responsibility would certainly constrict her freedom and vulnerability in the supervisory relationship. As a result of the role-play, the supervisor decided to withhold the revelation of his sexual attraction and divert his focus to the effect of his attraction on the interaction with the supervisee. Because of this awareness and focus, he was able to foresee and prevent possible harm to his supervisee.

The supervisor appropriately used the context of the supervision-of-supervision group to clarify and guide his use of self. The meta-supervisory process provides an emotional container to explore the personal worries that are often denied or avoided to the detriment of our clients or supervisees (Charney, 1986). Thus, by working through his awkward, subjective feelings in an appropriate arena, he increased his level of safety and efficacy with his supervisee. Ideally, this isomorphic pattern trickles down to the therapist-client relationship.

Honesty is also not necessarily the best policy when the supervisor is on the other (hierarchical position of responsibility) side of the meta-experience. In this case, the supervisor's verbalizations and actions need to be professional and sensitive to the supervisee's unique character and personal history utilizing the rules, roles, timing, and setting of the supervisory context. The disequilibrium of professional responsibility in the supervisory relationship may inadvertently rekindle feelings experienced in other vertical relationships that abused power, fostered dependency, squelched initiative, or embodied other oppressive qualities. Therefore, control issues that develop in the supervisory relationship have the capacity to clarify and mitigate the power of past projections. Attention to these transferences in the supervisory relationship will undoubtedly increase the supervisee's sensitivity to the professional use of hierarchy in the therapeutic and client systems.

Self-reflection can provide signals that help clarify motivations that influence words and behaviors. As stated in the last chapter, the language of the self provides consultative guidance to the role, be it as a therapist or supervisor. For instance, in the example of the supervisor's sexual attraction to his supervisee, in *some* instances the supervisor's internal experiences could alert him to parallel issues of sexual attraction within the therapeutic or supervisory system. In such cases, the supervisor may help guide the supervisee to professionally handle potential boundary problems, which are often more prevalent with younger supervisees. In sum, the supervisor promotes the supervisee's professional growth by monitoring personal responses and using appropriate professional discretion to advance or restrain personal disclosures. In addition, the supervisor must establish a climate that will encourage the supervisee to bring vulnerable, professional concerns to the supervision session. These actions will both offer information and a model for the supervisee's clinical work.

WORKING WITH DIFFERENCES

Like supervisees, supervisors work and supervise in contexts with a plethora of personal and cultural diversities. Therefore, the question "With whom am I having the pleasure?" can help supervisors adjust each approach to the specific supervisory system. From the other side of the supervisory interview, the supervisees simultaneously ask a similar question: "Where is the supervisor coming from and how does the supervisor see me as a professional and as a person?" The answers to these complex questions will determine the range of possibilities in the supervision. The greater the self-esteem, communication, congruence, and role-flexibility (Satir, 1988), the better the probability that the supervisory relationship will be optimally open to exploration, learning, intervention, and development.

In order to deal with the previous bilateral questions, this chapter further explores the bottom floor in the professional's house. That is, it explores the impact of the self of the professional on the therapeutic or supervisory systems. Although restricting attention to the bottom floor arbitrarily limits the scope to the personal experiences of the supervisee, the theories, values, political climate, rules, roles, and other messages from the middle, top floor, and attic will significantly influence the world view on the bottom floor. Therefore, the bottom floor of the professional's house integrally interrelates with the rest of the house. The supervisor often needs to climb to the middle floor to better understand "with whom am I having the pleasure." Similarly, the essence of the clients' house links with the therapist's bottom floor. Obviously, therapists will variably respond to different types of clients and clinical problems. For example, African American clients, a Caucasian supervisee, and an African American supervisor will probably produce a different constellation of empathy, involvement, and expertise than if the supervisee were African American and the supervisor Caucasian. Therefore, supervisors need to discuss and discern the effects of the clients' culture in the supervisory system, workplace, and the rest of the professional house. Greater alignment in the professional house will foster a more coordinated and effective approach in the therapeutic system.

THE TALK ILLUMINATES THE WALK: COMMUNICATION AND BOUNDARIES

Imagine the following scenario: a Caucasian, inexperienced, middle-aged, male supervisee tells a Mexican, younger, experienced, female supervisor that he does not need help with any of his clients, did not bring a requested videotape, and refuses to schedule live supervision. How should the supervisor comprehend and deal with the supervisee's reluctance to show his work? What is getting in the way? Which elements are producing barriers to the interaction? Where have the shoes of each protagonist traveled? What will resolve impasses?

Most supervisors would see this supervisee as *resistant*. However, labeling him resistant does not help bridge differences or enhance understanding of the supervisee's position. The supervisor needs to understand the nature of the inexplicable boundaries of the supervisee. The following story told by Jim Guinan (personal communication, 1980) will illustrate the phenomenon of unseen boundaries.

Jim grew up on a farm in Michigan. His family owned horses that were free to roam and feed in a large pasture encircled by an electric fence. When the horses bumped against the fence, they received a jolt of electricity. The electricity taught the horses about the boundaries of the pasture. After several years, due to a drainage problem, it became necessary to move the fence several feet. After the fence was moved, the horses steadfastly refused to tread over the boundary of the former fence. Even without the physical reality of the fence, the horses still remembered the rules to avoid the electric shock. The horses' adherence to an imaginary boundary perplexed Jim. On many occasions, he fervently tried to pull the horses across the old, illusory boundary to see if the horses could learn the rules of their newly designed habitat. The level of the horses' fear and their obedience to the rules of the old story taught Jim about the profound power of unseen boundaries.

Most of us have experienced a relational shock or cold shoulder after crossing an undetected boundary. Perhaps something happened in the interaction that was too painful or difficult to assimilate. The cold shoulder frequently operates as a survival ploy to handle intolerable feelings. Satir developed a model of relational complexity, "The Ingredients of an Interaction" (Satir, Banmen, Gerber, & Gomori, 1991), to demonstrate the multiple layers of the communication process. These complex processes occur among and between the supervisory triad. The initiator and responder of an interaction intuitively process the following filters:

1. **Perceiver:** What do I see and hear?
2. **Meaning maker:** What meaning do I make of what I see and hear based on my past experiences and learnings?
3. **Feeling:** What feelings are activated by the meaning of the experience?
4. **Feeling about the feelings:** How do I feel (panicked, okay) about having the feeling?
5. **Defenses:** If the feelings are unacceptable, how will I defend myself?
6. **Rules for commenting:** What are my rules for commenting about my role, feelings, values, etc.?
7. **Communicator:** Based on the above process, what and how will I communicate?

These filters clarify the perceptual, conceptual, historic, emotional, motivational, and linguistic processes (and potential impasses) that occur in interactional sequences. The elicited data would offer information about how to handle and/or negotiate differences between the supervisor, supervisee, or clients.

For example, these ingredients can be applied to the previously mentioned interaction between the culturally different, middle-aged, male supervisee with the younger, more experienced, female supervisor. When the supervisee commented that he felt uncomfortable with live supervision, the supervisor may have perceived the comment as a challenge. She would have formulated this meaning based on her experiences and beliefs. Her interpretation to his challenge could be as diverse as her unique structure within the interaction with the male supervisee. Let us assume, for the sake of exemplifying the ingredients of an interaction, that her interpretation (*meaning maker*) of his reluctance to live supervision was a deep-seated fear of female authority. Let's presume that she *felt* threatened and undermined by his intransigent position. Instead of reacting to this threat by asserting her authority, she could have become aware of the *feelings about the feelings* that were aroused by the challenge to her authority. Let's assume that she felt inadequate when she felt undermined, but was able to withhold a *defensive* reaction, such as withdrawal or blame. Instead, she may have contemplated the nature of the escalating tensions of the challenge and hypothesized that the male supervisee could have had previous problems with female authority figures. Therefore, she could have decided to *comment about her feelings* of being underminded and describe her desire to develop a fair and productive supervisory relationship. If she *communicated* this message directly, nondefensively, and respectfully to the supervisee, her mature level of differentiation and congruence may help the supervisee become more individuated and less emotionally reactive (Bowen, 1978). The supervisee would intuitively process his experience of the interaction through his unique filters, and so on.

Although this process clarifies communication in the supervisory dyad, additional filters are necessary to decipher the messages of the two protagonists. For example, Gilligan (1982) and Tannen (1990) have effectively articulated the attitudinal and communication differences between males and females. Goldner (1988) addressed the therapeutic implications of this phenomenon in her famous article, "Generation and Gender." She discussed her colleague's, Gillian Walker's, inquiry about a Black male's "resistance" in a therapeutic interview: "What best explains your not wanting to tell me too much: that I'm White, female, or highly educated?" The man, married to a White woman, immediately responded, "Mostly that you are a woman. I'm used to White people and I don't care that much about education." Goldner exclaimed, "This exchange freed up the conversation so that sex, race, and class (in that order) were no longer forbidden subjects, but became the subject of therapy" (p. 29). Similarly, considering and perhaps discussing other cultural elements promote the inclusion of diversity in the supervision process. Figure 3.1 illustrates four distinct elements in the

Figure 3.1: *Elements in the supervisory system**

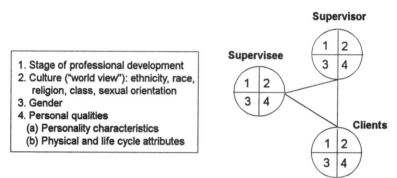

*This diagram, although different in content, is similar in form to Satir's model of the "Ingredients of the Interaction" (Satir, Banmen, Gerber, & Gomori, 1991).

supervisory triad. Each of these elements specifically shapes the experienced and perceived world view. Thus, supervising a professional's work with specific clients requires an infinitely complex map.

These elements work in tandem (like an internal family) to produce behaviors that adhere to the opportunities and perils of the environment. These behavioral messages may present decoding difficulties for the supervisor or the supervisee without the appropriate lenses to filter and clarify intent. Supervisors who employ multiple lenses may find the best angle for resolving the question about how to handle the culturally different, middle-aged, male supervisee with the younger, more experienced, female supervisor. The multi-purpose camera would have the facilities to present the wide angle view of the entire constellation of elements and/or the telephoto capabilities for examining selected elements in greater detail. The supervisor may consider a similar question to the one that Gillian Walker asked, "Is the supervisory impasse due to my cultural difference, age, gender, level of expertise, or personal characteristics?" A supervisor who considers these elements may be able to work through or, at the very least, develop a better understanding of the problem. The consequent understanding would provide mutual guidelines for respecting the unique experiences and contributions of each individual. Such a collaboration will maximize the possibilities of developing a resourceful relationship while minimizing the chances of an antagonistic association.

Although a thorough discussion of each element warrants its own book or set of volumes, the following sections will highlight and illustrate the ramifications of each element in the supervisory process.

STAGE OF PROFESSIONAL DEVELOPMENT

Therapists

Is a beginning, first-year practicum student comparable to one who is completing internship? Likewise, are the supervision needs of a recent graduate student similar to the needs of a professional who has several years of experience? Should a supervisor treat them similarly or modify supervisory goals and interventions based on their level of experience? Becoming an autonomous and mature psychotherapist is an acculturation process that begins with the dependent and uninformed role of beginning student. The very existence of stratified academic requirements (practicum, advanced practicum, internship) and postgraduate licensure and training programs is a testament to the sequential needs of aspiring professionals. Despite the significant impact of theoretical orientation, clinical setting, and trainee diversity, trainees' levels of apprenticeship significantly shape their developmental tasks, problems, and needs. Therefore, supervisors need to discriminate the stage of the trainees' acculturation to the field of psychotherapy.

The stratification of different professional levels becomes quickly apparent in high voltage cases. For instance, a supervisee who brings his or her first case with suicidal ideation to supervision would naturally require a more directive and supportive supervisory approach than an experienced clinician working in a mental health crisis unit. The senior therapist may need a consultation about some particular circumstances or simply desire a place to discuss personal reactions and fears. However, in many cases, the senior therapist can autonomously continue working with the case. On the other hand, the novice therapist may need continual supervisory intervention. Thus, the supervisor would be in a more consultative role with the senior therapist and in a more directive, teaching role with the novice therapist. The supervisor would need to closely scrutinize the novice therapist's assessment and determination of suicidal lethality and the methods that the therapist used to increase safety in the system. While the senior therapist will usually set clear and efficient goals in a difficult case, the novice therapist may not have the necessary knowledge and experience to set appropriate goals. Therefore, the supervisor needs to closely monitor problematic cases and directly intervene when the level of anxiety becomes too stressful for either the clients or the therapist. Direct intervention may include referral, cotherapy with an experienced clinician, or serial consultations with cases that are too difficult for the novice therapist to handle alone.

The goal of the supervisor is to combine direction and autonomy, support and challenge, and focus on client and therapist dynamics according to the appropriate level of therapist development. As therapists mature, they become more better able to work autonomously, to respond to challenges in the formulation and intervention of their clinical work, and to acknowledge and change their role in the therapeutic system. However, there is significant variance in the stages of professional maturation. First, labels like "novice" or "experienced" cover a great deal of territory. For instance, novice therapists range from those who have difficulty listening to their clients to those who can clearly formulate a problem and treatment plan. Second, a therapist may be expert with specific types of clients but not with others. Third, cultural, gender, and personal factors will affect professional maturation.

The literature on counselor development (see Worthington, 1987, for an excellent review) enumerates characteristics and supervisory issues in the stages of professional development. Powell and Brodsky (1993) have succinctly summarized the therapist characteristics and supervision issues of Stoltenberg and Delworth's (1987) integrated developmental model for supervision. This model, which builds on the previous work of Hogan (1964), Hunt (1971), and Loganbill, Hardy, and Delworth (1982), looks at each of three expertise stages in relation to three domains: autonomy, self and other awareness, and motivation (understanding of the role of the therapist and the process of therapy). In each stage, the three domains encompass eight competencies (intervention skills, assessment techniques, interpersonal assessment, client conceptualization, individual differences, theoretical orientation, treatment goals and plans, and professional ethics). My "road maps" deal with domains and competencies from a different perspective. The professional and client houses described in Chapter 2 deal with the domains of self and other awareness, therapist's role, and the process of therapy. The therapist's competencies are explored in my quadratic model (ideology, use of self, technique, and intuition/creativity) of supervisory dimensions in the next chapter.

The metaphor of the supervisor as parent of the supervisee (Powell, 1993) aptly fits the integrated developmental model for supervision. Novice or level 1 counselors have many child-like characteristics. They usually welcome the guidance and direct interventions from the supervisor and so are an easy and enjoyable group to supervise. On the other hand, they need to be closely monitored or else they may get in trouble. Novice counselors, like children, need nurturance, support, protection, and limits.

Like adolescents, intermediate or level 2 therapists experience rapid and tumultuous growth. Their needs are much more complex than those of the novice therapist. They desire autonomy at times but still need the supervisor's structure and support with difficult cases. They have developed a therapeutic methodology but have personal and methodological difficulty with clients with deep pathology and resistance. Instead of taking over the rudder, the supervisor needs to clarify the hazards, provide encouragement, and help them find and navigate their own course through rough seas.

Finally, level 3 or senior therapists act like adults. Having weathered the storm of adolescence, they have developed a clear professional identity. As mature adults, they willingly examine themselves, make necessary changes, and hence become more differentiated. They function well independently, are able to handle difficult clinical challenges, and have clear objectives in supervision. They require a collaborative form of supervision that will respect their experiences yet challenge them to be more coherent and expansive in their approach. Their devotion to professional excellence creates an interesting and challenging supervisory experience.

Besides modifying supervisory interventions based on developmental needs, the supervisor must consider when and how to move the supervisee from one stage to another. For instance, in live supervision the supervisor may give extra space for the increasingly confident novice therapist to overcome difficult moments in a session. The supervisor of an intermediate therapist may supervise mostly through questions rather than directives in order to promote formation of a personal style. The supervisor of a senior therapist may encourage the development of a collegial relationship by requesting help with his or her own cases.

Development is not a linear, discrete process. Stoltenberg and Delworth (1987) and others have commented that the therapist's structural changes in the various levels must accommodate regressive experiences. For instance, if a senior therapist develops burnout, the agitated scrutiny of professional identity experienced in level 2 may recur. Thus, the developmental process resembles a spiral rather than a straight, inclined plane. Periodically, supervisees should be encouraged to revisit familiar problems from a new perspective. The benefit—or some might say liability—of our profession is that, once we get comfortable with an approach, a new clinical puzzle pushes us to consider other options. Thus, professional development is a continuous evolutionary process.

Supervisors

Supervisors, like therapists, cultivate their skills through stages. Although Stoltenberg and Delworth (1987) enumerate three levels of supervisory stages I will describe only two: beginning and advanced. In practice, supervisors are either supervisors-in-training or full-fledged supervisors. However, certified or licensed supervisors, like senior therapists, need continued education and consultation for supervisory dilemmas.

To continue with the family metaphor, beginning supervisors are like new parents. They have added responsibility, newfound status, and the opportunity to pass the baton of knowledge and expertise to others. Adjustment to this role may create a great deal of insecurity and anxiety. "Do I know enough to help the supervisee?" "What if I make a mistake?" "Will the supervisee think I am credible enough to give assistance?" These and other questions are commonplace. Often the beginning supervisor is an intermediate therapist. Therefore, the supervisor may be assisting a novice therapist while simultaneously questioning his or her role as a therapist in the turbulent intermediate phase.

I have worked with level 2 intermediate therapists as supervisors for level 1 or novice therapists for the past five years. For the most part, this has been a very favorable match, since the supervisors-in-training (who are simultaneously in supervision) are extremely sensitive to the dynamics and feelings of novice therapists and the supervision process. Empathy and respect have been very important ingredients for the success of these relationships. However, occasionally too much empathy has hindered these supervisors-in-training in attaining the professional distance necessary for a meta-position. Supervision-of-supervision groups reinforce the need and the ethical responsibility to develop a hierarchical role. Role clarity contributes to the formation of healthy boundaries, parameters, and objectives in the supervisory process. Table 3.1 delineates polarized characteristics of the beginning and the seasoned supervisor (Ellis & Douce, 1994; Powell, 1993). The polarities arbitrarily demonstrate the different levels of supervisory expertise; in reality, the attributes of beginning and advanced supervisors are not nearly so absolute.

The developmental levels of the supervisor and therapist intersect in the supervisory process. A very advanced therapist may have lost touch with how to work with a novice therapist. On the other hand, a level 3 or senior therapist may resent being supervised by an intermediate therapist. Clients are also involved. They may be protective of their novice counselor and join forces to sabotage the supervision process. Or the supervisor may overfunction and unnecessarily assume too much responsibility for the clients' therapy. A clear hierarchy, where the supervisor facilitates the therapist's development and the therapist in turn facilitates the clients' development, should be established early in supervision.

CULTURAL CONSIDERATIONS

Culture is like air. It is all around us and we are immersed in it, whether we notice it or not. Culture unconsciously and intuitively shapes our definition, experience, projection, and expectation of day-to-day living. Culture is a primitive phenomenon—even the embryo responds to the relational culture of nurture, safety, and expansiveness in the womb. Perhaps only the insane

TABLE 3.1

Characteristics of Beginning and Advanced Supervisors

BEGINNING SUPERVISOR	ADVANCED SUPERVISOR
Lacks substantial knowledge of supervision theory and methodology	Well-informed about supervision theory and methodology
Overuses one approach to supervision	Implements diverse approaches suitable to specific instance
Anxious in the role of supervisor; overidentifies with therapist role	Understands role and responsibilities in the supervisory process
Intervenes largely by being the expert clinician	More apt to use the resources of the supervisee
Engages in power struggles with the supervisee over the right way	Able to connect and work with the supervisee's world view
Underemphasizes or overemphasizes the person of the therapist in supervision	Discriminantly explores the personal/professional interface when it is relevant for clinical issues
Overreacts to the supervisee	More aware of and able to utilize personal reactions in the supervision process
Experiences diffuse boundaries and inability to confront supervisee	Able to use clear boundaries to keep the supervisee appropriately on task
Ignores cultural differences and learning styles of the supervisee	Respects cultural and learning idiosyncrasies
Works with supervisee in isolation ignoring ecological context	Considers all of the floors in the professional and client houses
Content-oriented	Works with process, including the parallel process between the therapeutic and supervisory systems

temporarily escape culture through a life that disqualifies definition, predictability, and identity. For the rest of us, culture is in our food, bed, closet, home, wallet, friends, work setting, hobbies, media, entertainment, body shape, breadth, movement, communication, bones, etc. For the purposes of this chapter, the use of the word culture will encompass racial, ethnic, religious, sexual orientation, and socioeconomic classifications. Although the content and experience of each classification are quite dissimilar, there are many commonalties around inclusion-exclusion, acculturation-uniqueness, and control-suppression issues.

Getting a handle on culture (particularly in a few pages) can be done in a manner that is omnipotent or trite. Sue (1994) described two methods of dealing with culture: (1) attempt cultural proficiency in each of the racial, ethnic, religious, sexual orientation, and socioeconomic classifications and subdivisions in the world (for the omnipotent), or (2) minimize cultural implications by adopting a universal perspective (for the trite). Certainly, psychotherapy has historically erred on the trite side through the limited consideration of problems and resolutions from a patriarchal, Eurocentric perspective. However, excessive attention to cultural specificities can also create misinformation and relational interference by fostering cultural exclusivity, stereotypes, and an unwieldy amount of data.

The shrinking world and the resulting pluralistic society have forced therapists to consider complexities of the minority experience in the majority culture. No longer can we exclude the phenomena of racism, prejudice, acculturation difficulties, and socioeconomic barriers from therapy. Similarly, we cannot exclude the rich resources of the idiosyncratic values, customs, and mores of the minority culture from the clinical context. Thus, we have to consider the bicultural plight of appreciating and maintaining difference and diversity while coexisting and contributing to a multicultural society (Pedersen, 1991; Sue & Sue, 1990).

The figures in chapter 2 indicate cultural influences on each floor of professional and clients' houses. Supervisors presented with problems that occur inside the houses or at their intersection should consider the context of the multiple cultures that influence the problematic behavior. In particular, the supervisor needs to consider, acknowledge, relate, and work with the cultural voices that influence the therapy. The meta-position of the supervisor promotes the necessary perspective for listening to the cultural voices, viewing the cultural nuances, and smelling the cultural discomforts. The supervisor cannot be smugly removed from the cultural story because he or she is a pivotal player in the professional house; therefore, the supervisor's cultural orientation and values will significantly influence the relationships in the supervisory and therapeutic systems.

One way to decipher and augment the cultural influences of supervisor, therapist, or client is to make culture the *identified patient* (Ho, 1987; Szapocznik & Kurtines, 1993). The abstract punctuation of culture as the identified problem encourages the protagonists phenomenologically to explore cultural impact with a minimal amount of blame and defensiveness with each other. For instance, Cook's (1994) questions about racial awareness demonstrate how cultural considerations can amplify supervisory case discussion: "At what point did you notice the client's race? What did you think about it? How did you feel about it? What did you do in response to the client's race? How did you feel as a (supervisee's race) person in relation to the client? How do you think the client responded to your racial appearance?" (p. 138).

Such an exploration in supervision offers the supervisee the opportunity to explore, understand, and better integrate personal values, biases, prejudices, stereotypes, and experiences. Furthermore, increased cultural awareness will foster the development of a professional identity that can appreciate and work with diversity. On the other hand, supervision that avoids cultural investigations minimizes cultural information and experiences, limits directness and honesty in the supervisory relationship, and models similar avoidance to the supervisee.

> Supervisors who are committed to competent training must be willing to withstand their own awkwardness and discomfort in dealing with race as they teach their supervisees to "break the silence" in revealing and openly discussing racial identity attitudes. If we are to achieve authenticity in our therapeutic and supervisory relationships, we must relate to one another from our whole selves, which includes our racial selves. . . . Race does not have to continue to be avoided as a social stigma; it can be a focus of development in supervision as are other aspects of supervisees' personal and professional identities. (Cook, 1994, p. 139)

As figure 3.1 illustrates, the cultures of the supervisor, therapist, and clients interact. These interactions can create interesting constellations in the supervisory process. Since the supervisor has a hierarchical role, the manifest and latent issues of majority dominance may influence the supervisory interactions. For instance, an exacting majority supervisor may inadvertently recreate feelings of control, suppression, and subsequent withdrawal in a minority therapist. If the supervisee becomes increasingly passive and withdrawn, this could, in turn, increase the control and involvement of the supervisor. On the other hand, a minority supervisor may erroneously interpret a majority supervisee's resistance as being primarily racially motivated. The supervisor's misinterpretation may cause defensive behaviors that increase the supervisee's resistance. These misinformed, complementary relationships can quickly escalate into mistrustful, dysfunctional relationships. The clients, at best, lose the benefits of positive supervisory input; at worst, they could become scapegoated, neglected, or triangulated as a result of the supervisory dysfunction.

Since many minority supervisees have experiences with prejudice and racism, they are usually more sensitive to diversity issues and problems than majority supervisors. Their heightened cultural sensitivity and knowledge should be incorporated into supervisory discussions involving minority clients. In addition, supervisors should openly discuss the experience of cross-cultural supervision (supervisors and supervisees of different cultures), thereby establishing a cultural team approach that fosters respect and understanding. Most authors agree (see, for example, Bernard's 1994 summary article) that the responsibility for initiating multicultural discussions and monitoring cultural identity and tolerance development rests with the supervisor.

Despite the relevance of culture, supervisors must not emphasize cultural identity at the expense of clients and, secondarily, supervisees' development. In other words, political correctness should not override concern for the context and stage of treatment and training. "The integration of openness to culture with clinical skills entails not allowing ethnicity to become an ascendant and overriding consideration" (Montalvo & Gutierrez, 1988, p.184). Cultural identity is the music in the background that interacts with the other factors I have described. This cultural music deserves our respect, curiosity, and attention. However, since there are an infinite number of musical variations even within cultures, we should not presume to understand all of the nuances of cultural music, even that of our own ethnicity. We should consider when the background cultural music should be brought to the foreground to enhance the movement of the clinical and supervisory process. The following two supervision anecdotes illustrate the flexible consideration of cultural diversity.

Culture Before Acculturation

My friend, Lars Brok, M.D., asked me to supervise a political case during my visit to his inpatient psychiatric clinic in Rotterdam, the Netherlands. An illegal immigrant, who had entered the Netherlands from Surinam ten years earlier, became psychotic upon arrest by the police for being an illegal alien. The Netherlands' policy is that individuals will not be deported as long as they are receiving medical care for an illness. This created a classic double bind for the patient: If he improved he would be deported, and if he remained psychotic he would be confined to a psychiatric hospital. Additionally, he was terrified to return to Surinam because he had been involved in a violent insurrection there and risked imprisonment and bodily harm upon his return.

The session included the patient, his brother-in-law, his individual therapist, and Dr. Brok, who was the family therapist. I remained behind a one-way mirror with a Dutch translator who happened also to be from Surinam. The patient, who acted catatonic, would not verbally respond to questions and avoidantly stared at the floor. Lars conducted the session through the brother-in-law, who played the part of the patient's lawyer as he discussed his past and current problems. As an illegal alien, the patient had remained underground and therefore was both in and not in the Netherlands. His illegal status and political problems in Surinam made the difficult process of immigration ever so much more intense. The patient was remotely connected to his family, his home country, and the Netherlands. The only place he officially belonged was in the psychiatric hospital, but the future of the treatment was very unclear. Lars admirably tried to sort out the political complexities of this case. Although a great deal of information was acquired during the family interview, the stalemate with the patient remained.

SUPERVISOR: [via the telephone intercom] Lars, you are not a politician. You are a therapist. It is impossible to do therapy with this political dilemma. See if you can get the patient to talk about his life before he came to the Netherlands. Perhaps those issues will present a relevant and safe place for the patient to begin the therapy.

THERAPIST: [to the patient] Pick two objects [from a large table stocked with dozens a metaphorical objects]: one to represent yourself in the present and another to represent yourself before you came to the Netherlands when you were in Surinam.

[Patient picks a plastic, small, grotesque dinosaur to represent him in the present and a large bear with a leather jacket to represent the self in Surinam.]

THERAPIST: Please tell me about the bear.

The patient related that his father gave him a similar bear when he was a young child. After he began talking about his parents and the uncomplicated life of his childhood, the floodgates opened and he sobbed. The room became very still as the patient momentarily left his political problems and got in touch with the pain of his losses. Lars's deft work with a symbol of the patient's childhood also deeply touched the brother-in-law. He became much more empathic and involved with the plight of the patient and promised to bring the patient's two sisters to the next meeting. He also indicated that it might be possible to send for the parents in Surinam.

This case demonstrates how the political, cultural, familial, and psychological can all come together. The interplay of these variables guides the exploration, understanding, and attempted resolution of the existential issues occurring in the emigration and immigration processes (Sluzki, 1979). In addition, the case shows how using the patient's familial and personal resources facilitates the treatment process. Such consultative resources can advance treatment goals more effectively than reliance on professionals and institutions alone (Andolfi & Haber, 1994).

Sexual Orientation in the Therapy Room?

A novice therapist, a member of the gay-lesbian-bisexual community, brought to supervision questions about whether to disclose her lesbian sexual orientation to a female heterosexual, Christian client. She felt that she was being hypocritical by hiding her sexual identity. Videotape of a session revealed the therapist to be much more withdrawn and cautious with this client than with her gay and lesbian clients. She pointed out that her supervisor's sexual orientation was evident by his picture of his wife on his desk—so why shouldn't she declare her sexual orientation? The supervisor, an African American male, empathized with her predicament of being a minority therapist with primarily majority clients. The supervisor, like many experienced African American therapists, appropriately raised racial dynamics when they seemed to affect the therapeutic relationship. Putting racial dynamics on the table mitigated the chances that unspoken racial myths, projections, and stereotypes would undermine the therapeutic relationship. However, his minority status was evident by his skin color, whereas her sexual orientation was not clearly apparent. What should his approach have been with the supervisee?

The bottom line is that the supervisor should act in the best interests of the client and, secondarily, the professional growth of the supervisee. The supervisor trusted the supervisee's integrity and professional concern for the welfare of her clients. Therefore, he decided to clarify the personal dilemmas that were disturbing the supervisee's effectiveness with this case. Upon further investigation of the supervisee's reaction to this client, as opposed to other heterosexual clients, he discovered that she was unnerved by the woman's Christian religious beliefs. Due to her lesbian sexual preference, the supervisee had experienced religious guilt and rejection by her church. Therefore, the cultures of sexual and religious orientations powerfully influenced the therapist's experience, perspective, and connection in the therapeutic relationship.

He used the supervisory arena to sort out the voices of religious guilt and inadequacy that the supervisee experienced so that she would be less encumbered in her present relationship with her client. He set up an empty-chair dialogue where one chair represented the supervisee's sexual orientation and another her religious values. Both dialogued with the professional chair of the supervisee and with the client chair. Giving voice to these different personal influences helped the supervisee separate her need to defend her sexual orientation to the church from the needs of the client. She felt better able to connect with the needs of the client rather than putting the issue of her sexual orientation between them.

Interestingly, in the subsequent supervision session in front of the supervision-of-supervision group, the supervisee brought in a complex case that involved a litigated issue of sexual harassment of a gay male. She was determined to work with his grief, anger, and posttraumatic stress. However, she was very worried that her sexual orientation would limit her credibility in court and expose herself and partner to media attention, thus threatening job security. So once again, in a different case, the personal and societal trials of a minority practicing therapy in a majority culture came to the foreground. The supervisor, who had experienced and overcome racial prejudice, encouraged her to fight the system. In this vein, he staged a psychodrama where he had her alter ego (her uninhibited self) express her feelings to her image of the court.

While the supervision session proved to be cathartic and affirming for the supervisee, the image of the client never became involved in the psychodrama. From behind the one-way mirror where I sat with the supervision-of-supervision group, I asked the supervisor to position the client in the psychodrama and then to take a position between his supervisee and the court so that she would feel free to work with her client. The supervisee felt relieved to have the supervisor's protection from the intimidation of the court. She told the client in the psychodrama that she was responsive to his needs and did not fear the court anymore. After processing the experience of the psychodrama, she invited the supervisor to join her and the client in a consultation to process the issue of legal involvement. If this case came to trial (which it did not), they agreed that the supervisor would be the one to provide professional representation to the court. As in the psychodrama, the supervisor's material support enabled the therapist to be more attentive to the needs of the client. This support would probably become less necessary as this novice therapist gained more experience in dealing with therapeutic issues that raised anxiety about her sexual orientation. Since we live in a homophobic culture, homosexual therapists have a more complex developmental process than majority therapists. Supervisors need sensitively and fairly to guide homosexual and other minority therapists in finding a healthy professional identity that can integrate reactions to their minority status.

Both supervision anecdotes demonstrate that the culture of the institution, supervisor, supervisee, and clients must be considered in each case (Elizur, 1993). The information about culture exists whether it is requested or ignored. The issue is how to use it for the welfare of the clients and supervisees. If this knowledge is considered too personal for supervision, where can it be discussed?

PERSONAL QUALITIES

Brad Gilbert, Andre Agassi's tennis coach, recently commented that a coach must see the world through the eyes of the player. The coach can add perspective to the player but he cannot dictate style. This is particularly true of Gilbert and Agassi, as they play radically different types of tennis. Gilbert relies on psychology and guile, while Agassi prefers to overpower his opponents. Gilbert has helped Agassi improve by incorporating tactical strategy into his natural power game. Therefore, the coach's preferred style must coalesce with the player's preference, aptitude, and ability. Although Gilbert sensibly credits Agassi for his vast improvement, Agassi also returns the compliment by crediting Gilbert's tutelage for his development of a more creative and flexible tennis game. I would expand Gilbert's comment to include the need for the player to incorporate the eyes of the coach. (This explains why most of the top players pay substantial sums of money for the eyes and brains of a touring coach.) The player's inside perspective and the coach's more distant viewpoint collectively add a depth perspective that integrates both passion and wisdom. This integration has made Agassi and Gilbert a winning combination.

In addition to style, aptitude, and capability, the player's physical capabilities need to be considered. A quick, small, fit player would dictate a steady, retrieving game, whereas a taller, slower, bulkier player would impose a power game that finishes points quickly. Since Gilbert wanted Agassi to play a more consistent style of tennis, it was also necessary to improve Agassi's conditioning to handle longer matches. By enhancing his physical endurance, Agassi approached the rallies more patiently. However, tennis matches do not exist merely between the coach and the player, but include another player. Therefore, the coach must carefully consider the unique strengths and weaknesses of the opponent when planning for the match.

Analogously, the supervisor works through the character and the body of the supervisee within the clinical context. It is important for the supervisor to consider, activate, and modify the mannerisms, communication style, and flexibility of the supervisee's character. The supervisor needs additionally to consider the shape, age, agility, and experiences of the supervisee's body. For instance, a powerful looking and acting male supervisee might need help accessing his soft and sensitive side with some clients. On the other hand, a nurturing and extremely empathic female supervisee may need occasional guidance to avoid a caretaker role in certain clinical situations. These male and female stereotypical (but not uncommon) examples do not mean that effective supervision will mostly help strong, male supervisees find their soft side and assist nurturing, female supervisees formulate less permeable boundaries. Strengths need to recognized, respected, and utilized (like Agassi's backhand) and weaker qualities developed in order to expand the therapist's professional repertoire.

Personality Characteristics

Consider this experiment*: Allow a picture to emerge of a supervisee (or yourself as a therapist). Picture images of the supervisee's typical clothing, grooming, posture, eye contact, sense of humor, communication style, comfort level, client interactions, favorite positions in the clients' house, and ability to handle anxiety. In addition, view other images that you know about your supervisee, such as his or her relationship with family, friends, colleagues, any hobbies, and any other images that have caught your attention. As you review these images of your supervisee, appreciate his or her unique constellation of personality characteristics. Notice the level of influence and usage of each characteristic. Identify six characteristics that stand out. Use the shorthand language of metaphors to describe these parts. Perhaps you can identify these parts as famous people (Mother Theresa, Albert Einstein), occupational types (cab driver, physical education teacher), or animals. After you select metaphors for each part, picture the constellation of these six metaphors.

These six metaphors represent a wider range of characteristics than the uniform identification of a giving, intimate, unconditional, positive, soft, helpful therapist. Although those positive traits usually establish effective therapeutic relationships, opposite characteristics, such as occasional withholding, distance, conditional acceptance, skepticism, firmness, and confusion, can be useful in certain clinical circumstances. Perhaps the supervisee's less typical therapeutic qualities, if not identified already, can become part of the six metaphors.

Now that you have identified the six metaphors of a supervisee (or yourself), imagine them as a group. These parts can be viewed as an internal family of the supervisee. See how they get along. Which ones are in conflict and which ones form alliances? Can they resolve conflict or do they become stuck? Can they work together as a team or do they operate independently? Do they respect one another? Which parts become leaders in the group and which ones have the most energy? What do they each contribute to the group? Which ones do you like and which ones are the most disturbing? Notice anything else that seems relevant about this group.

Now imagine this internalized group of metaphorical parts as a group of consultants watching your supervisee (or yourself) in a problematic clinical interview. What does each think about how the supervisee is handling the case? What does each of them suggest to the supervisee? Do they disagree? See them staff this case among themselves. What occurs in the case staffing?

---

*This exercise simulates Virginia Satir's Parts Party (Satir et al., 1991).

Can some of them agree? Which metaphors seem to be in charge? Can the group find any consensus about the problem and the solution to the therapeutic impasse? What specific changes in the supervisee's position and way of being in the therapeutic system would they suggest? Picture the outcome of a couple of their suggestions for changes in the manner the supervisee handles the clinical case. How do these suggestions affect the therapeutic system? How would they need to be modified in order to be more useful? How could you, as the supervisor, access the useful aspects of these latent resources? What cautions need to be considered? How could you help the supervisee learn to integrate disowned traits in the therapeutic interview with previous accessible strengths?

Although many therapists present themselves as singularly benign, we, like our clients, have multiple aspects to our personalities. These aspects can be used destructively or therapeutically. The supervision session is an ideal setting to explore many different characteristics of the supervisee. The cultivation of these characteristics in the supervisory session can benefit the supervisee's work in the clinical milieu. For instance, many supervisees possess a delightful sense of humor that never makes its way into the interview. Others seem remote despite emotional connection with the client's story. These supervisees need to learn how to *show* their involvement. The greater the ability to incorporate multiple characteristics into the interview, the greater will be the supervisee's flexibility in connecting with clients.

Questioning the therapeutic utility of the supervisee's characteristics carries a necessary risk for both the supervisor and supervisee. A supervisee showed me a videotape of a second marital therapy session that she hated. The session involved her taking the husband's genogram. This extremely positive and nurturing therapist detested the husband's whininess and weakness. Embarrassed by her negative feelings towards the husband, she assured me that her emotional reactions did not come through in the session. The videotape, in fact, portrayed her as involved, caring, and attentive. The husband's story involved multiple losses, including his parents' divorce when he was four, his father's murder when he was six, and his mother's subsequent alcoholism. The couple's presenting problem was their anger with one another and feelings of worthlessness.

Surprised by this therapist's negative reaction to the pathetic husband, I initially tried to extinguish her wrath by rationalizing his whininess as due to his losses, emotional deprivation, and feeling of unworthiness. This ploy somewhat increased her level of empathy by increasing her guilt. "I know I should feel sorry for him and not blame him, *but* . . . " Then it dawned on me that the *but* could have more therapeutic importance than empathic responses. Exploration of her anger revealed that she felt overwhelmed by the burden of emotionally taking care of the husband. She professionally responded by attending to his wounds and fragility, but her emotional response was that of annoyance and disgust. Her reactions paralleled the feelings of the wife. So instead of eliminating the "but," we looked at ways that her anger could help direct interactions with the husband. Her anger became resourcefully employed as a reminder to help the husband take responsibility for his pain rather than expect others to cater to him. Her anger became reframed as a signal to lean back in her chair and withdraw from overinvolvement with his pain. This gave her the freedom to explore other ways of connecting with the husband. Her newfound ability to attend to her *negative* feelings enabled her to look forward to working with the couple.

Supervisory attention to the supervisee's personal and professional characteristics models the purposefulness of interpersonal and intrapersonal introspection. In actuality, we portray many characteristics during each day. Sometimes just looking at the names on my daily calendar engenders feelings of heaviness, lightness, defensiveness, freedom, intimacy, distance, among others. We function differently depending upon the nature of our clientele and their demands. On the other hand, we have some consistent approaches and mannerisms that enhance or detract from therapeutic relationships. Supervision should be a setting to refine, challenge, and add to our repertoire of personal characteristics.

> We must also be able and willing to view ourselves in context, and, therefore, as bringing to the therapy our own baggage from the many contexts in which we have carried out our lives. These include our family of origin, present family, ethnicity, religion, developmental stages, personal preferences, style, and so on, as well as professional expertise, environment, and preferences. We stand to benefit not only personally from becoming aware of these things about ourselves, but also from learning how our models of reality may shape the therapy that we do with different clients; how, in other words, specific aspects of the therapist interact with specific aspects of particular clients to form the structures of the therapeutic relationship. (Kantor & Kupferman, 1985, p. 243)

Physical and Life Cycle Attributes

While the supervisor has minimal influence in the physical appearance and the life cycle experiences of the supervisee, he or she must address the impact of these physical realities on the therapy session. Physical appearance and life cycle stage can result in positive and negative transferences and countertransferences. For instance, an older supervisee may trigger parental transferences with adolescent or young adult clients, whereas a younger one may become the object of romantic idealizations. A younger supervisee, on the other hand, may project parental transferences on older clients. If the supervisor notices that the supervisee is acting uncharacteristically in sessions, it is quite legitimate to ask: Does this person or relationship dynamic remind you of anything in the past? The answer frequently uncovers unfinished family-of-origin issues. These issues need to be explored and worked through so that the supervisee can approach clients more productively.

A supervisee, a young male, had a great deal of difficulty with the father in a two-parent family with three adolescents. The father, who looked formidable, took a tough love approach that had resulted in one son's being sent to a juvenile correctional setting. The mother and siblings were very remorseful about the boy's being sent away. The therapist attempted to get through father's denial of any feelings toward his son. This resulted in a stalemate—father's denial and therapist's pursuit. Supervisory interventions did not enable the supervisee to connect with father without indirectly challenging his position in the family. In the supervisory meeting before the next therapy session, the supervisee discussed how father's irrational, controlling behaviors reminded him of his own father. He responded to his father's control with indirect rebellion and felt that he responded to the client father with similar emotions. In a similar vein, he admitted that he felt in a struggle with me because he was particularly sensitive to my evaluation of him. He exclaimed that he felt very stilted in both the therapeutic and supervisory systems. Therefore, we decided that I would not call him for at least thirty minutes with any supervisory input. In addition, I told him that, since I trusted him to be in charge of the session, he should censor or change any of my supervisory suggestions. In this way, I tried to promote his autonomy and avoid dissension and rebelliousness in our relationship. In the subsequent session the supervisee helped the father become much more accessible and open with his teenage daughter. As one might expect, the more relaxed the therapist became with father, the more cooperative the father became in the therapeutic process. Less control and dogmatism rippled through the supervisory, therapeutic, and family systems. Paradoxically, relinquishing control did not undermine the purposefulness of the professional and family hierarchies.

In another situation, a young male therapist worked individually with a female graduate student about an extramarital affair. The history of this woman revealed that her father had rejected her. The therapist felt that the client was infatuated with him. He did not know how to handle her affection because he wished to avoid repeating the rejection she experienced with her father. He used the supervisory process to develop objective responses to the client's bids to gain his favor. The client gave the therapist a present for his office. The therapist felt that this was a test of the boundaries of the relationship, the client's attempt to become special to the therapist. We decided to inform the client that, although professional ethics precluded his receiving gifts for professional services, the therapist could accept the gift on behalf of the center and would place it in the staff lounge. The client seemed to benefit from the therapist's providing caring and clear boundaries with her. Such powerful sexual transferences and countertransferences require a benevolent, grandparental supervisor to help parental therapists help their clients feel both supported and safe.

I had the pleasure of supervising a female supervisee who happened to have many children and grandchildren. Her life experiences enabled her to join easily with clients—from infants to senior citizens. The supervisee had experienced the prejudice of ageism, the mistaken assumption that older people cannot work with young or adolescent children. Her abilities to play patiently on the floor or to open herself to the insecurity of the adolescent world dispute any beliefs about the inevitable aging process as a hindrance to the development of effective therapeutic relationships.

Perhaps more difficulty occurs from the other direction: the young supervisee working with clients at a later developmental stage. The supervisee may have to overcome the clients' beliefs that a young, unmarried person cannot fully comprehend unencountered developmental crises, such as marital infidelity, empty nest syndrome, chronic illness, or death. The supervisor needs to explore the supervisee's reaction to the clients' doubts as well as uncertainties about handling new and unexperienced developmental issues. The house metaphor can provide a guide to help the supervisee consider working from different floors. For instance, if a supervisee feels like a grandchild to an older client, the supervisor could help the supervisee explore how to join the therapeutic system from a grandparental perspective. At times I have figuratively recruited a supervisee's grandparent(s) as consultants to help him or her know how to work with the problems of older clients. "If your grandparent had the wisdom and know-how to supervise your work, how would he or she help you connect and guide this couple facing retirement anxiety?" "What position would your grandparent suggest that you take with this problem?" Such grandparental or parental consultative voices have enabled supervisees to tap into useful associations and thereby increase understanding and role adaptability.

The supervisor must objectively scrutinize the physical attributes and resulting projections of the supervisee in order to accomplish the clients' and supervisee's goals. This scrutiny must encompass physical challenges.* Crutches, canes, and seeing-eye dogs must become part of the field of

---

*I gratefully acknowledge the contribution of Frank Fite, M.Ed., to this paragraph.

supervision. The supervisor needs to accept the supervisee's disability and help to incorporate it into the session. For instance, when supervising a visually impaired therapist, I worked with him to enlist the family members as his eyes in a family therapy session. During a session with a family consisting of separating parents and two children, the supervisee asked each family member to produce a nonverbal sculpture that depicted the parenting of the two children. The supervisee recruited the identified patient, who was up to this point mostly nonverbal, as his eyes in the session. The comments of this typically silent female teenager were extremely profound and moving. The therapist's request for help with his visual impairment enabled the parents to hear their daughter's thoughts about the family. This case illustrates how an impairment in the right hands can become an asset. The supervisor must work *with* the impairment and avoid overcompensation and denial of the effect of the disability. On one hand, supervisees who have worked through the psychological effects of their disabilities can teach us a great deal about resilience, respect and compassion for physical and psychological hardship, ability to offer a novel perspective, and a comfortable humility in incorporating and appreciating clients' resources. On the other hand, disabled supervisees require similar supervision as other supervisees who are committed to improving their professional skills.

Ageism and *lookism* are culturally bound constructs with enormous subjective variance. Nevertheless, first impressions begin the formulation of distinct relational patterns. The supervisor must help the supervisee notice and deal with unproductive patterns. Since the issues of age and looks have such prejudicial influence in our culture, supervisors must address these issues with great sensitivity and respect for diverse possibilities. Supervisors, of course, must appropriately address their own biases and reactions to supervisees with different ages, physical appearance and capabilities, and life cycle experiences. The issue of biases, stereotypes, and value dilemmas also affect the way that supervisors handle gender differences in the supervisory and therapeutic relationships.

GENDERED SUPERVISION*

Gendered Houses

A definition of the gendered self emanates from biological, sociological, political, psychological, and interpersonal experiences. Often, this defini-

---

*This section was authored by Elizabeth Ridgely, M.S.W., C.S.W., Executive Director and Director of Training for the George Hull Centre for Children and Families. Since my male perspective has no doubt appeared throughout this book, I felt that it was particularly important for this section to be written from a feminine perspective.

tion of self is taken for granted and as such is unnoticed. We are what we are. We are who we are.

The perceptions and experiences of gendered positions on different developmental floors of both professional and clients' houses prompt the need to discuss gender in supervision. The subject of gender leads to personal and political issues, since one's therapeutic position in the houses is formed by biology, the family, and the wider culture. Therapeutic curiosity about gendered arrangements on the generational floors leads to an expanded understanding of each individual. Understanding the individual then leads to a broader understanding of the gendered rules of the system, across the floors, and the relationship between professional and clients' houses.

Gendered supervision invites the supervisee to notice the unnoticed, to expand the self from its usual gender stereotypic responses into atypical gender participation and organizational responses. By supporting the supervisee's capacity to rethink and challenge assumptions of gender, gendered supervision introduces a new map for the exploration of experiences and relationships of women and men.

The main idea in supervision is "tourism." Men and women do not know the world view of the other. In therapy and in supervision, it is essential to research this as one would when travelling in a foreign country. Curiosity about the other, without assumptions, is helpful in the therapeutic process. In spite of the popular literature on this topic (Tannen, 1990; Gray, 1994), naiveté about the opposite gender has prevailed in therapy. For a male therapist to be taught by a woman client about her experiences as a woman—and to restrain himself from wanting to correct these experiences—is a challenge not unlike gender clarification in marriages. Add working with the female on her presenting dilemma to this context and the process becomes more challenging. Similarly, women must work with men from their frame of reference and forego female logic that defines problems and solutions in ways that are not understandable to men.

Driven primarily by a major shift in the larger culture that put women permanently into the workforce, research into differences between men and women has been undertaken, published, and discussed throughout the past two decades. Such an enormous change rearranged gender roles outside and inside the family. Gendered roles and gendered power went into acute flux, changing the lives of men, women, and children. Such massive social change required new solutions for the family. Definition of the self through gendered assignments took on new meaning as more men became involved in nonpaid household work (e.g., laundry) and more women developed expertise in paid work (professions). This sounds simple enough, but the complexity did not escape any family who tried to find a more equitable balance of housework, child care, financial management, and decision making. The formula of man as "provider" and woman as "caretaker" died externally for some men and women, but survives in the intrapsychic vestiges of role identity. So embedded are these concepts that the exchange of functions produced significant conflict and despair in families. There were few models in the upper and attic floors that could guide men and women in a flexible and equitable gender identity. Often, disapproval of the change was not only covert but also overt. Families should stay the same. Women, at home. Men, at work.

If women experienced depression, exhaustion, and confusion about identity, their mothers were at a loss to offer advice or support. Their daughters' family life went well beyond their experience. Similarly, if men complained of confusion, depression, loss of identity, insecurity, and loss of control, their fathers could not offer relevant advice because they had experienced a more patriarchal culture. Family therapy, for the most part, was slow to respond to the social and political changes that forced adaptation within the family. Discussing men, women, and power requires an expanded vision of marriage and family; as the literature shows, each session becomes as much about the political as the personal. "The overall goal of family therapy is to change the institution of the family so that women and men who choose to participate in family life can do so cooperatively as equal and intimate partners" (Wheeler et al., 1989).

In this delicate operation, the gendered houses of both the supervisor and the supervisee become an important point of reference for the supervisory process. As supervisors and supervisees connect their own personal experiences with clinical and supervisory issues, personal values and professional interventions intersect. The supervisory process needs to take into account differences and ambivalence about gender values on all floors and in all houses.

The supervisory process affords the opportunity for uncovering and expanding the options of the gendered professional self, a therapist who combines personal gendered experiences with professional exploration of developmental impasses. Although the focus in supervision remains primarily with the professional, personal biases and proclivities must be examined as well.

Gender and World View

Just as gender organizes families (Goldner, 1988), so, too, does it organize supervision. Nevertheless, gender differences are not usually discussed at the beginning of the supervision contract. Focusing solely on the formulation of the problem or a solution, without considering gender issues, blurs the perception of political, social, and personal variables that interfere with the client, therapeutic, and supervisory systems. The following statements establish a context that reduces the gender blur:

- "I am a woman. You are a man. We will have different world views that both accompany and transcend our education and training. No doubt, the differing world views will become apparent in the area of entitlement and participation inside and outside of the family. We will explore these different world views within the context of learning from and about each other and from and about the families we work with. I have found that ideas surrounding entitlement and participation become apparent as finance, childcare, and decision making are explored in both therapy and supervision."
- "We are two men and have no female brain here to help our work with the mother of the family."
- "We are two women with no male brain to work with the father."

Whatever the gender combination, the issue must be addressed.

In order to deal with gender or cultural imbalance, Waldegrave (1990) describes a process of accountability, where men who treat women consult with a woman during the treatment process and vice versa. The same concept applies when working with cultural differences. For example, a white therapist working with a Maori family will consult regularly with a Maori consultant. The consultant does not have to be a professional colleague but must be Maori. These efforts check gender bias and/or culture bias.

The effect of culture on gender is part of the supervisory process. It is especially unusual in Canada, for instance, to have a culturally homogenous supervision group. More frequently, multiple cultures (supervisor, supervisee, group members, and clients) work together toward change—all with specific world views on gender. The interesting part of the supervisory process is noticing differences. Respect and curiosity for the personhood of the supervisee foster coherent approaches that fit therapeutic style. The following statement made by a male, El Salvadoran, psychiatric supervisee to a female, Canadian, social worker supervisor revealed the confusion of all the "abnormal" hierarchies: "You will have to remember that I am a Latin male." The ensuing discussion of what it meant to be a Latin male and a Canadian feminist woman began a discussion of gender issues that transferred directly to the confrontation of gender issues in clinical interviews.

The gendered conversation between supervisor and supervisee serves as a therapeutic model. The following hypothetical monologue demonstrates the therapist's openness to exploring the values inside the clients' house.

"Hello, my name is Lewis, originally from El Salvador. You will have to teach me about your family. How does it work for men? For women? For sons? For daughters? How does it differ from your parents' house? How do these things affect the problem that brought you here? How do you want to change this? Do you want to change this?"

We are all culture bound until otherwise directed. Our world views benefit and change from constant examination in relation to others. Theorists of culture would suggest that women know more about men than men know about women. This idea comes from evidence that the subordinate culture knows more about the dominant culture. For the subordinate culture to survive, it has to "know" the ways of and to adapt to the dominant culture. Therefore, the George Hull Centre Family Therapy Training Program* in Toronto established a policy that the ideological preference for coteaching is with a woman and a man. In addition, the program also maintains that if this teaming is not possible, then two women will teach together but not two men. This difference is based on the ideas that (1) two men know less about women than two women know about men, and (2) the effect of two men working together as supervisors can be intimidating to women supervisees, on either a conscious or an unconscious level.

In the case of supervising the other sex, the supervisor needs to become like a tourist who asks for directions about the gender assumptions, experiences, and world view. What was it like to be a man or woman in this family? How did you feel about discussing the issues of puberty and sexual development? How did you handle your value differences? How was this man socialized as a boy to assume the mantle of manhood? How does this affect his view of other men and of women? How can I help you develop more empathy for the clients' experience?

World view is also developed and influenced by teachers. When a supervisee explores the genogram of supervisors (as discussed in Chapter 1), in addition to seeing the development of theory, he or she can better understand the gender of the teacher. This leads to improved chances for gender balance in the mentoring area. As the number of women supervisors increases, teachers can be chosen for gender as well as reputation.

Gender and Supervision

Gendered conversations in supervision begin when the referral problem is discussed prior to the first session with the family. What might be the

---

*Daniel Bogue, M.S.W., C.S.W., Martha Howard, M.S.W., Catherine Martin, M.S.W., C.S.W., Angela Ragazzi, D.C.S., Elizabeth Ridgely, M.S.W., C.S.W. (Director), Stephen Weiman, M.S.W., C.S.W.

gendered difficulties that the presenting symptom is attempting to address? What might be in the normal range of gendered difficulties with two working parents and three schoolaged children? What might be specific to this particular family? Where are the losses in the house? These conversations are the heart of supervision as political views (gender perspectives) are shared. The enormous impact of such views on the family treatment is the key issue. The positions of the supervisor and the supervisee must be clarified and not projected onto the family.

In one instance, a young couple with two small children were discussing the financial arrangements in the family. The husband said that this was absolutely no problem. They had a joint bank account into which he put his paycheck and she took out what she needed to run the household. He was working fulltime and she had reduced her work to part time because of the children. The presenting problem was marital dissatisfaction and not feeling as together as a couple as they did before the birth of the children. Their love story had become diminished by fatigue, additional responsibilities, babysitters, and very different gendered lives.

As the male therapist/supervisee continued the discussion of money, the wife proclaimed dissatisfaction that she could not write the check to pay the mortgage. The husband immediately answered that they would lose the house if she were in charge of the mortgage. It was essential that the mortgage be paid by him directly. The supervisee, a male psychiatric resident married to a professional woman who earned twice the salary that he did, stated that he absolutely understood the husband's position and he too paid the house mortgage in his marriage. This was the man's job—to provide shelter. Subsequent discussion of gendered roles in supervision and in therapy resolved this stuck point for the family by altering the therapist's and husband's sexist collusion of values.

In general, in supervision men need to develop increased comfort with relational aspects rather than relying on "doing" and "taking over." The following example portrays the male therapist's proclivity for doing rather than listening or being. The instinctive urge to bring order to a female household of mother and two adolescent daughters, seen by the male supervisee to be "enmeshed," overlooked the connectedness of the women and the developmental task of differentiation. He was encouraged to overlook for the time being the need for hierarchy and clearer decision making, and instead to explore each woman's issues around developmental tasks, past experiences with abusive men in the family, and the death of the mother's mother when she was 14 years old. The male supervisee was coached to understand that this group of women bonded together as a functional strategy of emotional development in spite of loss from the upper floor and danger from the horizontal floor. With the daughters in adolescence and now physically safe, connection that would foster differentiation was required. The supervisee's anxiety, increased by the absence of a man in the household, lay in the concern that there was not "enough" differentiation. In this instance, the supervisory experience expanded the supervisee's repertoire by helping him understand and tolerate the affiliative needs of his female clients.

For women, supervision more often involves learning to assume a position of influence. Most women readily employ relational skills that take into account the needs of all parties. These relational skills can be a liability when a beginning therapist dutifully responds with deference, passivity, and emotional responsibility for fear of being offensive or exclusive. Too much reliance on these skills can result in more process than direction and more support than activity, with the overall effect of maintaining the status quo. Many women supervisees need to learn to discover and incorporate the voice of assertion and direction. The message of feminine strength is vital for many female and male clients.

One supervisee persisted with inclusiveness to the point of repetitive conversations. I assigned her the task of bringing a bag of her most valued possessions to the next session. Having her choice possessions beside her represented and reinforced her ability to take a position, to clarify her sense of belonging outside of the family, and to risk making decisions for the benefit of the client system.

The information about gendering of houses is crucial for both the treatment process and the supervisory process. Issues of identification, projection, transference, and countertransference all lead back to the organization of relationships between men and women and boy and girls. "Gender and the gendering of power are not secondary mediating variables affecting family life. They construct family life in the deepest sense" (Goldner, 1988).

CONCLUSION

This chapter attended to the unique dynamics of each individual involved in the supervisory relationship, specifically stage of development, culture, gender, and personal idiosyncrasies such as personality, life cycle, and physical characteristics. The supervisor needs to consider the interplay of these in a context-sensitive way, taking into account the person of the supervisee, the clients' idiosyncrasies, the specific professional setting, and the supervisor's position in these systems. With such awareness, the issue of what to do in supervision becomes quite apparent.

4

Supervisory Dimensions

WHAT DO YOU WANT TO WORK ON TODAY? What are your goals with these clients? What goals do you have for your professional development? What is getting in the way of your clinical work and professional development? How does expertise in this particular area relate to our supervision contract? How has your proficiency improved since our last meeting and since the inception of our supervisory relationship? Are expectations clear about what abilities should be mastered and how they will be evaluated?

This chapter categorizes psychotherapy aptitudes into four domains: ideology, use of self, methodology, and intuition. These dimensions can be immensely useful in the supervisory process because they provide a compass that indicates specific directions for the mastery of therapeutic expertise. Thus, this chapter concentrates on the *what* (competence), whereas the previous chapters have dealt with the *where* (context of the clients' and professional's houses) and the *who* (personal idiosyncrasies). Although contextual and diversity issues crucially impact the parameters of supervisory possibilities, the focus on specific conceptual, technical, personal, and intuitive skills provides clarity of purpose and direction in the supervisory relationship.

Supervision can embrace clinical and professional progress simultaneously by enhancing therapeutic aptitude with effective case management.

Thus, the ultimate supervisory question is: Which competencies will help the supervisee work most effectively with the problems of a specific case in his or her general caseload? The answer to this highly subjective question reflects less on the supervisor and supervisee's academic discipline than their idiosyncratic theories about the nature of illness, health, change, and the interventive role of the therapist. In fact, the fields of family therapy, social work, psychology, counseling, and psychiatry have each been unable to develop a comprehensive model of supervision (White & Russell, 1995). Competing supervisory models within each field differ tremendously with regard to the competencies deemed necessary to practice therapy. Likewise, these distinct models require supervisory interventions that differ in focus, style, and content.

One such difference is clearly exemplified by the debate about whether the therapist's family of origin should become part of the supervisory framework (Friedman, 1991; Haley, 1988). Friedman feels, as do most Bowenian supervisors, that it is imperative to explore the supervisee's relationship with his or her family of origin in order to foster personal differentiation. Bowen believed that coming to terms with one's own family was the most effective way to develop a helpful, differentiated presence with client systems. Haley, on the other hand, argues that the supervisor should use directives to enhance the therapist's clinical work. Furthermore, Haley believes that the concentration on the supervisee's family-of-origin problems, if not unethical, could erroneously encourage family-of-origin work with clients regardless of the clinical problem. The vast ideological differences between strategic and Bowenian therapists are also reflected in contrasting supervisory methodologies. Bowenian supervisors coach supervisees in the exploration of and differentiation from clients' and personal family-of-origin dilemmas, whereas strategic supervisors typically conduct supervision behind one-way mirrors so that they can direct the skill acquisition process.

Liddle (1988) suggested that the concept of isomorphism could provide a unifying principle of supervision embracing differences as wide as Haley and Friedman's. Liddle maintained that isomorphism presents a framework that considers the similarity of the form and process of two different relationships, such as therapy and supervision. The form and process of isomorphic systems are analogous even though there may be vast differences in the content of the interactions. Thus, the theories of development, dysfunction, health, change, and intervention apply to both therapy and supervision, whereas the specific skills taught in each domain would be quite different. For instance, Haley contends that both therapists and clients learn new behaviors through direction in skill acquisition. However, the specific types of skills that supervisees acquire for conducting therapy may be far different from the clients' skills for resolving personal and relational difficulties. Therefore, the principle of isomorphism relates to the internal validity of different theoretical and supervisory models. An isomorphic model of supervision provides a coherent methodological approach, so that the supervisee does not have to contend with confusing "do as I say, not as I do" messages.

Internal consistency in various therapy and supervision models also contains a fundamental limitation. The uniformity of observations and interventions, by definition, limits the range and scope of therapeutic and supervisory possibilities. The Bowenian supervisor could remain too distant from actively managing the problem, whereas the strategic supervisor might avoid family-of-origin issues that contribute to the supervisee's anxiety and ineffectiveness with similar family patterns. Moreover, the strategic supervisor may lack the benefits of the Bowenian's theoretical sophistication, whereas the Bowenian supervisor may be deficient in the eloquent application of strategic techniques that quickly reorganize a dysfunctioning system. A comprehensive supervisory model that incorporates the virtues of multiple approaches provides an optimal degree of resourcefulness and flexibility in the supervision process. Lebow (1984) aptly summarized the attributes of an integrative model of supervision:

- It arms trainees with a wide array of avenues from which to pursue change in their clients.
- It more easily enables trainees to match intervention strategies with their own individual personalities, resulting in a better practitioner/practice fit.
- It exposes the trainee to many different models of therapy and thus increases the trainee's ability to communicate with therapists of different theoretical orientations.
- It encourages a more open attitude about existing methods of treatment.
- It encourages the formation of a more flexible and knowledgeable therapist.

THE SEARCH FOR A COMPREHENSIVE
MODEL OF SUPERVISION

White and Russell (1995) used a Delphi study to identify the variables that contribute to successful supervisory outcome for marriage and family therapists. These authors felt that the identification of these variables was an initial step toward the formation of a comprehensive model of marriage and family therapy supervision. Such an eclectic model could not only inform the work of a variety of marriage and family therapy supervisors but also add to the generic supervisory models of other approaches, such as the developmental model (Stoltenberg & Delworth, 1987), ecological systems model (Brofenbrenner, 1989), social casework model (Kadushin, 1985), and the previously mentioned isomorphic model (Liddle, 1988).

A relevant model would need a classification general enough to provide an overall taxonomy of requisite therapeutic skills and specific enough to incorporate meaningful contents of particular approaches. White and Russell's study of experts in the marriage and family therapy field elucidated four clusters of important supervisee (and supervisor) variables: personal characteristics, knowledge, attitudes, and skills. In a review article on supervisory contributions to treatment efficacy, psychologists Holloway and Neufeldt (1995) found these related factors to be of utmost importance: good relationship skills, clear and relevant conceptualization, appropriate treatment timing decisions, and skillful interventions in a manner consistent with theoretical orientation. Thus, across the two fields (psychology and marriage and family therapy), there was a good deal of consistency in conceptions of what constitutes effective supervision focus. Both empirically based discussions agreed that a composite of personal, conceptual, intervention, and artistic (attitude and timing) skills were necessary for effective supervisory and therapeutic outcome. Cleghorn and Levin's (1973) often quoted model of perceptual, conceptual, and executive learning objectives for family therapists supports this composite theoretically. Tomm and Wright's (1979) excellent elaboration of Cleghorn and Levin's seminal work clearly correlates with the four previously stated variables. In order to easily make the comparison, Cleghorn and Levin's objectives are **bolded in italics** while the categories of the preceding literature review are (**parenthetically**) **bolded** in Tomm and Wright's comment:

> The **perceptual** aspect refers to the therapist's ability to make pertinent and accurate observations (**artistry**). The **conceptual** aspect refers to the process of attributing meaning to observations or of applying previous learning to the specific therapeutic situation (**conceptual**). . . .
> The executive skills also comprise two components, namely, the therapist's **affective response** (**relational**) and his/her **overt intervention** (**skills**). (pp. 228–229)

In a comprehensive study of beneficial attributes of beginning marriage and family therapists, Figley and Nelson (1989) supported the construct validity of Cleghorn and Levin's perceptual, conceptual, and executive learning objectives. However, they found that different family therapy models resulted in markedly different proportions of focus and skill development in the different objectives (Figley & Nelson, 1990; Nelson & Figley, 1990). Thus, they demonstrated that the different models can be compared along these learning objectives. However, the weight of desirable therapy skills in the various objectives may be discrepant. Therefore, divergent therapy and supervisory models such as those of Friedman and Haley can be compared in an comprehensive model that accommodates discrepant modalities. This adds an external dimension of comparison that complements the internally consistent isomorphic approach.

Finally, Antony Williams's (1995) goal of increasing clinical wisdom in his integrated supervision model likewise involves four comparable domains: *theoretical and technical knowledge, procedural knowledge* (flexibility in applying theory to practical work), *judgment* (self-knowledge, inner sense of ethics), and *perspicacity* (to be intuitive, spontaneous, systemicly understand actions, see through things, see patterns).

In summary, there is an accumulation of theoretical and empirical support for a typology of requisite therapeutic skills in the following areas: ideology, methodology, use of self, and intuition. Supervisors might well consider what they will emphasize within this framework. In addition, such a typology can provide a shorthand language for mapping and comparing requisite skills. Jungian psychotypology provides a quadratic model of psychological functions (thinking, feeling, intuition, and sensation) that correlates with these four areas.

JUNG'S PSYCHOTYPOLOGY

There is a great deal of face validity between the preceding learning objectives and C.G. Jung's (1976) description of psychological functions from his well-known theory of psychological types. Moreover, this theory has been one of the most substantially validated theories of psychological functioning. Psychological types have been the subject of the popular Myers-Briggs Typology Inventory (Myers, 1962), as well as the Gray-Wheelwright Jungian Type Survey (Wheelwright, Wheelwright, & Buehler, 1964). My early work with this theory clearly demonstrated different learning styles, preferences, communication patterns, and stratification of specific capabilities (Haber, 1978a, 1980; Haber & Cooper, 1980). In sum, this schema has proved that there are "different strokes for different folks" and that these differences can inform and complement other theoretical approaches (Haber, 1978b). Furthermore, the Center for Application of Psychological Type, located in Gainesville, Florida, has compiled literally thousands of studies of Jung's theory of psychological types that have explained phenomena as diverse as career preferences, academic success, outcome of counseling, morality, and theoretical preferences of therapists.

Jung's typology was formulated, in part, as a result of the Sigmund

Freud–Alfred Adler schism. Jung, who left Freud's psychoanalytic circle a few years after Adler, was perplexed by the nature and passion of Freud and Adler's disagreement about neurosis. Equally remarkable to Jung was the fact that some of his patients fit the Adlerian social model while other matched the Freudian libidinal model. Therefore, Jung attempted to present a theory of psychology that could include both Freudian and Adlerian viewpoints (Singer, 1973).

Initially, Jung proposed that there were two basic attitudes of behavior: extroversion and introversion. The extrovert naturally seeks means of communication and expression while the introvert gravitates toward self-understanding. The object in the environment largely determines the focus of the extrovert, whereas the subject (one's own being) fundamentally interests the introvert. Therefore, the extrovert more effectively handles the environment, while the introvert excels in self-understanding. Since the extrovert does not process phenomena as deeply as the introvert, the extrovert typically responds more quickly in conversation than the introvert. This may result in the introvert erroneously appearing less interested or intelligent than the extrovert. Jung emphasized in many writings that neither attitude was preferable; in fact, we are a mixture of the two. However, Jung theorized that individuals naturally developed a predominant external or internal orientation.

Jung, realizing that introversion and extroversion did not account for the tremendous variance among individuals with either attitude, spent ten years deciphering these intra-attitudinal differences. He used common terms to distinguish four basic functions of orientation: thinking, feeling, intuition, and sensation. Jung noted that people differed in the way that they perceived and judged experiences. He described sensation and intuition as the irrational, perception functions, and thinking and feeling as the rational, judging functions. Although Jung's terms are pleasingly simple, he did not use them as we might ordinarily. In particular, feeling may be commonly seen as irrational; however, Jung described feeling as a method of coming to terms with the issue of personal value. Therefore, feeling types judge by the personal value of an experience, whereas thinking types judge by objective principles. In contrast, sensation types perceive experience through the physical and practical reality of the senses, while intuitive types perceive the patterns, images, and possibilities of the experience. Jung (1968) briefly characterized the totality of the functions: "Sensation tells us that a thing is; thinking tells us what that thing is; feeling tells us what it is worth to us; and intuition tells us what we can do with it" (p. 14).

Although everyone has the capacity to use all four of the functions, like the extroverted and introverted attitudes, each individual relies on one of the functions more than the others. Jung called this the dominant function.

Myers (1980) compared the dominance of the function to the dominance of left- or right-handedness. The dominant hand gets much more attention and practice than the nondominant hand; thus it develops additional expertise. Nevertheless, the nondominant hand complements the dominant hand by lending additional support. The complementarity breaks down when the two hands do not cooperate or when they fight for dominance. For example, it would be very confusing for a baseball player to not know whether to throw a baseball with the left hand or right hand. Therefore, two hands do not have to be equally strong and dexterous to function adequately; rather, they need to work cooperatively as a balanced and coordinated team. The parts work for the benefit of the whole. Similarly, the dominant function requires auxiliary functions to perform complex tasks. If one of the judgmental functions (thinking or feeling) is dominant, then the auxiliary function would be a perceptive function (sensation or intuition). Successful behavior and understanding require both perception and judgment.

Jung called the least frequently used function as the inferior function. He said that this function existed in the shadow or the unconscious of the personality. The inferior function is diametrically opposite to the dominant function (see figure 4.1). In Jung's dialectical approach the opposite functions (or attitudes) are in a psychic equilibrium. More conscious control of one means less conscious control of the opposite. For instance, a right-handed person will have less conscious control with the nondominant left

Figure 4.1: *The four psychological functions.*

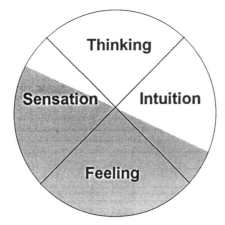

Thinking is the superior function, with intuition as the auxiliary function in this diagram. The shading signified the unconscious aspects of the psychological functions (Jacobi, 1962).

hand than with the more differentiated, right hand. In figure 4.1 the dominant function is thinking; thus, feeling is the inferior and least conscious function.

> As a rule, the inferior function does not possess the qualities of a conscious differentiated function. The conscious, differentiated function is generally directed by intention and the will. If you are a real thinker, you can willfully direct your thinking. Thus, have the capacity to control your thoughts. You are not the slave of your thought. . . . The inferior function is always associated with an archaic personality in ourselves; in the inferior function we are all primitives. . . . Thus, the dominant thinking type is afraid of being caught by his inferior feeling because he is the helpless victim of his feelings. (Jung, 1968, p. 19)

In figure 4.1 intuition is the predominant auxiliary function, but sensation can also be consciously used. In this case, the thinking person complements reasoning power with intuition and, to a lesser extent, sensation. Intuitive and sensory perceptions help the thinker direct the better developed ability to judge the situation analytically. Otherwise, the thinker would aimlessly think for the sake of thinking without discerning or regarding the environment.

Although each psychological function exists in a dynamic and idiosyncratic equilibrium with the other functions, the following brief summary separately characterizes the qualities of each function in order to differentiate its role in the supervisory process.

Thinking

Thinking types make judgments based on rational logic. Thinkers employ excellent analytical abilities to weigh facts and hunches and predict consequences. They approach information and principles objectively and impartially. They have an easy time grasping abstract theories and enjoy acquiring knowledge. Their linear approach to phenomena helps them see the temporal relationship between the past, present, and future. Thinkers' inferior function is feeling. If completely ignored, feelings may break through unexpectedly. Lacking contact with their feeling side, thinkers may seem cold and impersonal.

Bowen's systems theory reflects an approach of a prototypic thinker. His model has a comprehensive, clear, and thorough logic. The goal of differentiation fosters a familial and therapeutic position that rationally handles emotional and anxious responses to problematic triadic relationships. The Bowenian school looked to facts and theories of natural science to support its principles. Bowen aptly used his thinking as a way of disclosing his own family patterns and required the same of his trainees. He felt that a logical, unemotional approach to the exploration of triangulation and family fusion would provide great safety and efficacy in the personal journey toward increased differentiation.

Feeling

Feeling types make their choices and judgments based on personal values. Rather than looking for the "right" approach, feelers consider human values, motivational issues, harmony, trust, and positive regard. They enjoy pleasing others and likewise are sensitive to their emotional experience. Their sensitivity aids them in understanding and joining with others. They are usually good communicators and have an uncanny ability to set the emotional tone in a group. If they have not developed the other functions, feelers can become trapped in their emotions—for example, relentlessly holding grudges. If their thinking is primitive, they may be prone to a lack of cognitive control, even to the point of obsessive thinking. Undeveloped thinking in feelers may also lead to the impression that they are flighty, disorganized, and lack strong convictions.

Virginia Satir exemplified the feeling type. Her approach deftly used congruent communication and developed self-esteem. No one was a stranger to her for long, as she quickly and deeply developed relationships, even in chance encounters. Her charismatic ability to generate enthusiasm was evident in her public and professional presentations. Although she was a brilliant lecturer, she preferred to teach through human contact. Her approach to training was through the "person of the therapist." Not only did she experientially work with the multigenerational stories of her trainees, but she frequently remembered their personal issues and inquired about how they were managing their lives. Her ardent desire to make a personal humanistic impact in the world was more important to her than mapping time for professional publication. She preferred to disseminate her ideas through workshops, "process communities," or the Avanta Network, the training organization that she founded.

Intuition

Intuitives perceive data like artists. They tend to be imaginative, nonconformist, and holistic in their orientation. They have a keen ability to see patterns and the relationships between events and their rich internal world. In this sense, they have an intuitive ability to see the Gestalt, the holistic, the big picture that extends beyond what is actually presented and experienced. Intuitives have an acute capacity to see the possibilities in a situation. From a temporal point of view, they can envision the future better than the other types. For instance, looking at a tree, they would notice how the tree fits in the environment or perhaps imagine how the tree could be transformed into a tree house. They trust their unconscious ability to make sense of a situation and tend to be very spontaneous. In the work situation, intuitives prefer the novel and abhor the routine aspects of a job. "The sensation person depends on *perspiration* where the intuitive person is more likely to depend on *inspiration*" (Kiersy & Bates, 1984, p. 19).

If intuitives do not have adequately developed sensation functions, they may be prone to impracticality and impatience with finishing projects. They can be very unreliable and irresponsible. Extremely one-dimensional intuitives may be insensitive to their physical limitations as well as the restraints of the outer world and fall prey to self-denial, disassociation, and delusion. In these extreme cases, they rigidly adhere to their fantasies in the face of contrary realities.

Carl Whitaker was an intuitive type. His credo of "process not progress" emphasized his trust of his primary process as opposed to goal-directed, rational thinking. His fascination with schizophrenia was partly due to his love of his own imagination; however, he frequently acknowledged that he was "smart crazy"—able to use his intuitive hunches in his work. His phrase "I had this crazy idea . . . " aptly demonstrates how he integrated his imagination into his work. He also fostered play in his therapy with both children and adults. He felt that playing with children early in his career taught him much more about therapeutic practice than traditional professional training. Toys and metaphors helped him learn how to work indirectly with process rather than concretely and directly with the problem. Although he used techniques throughout his life, it was not until late in his life that he was able to methodologically describe his symbolic-experiential approach.

Sensation

Sensing types perceive data by way of their senses. They see things as they are, closely observing facts, details, and beauty. Their reality orientation enables them to be very practical and dependable. They like techniques and proven approaches that they can apply in a trade. They much prefer the concrete to the abstract. They can handle meticulous detail, patiently remain with a task until its completion, and adeptly meet the demands of the milieu. Although they use past experience as a guide for attending to the environment, they are most responsive to the temporal reality of the present. If there is a problem, sensing types will attempt to solve the problem as it exists in the present, paying less attention to the inconspicuous past or future aspects. Their nuts and bolts approach to life lends itself to an uncomplicated, conventional outlook.

If sensing types do not have the ability to use their intuition, they may become immobilized in concrete reality. Von Franz (1971) said of these unidimensional sensors, "The future does not exist, they are in the here and now and there is an iron curtain before them. They behave in life as though it will always be the same as it is now; they are incapable of conceiving that things may change" (p. 28).

Although Jay Haley has traditionally been a theoretical iconoclast, his strategic approach reflects a sensing approach to therapy. His brand of directive therapy works from a present-centered, problem-focused orientation. Haley endorses a parsimonious approach to therapy; he does not attempt to overhaul the motor when a simple adjustment to the carburetor will suffice in getting the car back on the road. His goal as a supervisor is to help the supervisee devise appropriate techniques that will resolve the problem. Haley's background in Ericksonian hypnosis helped him learn direct as well as indirect techniques to manipulate the individual and/or the environment to promote change. Haley has developed his therapeutic model from his position as supervisor rather than the position as a therapist. Perhaps this is because the one-way mirror offers an ideal situation for using his observational, tracking, and directive abilities, rather than spontaneously responding to the therapeutic process. Although strategic therapy correlates with a sensing approach, I imagine that Haley himself is a thinking type with excellently developed sensing and intuitive functions. His directive, practical therapeutic approach reflects his conviction that therapy models should exist for the average therapist rather than for the extremely astute or creative. His ideological clarity helped him develop such an approach. Haley has been criticized by feminists for developing a hierarchical, directive approach rather than a collaborative, relational approach that is more compatible with female development. Perhaps this difference could be partially explained by Haley's preference for thinking over feeling.

The Jungian typology of psychological functions is a map that provides useful information about perception and adaptation to the environment. This map was never intended to be a discrete marker of native abilities; rather, it fosters a language to understand and categorize ambiguous behaviors. As seen in the case of Jay Haley, it is necessary to look at the specific constellation of the four functions rather than merely discerning the impact of the dominant and inferior functions. Jung (1976) forewarned his readers to consider psychological type tentatively.

Although there are doubtless individuals whose type can be recognized at first glance, this is by no means always the case. As a rule, only careful observation and the weighing of the evidence permit a sure classification. . . . Hence one can never give a description of a type, no matter how complete, that would apply to more than one individual, despite the fact that in some ways it aptly characterizes thousands of others. Conformity is one side of man, uniqueness is the other. Nevertheless, an understanding of psychological type opens the way to a better understanding of human psychology in general. (p. 516)

JUNG'S PSYCHOTYPOLOGY AND SUPERVISION

This chapter began with the premise that the supervision of psychological skills categorically falls into four basic areas: ideology, use of self, methodology, and intuition. The description of the Jungian psychotypology illustrated construct and face validity with these basic dimensions of supervision. The significant research on the Jungian typology demonstrates the relevance of psychological functions in many areas. However, one does not have to be well-versed in Jungian typology to utilize a supervisory map of these four areas. The commonsensical application of these dimensions can readily organize short- and long-term supervisory goals. These dimensions give the supervisor a map to assess the competencies of the supervisee in each of the areas.

Although particular theories and methodologies emphasize certain functions more than others, each domain carries a specific relevance. Therapy involves a combination of process (intuition and sensation): the **inspired**, *could be*, and the **pragmatic**, *how to*, as well as a composite of comprehension (thinking and feeling): the **conceptual**, *why*, and the **personal**, *I*.

Figure 4.2 illustrates the interface between the Jungian psychological functions and the supervisory dimensions. The gestalt of this map may be most easily grasped by the body metaphors of each dimension:

- Ideology (thinking) = head
- Use of self (feeling) = heart
- Methodology (sensation) = hands
- Intuition (intuition) = nose

The supervisor must realize his or her personal preference for using the head, heart, hands, or nose when conducting therapy and supervision. Additionally, the supervisor must assess the supervisee's ability to use the four body parts. If the supervisee is a "head" person, then it may be too drastic initially to get the supervisee to work with the heart. Perhaps such a supervisee would need to know *why* he or she should use the heart and how to use "the hands" (practice making self-disclosures) to get closer to the

Figure 4.2: *Supervisory dimensions*

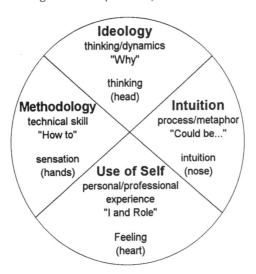

heart. Furthermore, the supervisor must assess the body parts that are emphasized in the supervisee's therapeutic modality. A Rogerian therapist will work predominantly with the heart to establish an empathic, therapeutic relationship. However, such a therapist may have conceptual difficulty with strategically directing the therapy (although Haley, 1976, has aptly described that even a Rogerian, "non-directive" therapist actually directs the therapeutic encounter through selective monitoring and reflection of only a minutia of the clients' verbal and nonverbal communications). Finally, besides juxtaposing the preferences of the supervisor, supervisee, and theoretical orientation, we must factor the preference of the clients into the equation. Thus, if when a family enters therapy one member is suicidal, the family may prefer to connect with the therapist's heart and hand before the head. On the other hand, if a family and therapist are deadlocked, they may be most receptive to following the nose in a new direction. Careful consideration of the head, heart, hands, and nose imbues an integrated approach to therapy and supervision that allows for multiple approaches to clinical and professional development.

Of course, the body parts ideally function as parts of a whole. The nose may warn the head of potential danger so that the head alerts the hands to protect the heart. Or it may alert the therapist to a client's fantasy or smell an association between a client and memories of a deceased relative. The head could organize that information by linking it to an analytic theory of countertransference or a transgenerational, systems approach. If the head feels the information could be useful to the clients, the head could send messages to the hands (and mouth) to share the disclosure. The heart could assist this process by letting the hands know the extent of the disclosure that the therapist can emotionally handle. Like our physical bodies, most of the functions of the body parts occur automatically. However, beginning therapists may need to focus on one body part at a time, so that they can selectively master its tasks before integrating it in the entire organism. Due to the dominant and inferior functions of psychological type, certain body parts will be more quickly and fully developed than others.

Ideology (Head)

Academia prepares emerging clinicians through instruction in theory, techniques, assessment, human and family development, ethics, diversity issues, and many other subjects that develop thinking about clinical issues. However, once clinicians begin their work, theory frequently falls to the wayside in favor of "seat of the pants" approaches. That is, beginning therapists conduct sessions without an epistemological frame of reference while they search for techniques or advice that will calm clients' (and their own) anxiety. This approach is natural for people who are jumping into cold water. The rationale for the proper form and execution of swimming strokes carries less weight than basic survival. Primitive feelings frequently result in bypassing the logic of the head in favor of panicky thrusting of the hands in a frantic attempt to remain afloat. In such situations, supervisors may be wise to give hands-on help. Once novice clinicians get used to cold water, they are ready to rationally understand and describe their experience. Theory then becomes a useful map.

In addition, theory is a shorthand language for the consideration and comparison of human nature according to models. Theory does not have to be gospel, but it does need to be informative. For instance, Jung's psychological functions could explain behavioral choices. If this theory fits the clinical territory, then there is a coherent direction. However, if the territory differs from the theory, then the map needs to be redefined in order to accommodate exceptions to the theory. Therapists who become wedded to theory can become extremely rigid and myopic. The other extreme, novice clinicians traveling without a map, is equally dangerous. Sometimes I sit behind a one-way mirror and wonder what books my supervisees have read that inform their therapeutic behaviors. A good task for a supervisor is to guess the theory from observing the interview rather than hearing the supervisee's description of the interview. With novice and intermediate therapists, what they say they do and what they actually do may not match.

One of my goals in supervision is to promote flexible coherency between the head and the hands.

In this vein, Liddle (1982) advocated that trainees compose an epistemological declaration of their theoretical position along dimensions such as life cycle development, health, illness, change, role of the therapist, and identification with specific theories and therapeutic modalities. This declaration defining the trainee's position can be referenced during the clinical work. Liddle argued that too many clinicians hide behind the cloak of eclecticism to escape the rigors of self-definition; they indiscriminately borrow pieces from different approaches without considering an integrated view of the whole. The epistemological declaration fosters the promotion of an integrated eclecticism.

My professional genogram in the first chapter illustrated the roots that helped to form a systemic-experiential integrated position. However, this position entailed a 20-year journey. Initially, I relied on a Gestalt perspective as a home base of operations. At that stage, I was usually able to define a clinical problem and a path of interventions from a Gestalt perspective. I would ask myself: "What would Mel Foulds do or what does Fritz Perls have to say about this circumstance?" My mentor and his reading list served to inject a clear consultant in my head. I agree with Perls' (Perls, Hefferline, & Goodman, 1951) assumption that it is better to read one book five times than it is to read five different books. Similarly, I prefer novice therapists who work from a single approach over ones who shuttle between different ideas. When intermediate therapists have assimilated a theoretical base of operations, then I encourage them to add and integrate complementary perspectives.

My head has also gotten in the way of my work. At times I have excessively relied on my thinking to understand and correct irrational processes. Whitaker often mused about the irrationality and craziness of considering life's problems from a rational and orderly perspective. While he (1976) favored a discriminating application of the personal instincts of the professional, he cautioned that theory can actually be a hindrance in clinical work. Furthermore, he had an ambivalent relationship with therapeutic techniques, as evidenced by his frequent comment that "techniques are something to do until the real therapy happens." His phenomenological position challenged the assumption that the head alone can figure a way out of an impasse. My attempt to think my way through dynamics and intervention strategies all too frequently resulted in my becoming distant from the clients' and my experience. Although I do not adopt Whitaker's extreme atheoretical position, the head must live in configuration with the other parts to effectively function. Thus, I still use my head to generate hypothetical constructs that organize my thoughts in the clinical context, but I am more quickly responsive to my phenomenological experiences and clients' reactions to my ideas.

Methodology (Hands)

Whereas the head judges information based on facts and theories and the heart by values, experiences, and relationships, the hands pragmatically work with information to facilitate goal attainment. The hands apply their guile to benignly manipulate the circumstances that maintain impasses. The hands do not ask, "Why?" or, "How am I?" Rather, the hands concretely respond to "what to do" and "how to do it." When a computer, car, or sinuses fail to function properly, ideology and feelings become less important than the agility of hands that can correct such problems. Of course, agile hands also need to incorporate knowledge and relational abilities in order to effectively complete their tasks. Nevertheless, deft hands quickly receive recognition for their expertise because they can adroitly maneuver in territory foreign to the average person. Although the process of fixing cars and computers is a learnable skill, workers who have developed these vital techniques and skills seem like magicians to those who have not acquired such talents. Similarly, many therapists take their psychological and relational skills for granted even though clients pay good money to benefit from professional knowledge, relational abilities, and transformation skills.

In the desire to help distressed clientele, the hands eagerly aspire to learn scientifically proven methods that will improve their efficacy. The behavioral psychology movement evolved as a science-based method to augment the idiosyncrasies of analytic and experiential approaches. Many successive approaches to behavior modification — such as biofeedback, hypnotherapy, strategic therapy, neurolinguistic programming, and solution-oriented approaches — focus on specific skills and techniques for various problems. In this day and age of managed care, the medical approach of insurance companies demands that therapists practice psychotherapy with clear methodologies and outcomes for diagnostically prescribed symptoms. If psychotherapy is a combination of art and science, the science part is now receiving widespread support. For example, insurance companies covet standardized treatment protocols that can treat complex problems such as alcoholism, phobias, and depression in a preset amount of time. Therefore, quick hands are being rewarded with increased managed care contracts and referrals.

However, brief approaches do not have the corner on techniques. All therapy approaches employ techniques. It is impossible to conduct a therapy session *without* using your hands. Everything that happens from the moment of greeting our clients to the moment of saying good-bye can be considered skills. The issue is not whether to use skills, but how to use them effectively. Even approaches that do not espouse the use of techniques, such as existential, Jungian, and Bowenian approaches, employ an array of techniques that help the therapist conduct the therapy. Even seemingly inconsequential statements, such as "What do you want to do here today?" or a clarification of a response, are techniques.

Expert therapists use techniques spontaneously and adjust techniques to fit particular circumstances. Novice therapists, on the other hand, memorize techniques and apply them indiscriminately even in situations that do not call for such tools. For example, a novice therapist might initiate an empty chair dialogue with an unwilling client. A therapeutic impasse could ensue if the novice therapist were to persist with that technique. The reluctant empty chair enactor could then be seen by the therapist as resistant. In such common scenarios, clients are asked to fit the therapist's techniques, when the therapist lacks methods to fit the clients. The other side of rote and indiscriminate application of techniques is avoidance or refusal to provide expert guidance in dire clinical circumstances. The issue is not whether we provide help, but how we do it. Techniques do not mean that we have to advise our clients how to live their lives. But techniques can help clients experience and think about their lives with a fuller range of options. Thus, novice therapists need to learn contextual methods for the clever and relevant use of their hands. Not only do they need to know the rudimentary skills to drive, but they also need to know how to read traffic and weather conditions in order to proceed safely.

According to the literature on supervisee satisfaction, supervisees want supervisors who will guide them in the development of clinical expertise. Trainees want their supervisors to be expert and supportive (Allen, Szollos, & Williams, 1986), directive and advising (Rabinowitz, Heppner, & Roehlke, 1986), supportive and appropriately confrontational (Kennard, Stewart, & Gluck, 1987), instructive (Guest & Beutler, 1988), and helpful in dealing with clinical impasses (Liddle, Davidson, & Barrett, 1988). Williams (1995) summed up the need for adroit, supportive guidance in a supervisory relationship: "Perhaps there is no need for further studies to feel safe in the conviction that trainees appreciate being guided by someone with clinical expertise and being supported by that same person as they take their first professional steps" (p. 37).

There is little consensus as to the techniques and skills necessary to practice the craft of psychotherapy. The advantage of operationalizing desirable techniques and skills is that it forces the supervisor and supervisee to hammer out their divergent theoretical and methodological perspectives and to forge shared goals for supervision. This ensures a more ethical relationship for the supervisee because the supervisory expectations are clear. In addition, if the supervisor needs to evaluate the supervisee, then articulated learning objectives provide for a more defensible and fair evaluation. Even if the supervisee does not need to face formal evaluation, goals and objectives give focus and direction to the supervisory relationship. The supervisor can use the goals as the focal point in the triadic relationship between supervisor, supervisee, and the supervision process.

Many approaches agree that the therapist's functions organize into four phases: engagement, problem identification, change facilitation, and termination (e.g., see Tomm & Wright, 1979). The specific skills for each phase depend upon the particular school of therapy. For instance, Whitaker (1989) has often discussed the importance of the political process of establishing the "blind date" that begins the engagement stage of therapy. Other approaches begin the engagement phase differently. For instance, Haley (1976) emphasized the importance of clearly defining the problem in the beginning interviews; the Milan school advocates circular questions to introduce and reformulate hypotheses that can elicit new information and relational differences; a Rogerian, client-centered approach begins by establishing a therapy relationship through the communication of unconditional positive regard, warmth, understanding, and congruence; a Gestalt approach begins by directing attention to awareness of present experience; Andolfi begins by "marrying" the symptom or problem in order to reach existential dilemmas in the trigenerational family, etc. Each approach calls for different methodological skills in the engagement phase of therapy. The supervisor's method of expanding the dexterity and flexibility of the supervisee's hands varies according to the supervisory model. The supervisor's hands could guide the supervisee's hands via education, personal facilitation, consultation, direction, provocation, support, or symbolic exploration.

Minuchin and Fishman (1981) describe the method of training spontaneous therapists through the story of the training of the Samurai warrior. For a Samurai, the sword has to become a continuation of the arm in order to ensure survival. Therefore, the Samurai student has to undergo three to five years of instruction and dedicated practice to learn the craft of swordsmanship. After becoming a master artisan, the Samurai student is required to abandon the craft of fighting while pursuing expertise in an unrelated area, such as calligraphy or painting. Only after the Samurai student has achieved mastery in an unrelated intellectual area can the warrior pick up the sword again. The student becomes a Samurai warrior only after forgetting technique while integrating the application of the sword with the rest of the body.

The valuable lesson of initially learning techniques, rigorously practicing them, and then forgetting them so that one can fully participate in the present context also applies to the craft of tennis. Aspiring young tennis players rigorously practice strokes until they become unconsciously grooved and natural. The instruction and practice enable the player to apply the strokes confidently in match situations. However, grooved strokes do not usually offer enough variety for competition at championship levels. The championship players spontaneously and intuitively adjust to the novel aspects of the opponent, playing conditions, and the patterns of the match. Like the sword of the Samurai warrior, the tennis racket works best as an extension of the entire body.

Use of Self (Heart)

The heart beats with passionate subjectivity, whereas the head thrives in an environment of rational objectivity. Even when the head pretends to be neutral and objective, ideology cannot be separated from personal values and experiences. The language of the heart is both simpler and more complex than the language of the head—simpler because the heart opens tenderly to people who are needy, troubled, and vulnerable; more complex because the heart's nonverbal language combines unnamed, unrecognized, and often conflicting past and present feelings. These feelings need to be harnessed to resonate with the demands of the clinical situation. Therefore, beyond the heart's intuitive abilities to join, be involved, and offer hope in therapeutic relationships, the expanded use of self should be developed after the supervisee has mastered the rudimentary aspects of the head and the hands.

Using the heart does not mean assuming a unidimensional characterological position (no matter how benign) in the therapeutic relationship. Leaning forward in an attentive, listening position could be a useful skill, but empathy that flows from the heart reaches the client more powerfully than sitting on the edge of one's chair. As an empathic parent provides limits for a child, a therapist may express empathy for a client by firmly negotiating the boundaries of the therapeutic relationship. The therapist's heart connection to the client includes the necessary anesthesia and flexibility for dealing with the stressful aspects of the change process. The therapist's heart can be cold, warm, hard, soft, tough, tender, light, heavy, strong, fragile, serious, playful, grievous, joyful, proud, humble, ambivalent, certain, effervescent, sober, distant, close, pessimistic, optimistic, nonchalant, passionate, etc. The bottom line is that the therapist's heart (use of self) should be exercised for the direct benefit of the client. The supervisor should help the supervisee handle, increase, and hone his or her heart impulses for clients' advantage. "If a therapist has an increased range of postures that can be assumed, he or she will have increased the range of interventions possible, and will probably succeed with a broader range of clients" (Mazza, 1988, p. 94).

As the supervisor observes the supervisee over time, certain relational patterns and boundary profiles with different types of clients will become evident. The supervisor could use the recurring patterns as a reminder of the areas that the supervisee needs to expand. For instance, in two consecutive sessions a supervisee commented that he was afraid that his clients would drop out of therapy. This realization inhibited his freedom with these clients. His goal was to get through the hour without upsetting them so that they would come back the next week. If this had been an infrequent clinical position, then it would have made sense to proceed with either the head's view of the dynamics of the case or the hands' ability to handle this case differently. Instead, I wanted to challenge his heart. Since we did not have much time in the presession interview, I asked him succinctly to explain his pessimistic view about his clients' ability and desire to face and overcome their obstacles in therapy. The label *pessimistic* provoked him because it contradicted his theoretical philosophy. With minimal interventions in live supervision, he moved from being passive and protective with his client to becoming much more active and incisive. He was able to challenge one client's rigidity about her relationship with her fiancé. When it became apparent that the client's desperate attempt to enter the world of her fiancé was her method of mitigating the loneliness of her family-of-origin experiences, the supervisee was able to attend to the client's deep pain and isolation. By being less protective, he was able to respond to the emptiness in her heart. A therapist who is afraid of the workings of the heart inherently avoids strong feelings. In this case, the challenge and the support of the supervisor allowed the supervisee to face his client's pain. This resulted in his feeling much more optimistic about the possibilities for change with this client.

If this pattern persists, then it does not make sense to challenge the pessimism of the therapist repeatedly. Such challenges may create a "first-order" change that redirects the behaviors of a therapeutic relationship, but they do not instigate a "second-order" change that affects the underpinnings of the therapist's reflexive position in the formation of therapeutic patterns. The therapist's heart can habitually respond or cope with automatic survival mechanisms learned in the past, most often from family-of-origin experiences. Exploring this territory of the heart involves a detour from the immediacy of the clinical problem. However, this detour could be directly helpful to specific and habitual therapeutic impasses. There has to be a great deal of trust between the supervisor and supervisee for the successful journey through the detour. The supervisor must trust that the supervisee knows the difference between therapy and supervision and that he or she can handle the revelation of personal influences in the clinical impasse. The supervisee must trust the supervisor to work benevolently and professionally at the interface between the personal and the professional. In other words, the supervisee must be somewhat willing for the supervisor to explore the territory of the heart. The supervisee and supervisor must at least implicitly agree to the decision and the range of the detour. Quicker detours are generally better than longer ones because the supervisory relationship does not become lost in the detour. *All detours must begin and end with the professional, not the personal, issue.* Typically, I detour into a personal/professional interface issue only with professionals whom I know fairly well who are at least intermediate in their training and have developed a clear professional identity.

I had been supervising an extremely competent professional for nine months. She had been working with a female graduate student for much of that time. Due to the student's impending graduation, they were dealing with termination issues. My supervisee reported significant frustration with the termination process. She asked for techniques and strategies for a premature termination caused by the external circumstance of her client's graduation rather than the rhythm of a natural termination of the therapeutic relationship. When I asked if this was a *hand* or *heart* problem, she assured me that it was a *hands* problem. Yet, this was belied by the intensity of her voice, which implied that the problem rested in her heart. Techniques and strategies of termination seemed less significant than the emotional process of saying good-bye to her agitated client. Upon my questioning of her position and internal experience in the therapeutic relationship, she admitted that this was a heart problem more than a hands problem.

The detour began when I asked the supervisee to identify a person in her past or present life who could best help her deal with her heart problem with her client. She emphatically chose her mother. The room was configured by the supervisee so that her mother was imagined to be in an empty chair behind her while she faced her client in front of her. She told her mother that she was having trouble being with her client in her pain. My supervisee realized then that her trouble with her client's pain resembled her mother's fear and consequent avoidance of any pain in the family. My supervisee stated that she had often wanted to speak to her mother about her emotional pain, but her mother avoided confronting such feelings. The supervisee believed that her pain reminded her mother of her own pain. Therefore, my supervisee and her mother had developed an unspoken agreement to withhold sharing pain. This made my supervisee feel that her mother was emotionally unavailable to her. The mother, in the consultant role in the empty chair, on the other hand, was there to hear her daughter's pain. This empty chair dialogue fortified my supervisee's resolve to offer her client understanding and tolerance of her pain. The client no longer had to be "fixed," but could be phenomenologically accepted. Follow-up revealed that she felt much more personally present in the termination process, as she was able to say good-bye with great appreciation for the work that she had done in therapy. Paradoxically, as the supervisee faced her reaction to her client's pain, the client's resources became much more evident. She terminated with much more hope for her client's future.

In parallel process, exploration and attention to heart issues in the supervision process foster more congruence in the therapeutic relationship; that is, the detour to the therapist's heart can significantly change the therapist's clinical position. Grasping this fact experientially offers many advantages.

1. It teaches the power of differentiation firsthand, as the supervisee experiences the impact of the differential use of self in a relationship.
2. It demonstrates the use of the self as a reference point in the therapeutic interview.
3. Self-knowledge offers many inroads to relational knowledge, as the therapeutic relationship confirms or runs counter to the client's behavior in other relationships.
4. Exploration of and sensitivity to past experiences and relationships foster a process of internal consultation that guides the therapist in the clinical interview.
5. Use of self can model congruence, vulnerability, courage, and ability to change.
6. Conscious, differential use of self in the therapeutic relationship bridges the gap between therapist and clients in a way that promotes response-ability and thus engenders a deeper bilateral emotional commitment (Haber, 1990a, 1994a, 1994b).

Intuition (Nose)

"Intuition is when you know something, but, like, where did it come from?" (a 15-year old girl's definition of intuition in Goldberg, 1983, p. 31). The working of the nose presents a paradoxical dilemma for supervisors. Although vital for the maturation of a creative therapist, the nose does not learn by rational and formal discourse or training. *The nose knows.* Therefore, the supervisor has to awaken a primary process indirectly rather than through a direct, linear, cause-and-effect process. Even though the supervisor can ask a supervisee to stop on the road and smell basil leaves, the supervisee has to allow the smell to permeate the membranes of the nose. This is particularly true of less obvious smells, such as a subtle, distant change in the weather. The supervisor can raise awareness, but the supervisee must make the leap out of the clarity of the brain and into the obscurity of the nose. Therefore, many people have less developed access to their noses (and their hearts) than to their heads or the hands.

Societal adaptation to the production and information ages has required the head's cognitive skills and the hands' obedient mechanistic skills for survival. In more primitive cultures, noses were well-developed and invaluable as they warned of danger, helped hunt for food, and connected with the spiritual essence as symbolized by the breadth of life. Civilization, with its machines and electricity, has routinized life in a way that was unknown to cultures that followed the natural rhythms of the environment. Although the analysis of the scientific method has provided the world with many treasures, the price of advanced civilization has been very dear to the ecology, family, and the psyche. The quest for information and materialism has widened the distance from the primary process of human nature. Intuition, symbols, dreams, nonverbal messages, metaphors, and other right-brain processes provide a bridge to the power and wisdom of the primordial world. This pathway can guide humans in the world today (Haber, in press b).

The above paragraph should not be inferred as a call to go back to the good old days. To the contrary, intuition can help inform hypothesis-building, research, analysis, and production. Modern brain research on the distinct and conjoint properties of the left and right hemispheres has concluded that both linguistic analysis and intuitive, creative synthesis require the collaboration of the hemispheres for optimal results (Boss, 1987). Therefore, the relevance of rationality and irrationality is a *both/and* prospect, not an *either/or*. However, scientific analysis and intuition are balanced in the same way, partly because of the heavy emphasis on linear, cause-and-effect explanations by social, educational, and religious systems. Not too long ago, irrational and intuitive approaches were held with such suspicion, contempt, and fear that our civilization publicly burned witches and mystics at the stake in order to preserve the accepted logical order. Although witches are no longer burned, present society still holds intuition and non-logical processes suspect. Incremental graduate degrees and dedication to the study of science unfortunately correlate with increased distance from the amorphous creativity of unconscious processes.

"If we issue an open invitation and make intuition feel that visits are welcomed at any time, it can become a perfect guest, showing up on all the right occasions, dressed properly, and bearing felicitous gifts" (Goldberg, 1983, p. 155). The weaving of intuitive processes into the fabric of supervision and therapy initially necessitates that supervisors assess their personal relationship with intuition, the unconscious, and other illogical approaches. Whitaker exemplified the ability to teach and consult through the use of his whole person. His humor, puns, metaphors, stories, and "crazy" intuitive fantasies were his pathway into his "I" position. His dedication to his "I" position has helped students and consultees feel more free to find their unique "I" positions long after the workshop or the interview ended. His love of his right brain was contagious. However, it would be a mistake for the inexperienced therapist to allow intuition to ride unbridled in clinical interviews. Whitaker was able to take a strong "I" position because of his clarity of his role on stage or in the consulting office. The dialectic of the craziness of his "I" position and his professional role provided a fulcrum that fostered extreme creativity in a purposeful context. (For an excellent elaboration of intuition from a symbolic-experiential perspective, see Keith, 1987.)

Whitaker's genius, uniqueness, and 50 years of experience enabled him to feel safe with his craziness. Beginning therapists need to develop a relationship with the many facets of the nose before they excessively rely on it in clinical interviews. Supervision provides a perfect context to enhance and assimilate the information from the nose. The inexperienced therapist needs to sort out his countertransference from his intuition so that his right brain responses benefit the clients. Intuitive experiences are the property of the owner. They should not be seen as the truth, or even useful for anybody. Jim Guinan often said that his modus operandi with his intuition was simply to notice it initially, but to give it more credence if the same intuition reoccurred. The beginning therapist has to learn how to honor intuition rather than treat it as dogma by developing a censor for certain unconscious images, developing a sense of timing for employing messages from the nose, responding to the context of the therapeutic alliance, and employing intuition to promote the goals of the therapeutic relationship. Intuition and goals are not antithetical. In fact, the symbols and intuitions of the unconscious frequently mobilize the system toward growth.

A previously mentioned supervisee continued to be pessimistic about his clients' commitment to therapy, which resulted in great fear that they would prematurely terminate from the therapy process. He said that he would feel like a failure and a fraud should this occur. Self-reproach and his foreboding fear of failure generated tremendous internal pressure. He chose two figures from a collection of assorted miniature toys to represent how he coped with his feelings. An oblique mask represented his withdrawal and a slave-master with a whip portrayed the driven to succeed part. After working with family-of-origin antecedents around fear of failure, I asked him about where intuition was in his therapy model. Although he conceptually agreed that intuition should have a role, it seldom appeared in his sessions. He chose figures of a child and a woman to symbolize intuition. These figural representations offered alternatives to being overly driven or withdrawing. I asked him to apply the intuition of the woman and the child in the subsequent interview. He kept the figures on a table as a reminder of his objectives. In previous sessions, despite his negative interpretation of his clients' commitment to therapy, he formed a notably positive working alliance. However, his internal foreboding and self-reproach processes caused him to be quite cautious and constrained in his role as therapist. In the interview that followed the work with his family of origin and the symbolic figures, he used humor and intuitive associations about the leaving home struggles in a family. In the postsession interview he reported that he enjoyed using his intuition, but felt that the session was very choppy and uncoordinated. In fact, it was choppy because he did not follow up on the feelings and concerns that were aroused by his intuitive comments; however, I did not interrupt the session from behind the mirror because the client seemed to be profiting from the interview and I was concerned that my phone call would serve to make the supervisee more doubtful and cautious. He needed space from me as well as self-confidence to learn to use his nose. In the postsession supervision, we explored ways that his intuition could function as a consultant to his therapeutic (head, hands, and heart) role with his clients.

Supervision with more advanced trainees is an appropriate arena in which to harness the immense creativity of intuition. Besides, the nose offers the play and imagination that can offset burnout. Here are some ideas for developing domains of the nose.

- *Cotherapy.* The benefit of having two professionals working side by side is that one can mind the shop while the other has more free reign with unconscious processes.
- *Children.* Since children are naturally intuitive, their inclusion forces the therapy to become less rational and more symbolic.
- *Play.* Similarly, play offers the opportunity for the therapist and clients to become more associative.
- *Associations and fantasies.* If supervisees are asked to share their crazy inner life (whether in live or indirect supervision), they must become more generative and less rational.
- *Metaphorical objects.* Differential use of objects tangibly reminds supervisees to access different parts of themselves.
- *Humor.* Besides providing positive physical and psychological benefits, humor, with all its illogic, offers a different perspective on problems.
- *Role changes.* Asking the supervisee to play a different role (e.g., lead the session from the perspective of a 15-year-old) offers the opportunity to see the clinical relationship differently.

- *Quiet withdrawal.* Sometimes the nose needs an incubation period to sniff and ponder the situation. Therefore, teaching supervisees to withdraw helps them develop the necessary time and space to become more inventive.
- *Metaphors.* The figurative language of metaphors allows the therapeutic process to work with the amplification of different themes. The metaphor can control the organization and direction of the session.
- *Body experiences.* Sensitivity to body feeling (e.g., stiffness in the neck) can provide good clues to the supervisee's internal experience.
- *Paradoxical or dialectic thinking.* Seeing the world from the opposite angle enables the supervisee to be less rigidly loyal to a certain position.
- *Art.* Different art forms change the medium of the therapy or supervision and offer the opportunity to join differently as well as enjoy different perspectives.
- *Experiential learning.* The unrehearsed, "no right answer" aspect of experiential exercises opens up uncharted territory.

These methods can work in both the therapeutic and supervisory context. For example, the supervisor could supervise the process of using metaphorical objects in therapy or could include metaphorical objects in the supervision process, as was illustrated in the previous example. Of course, the nose may find other ways to integrate the creativity of irrational approaches into supervision and therapy.

CONCLUSION

This chapter has presented a schema for the consideration of the skills and objectives necessary to both the therapeutic and supervisory process. This chapter did not present an objectified framework because each supervisory relationship requires an idiosyncratic approach that considers the specific talents and limitations of the supervisor and supervisee. However, the schema gives a map to locate the preferences and deficiencies of both the supervisor and supervisee. Such a map can promote the acquisition of an implicit or explicit contract for the long-term and short-term activities and goals in the supervisory relationship.

To tie this in with the professional and client houses that were described in the second chapter, think of the head, heart, hands, and nose differentially operating in the rooms in the different floors of both houses. The supervisor can consider the head, heart, hands, and nose involvement in each of these settings and consider specific interventions that will benefit the supervisee and the clients. For instance, one supervisee may need guidance in methods (hands) for working with young children in the family house, while another may need help in contemplating ideas (head) in the work setting. In addition, the individual differences depicted in the third chapter (developmental, cultural, characterological, and gender) influence the participation of the various body parts in the houses. For instance, it may be too soon for a beginning therapist to adroitly work with the heart and the nose; on the other hand, it may be annoying for an advanced trainee to have the supervisor frequently guide his or her hands. The supervisor and supervisee will have to use the composition of maps in each chapter of this section to increase the flexibility and fit in the supervisory and clinical systems.

Before going on to the next chapter, consider a case that you are supervising or would like to bring to a consultation with a supervisor. Now let the head, heart, hands, and nose staff the case. Listen to their individual descriptions of the therapeutic relationship, the therapeutic dilemma, the solution, the help that each needs to function more adroitly, and any other comments. Now, notice how the various body parts work in unison. Are any of the body parts at war? How could they pool their resources? Review the assets and liabilities of each body part as well as the relationship of the body parts in the present clinical situation. See if you can come up with a plan for how some of the body parts could function differently in the future.

5

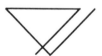

Ethical Supervision

ETHICAL SUPERVISION IS THE ULTIMATE ROAD MAP. The supervisor's ethical actions and responsibilities must consistently consider the best interests (rights and welfare) of the clients and the supervisee within the reasonable context of a professional relationship. The contemplation of ethics helps professionals locate and follow the moral pathway at the fork on the road. Lacking an ethical road map, professionals might make ill-considered or self-aggrandizing choices that would result in clients' and supervisees' suffering the consequences of mistrust and betrayal.

Supervisors and therapists must learn how to handle the responsibility of hierarchical relationships. The vulnerability of emotional and professional dependence creates an environment where abuses of exploitation, malevolence, and neglect can occur. The ethical codes of the various psychotherapeutic disciplines stipulate regulations that ensure the clarity and safety of vertical, dependent relationships. Like actual road maps, the ethical codes need to be kept in a convenient place for frequent reference when the route becomes confused or poorly marked. The codes provide an objective reference when intuition is insufficient for deciphering the proper path.

Frequently, situations that confront us in our offices are too obscure to be found in the ethical codes. Sometimes the ethical codes mandate double, conflictual actions, promoting two divergent roads as proper—a "damned if you do, damned if you don't" choice. Supervision provides an ideal context in which to consider the consequences of ethical choices at such forks in the road. Both dramatic and everyday ethical dilemmas should be discussed in the supervisory process, as the supervisor imparts a methodology for moral reasoning. In addition, supervisors must practice what they preach. This chapter considers both the supervisor's assistance with moral decisions and the conduct necessary for an ethical supervisory relationship.

TWO ETHICAL DILEMMAS

To Report or Not to Report?

During an initial meeting of a supervision group, a female group member requested assistance with a decision about whether to file an ethical grievance against a professional who previously had sexual relations with one of her clients while he was her therapist and minister. This triple (minister/therapist/lover) relationship existed for several years until the client discovered that the minister was having a sexual relationship with another parishioner. Prior to the group supervision meeting, the supervisee met with the client and her former therapist/minister. She reported that he was defensive and not very remorseful about the sexual exploitation. His cavalier attitude angered and worried the supervisee because she felt that he had no intention of changing his unethical behavior. Nevertheless, the client did not want the sexual exploitation by her therapist/minister to be reported to any licensing boards or professional associations, even though she knew he continued to take sexual advantage of other female clients and parishioners. The supervisee, who was incensed by the therapist/minister's unethical and abusive behavior, wanted to know whether she was bound to report the illicit sexual relationship despite her client's objections. Incidentally, the supervisee mentioned (without provocation or question) that her history of molestation, harassment, and a rape heightened her sensitivity to the effects of sexual abuse. What should be the supervisor's position with her dilemma? (The ethical deliberation of this case appears later in this chapter.)

What Should the Therapeutic Contract Be?

A male client requested therapeutic services at a university counseling center after a physical altercation with his wife while he was under the influence of alcohol. Since the university police responded to the physical altercation, the wife got a restraining order on her husband and the university discipline office intervened by evicting him from university housing. The discipline office referred the husband for individual therapy to deal with his recent suicidal ideation and drinking problems. The client's motivation to come to counseling was clearly to resume living with his wife and child. The supervisee, on advice of the supervisor, requested that the wife and a representative from the discipline office participate in a conjoint session with the client in order to clarify the boundaries and objectives of their relationship. The wife was adamant about her decision to file for divorce. She reported that her husband shook her in a way that made her fear for her life. She said that this fight was not the first one, but it would be the last time that she would allow herself to be physically intimidated. The university official firmly stated that the husband could not make any physical or phone contact with his wife for several months. The husband and wife mutually agreed on a plan for husband-son visitation.

Two weeks later, the wife changed her mind and requested that the university officials allow her husband to move back into the apartment. The student discipline office agreed to her request with the proviso that the couple regularly attend marital therapy. Should the wife be advised to participate in individual therapy sessions as well as marital therapy? Should the therapist only see the wife in individual therapy so that she could discuss her concerns without processing them with her husband? Should the husband be required to attend alcohol treatment and a support group for physically violent men? Should the therapist refuse treatment because the counseling center is ill-equipped to handle the diverse therapeutic needs of the couple? As the supervisor, how would you attempt to organize this case with the supervisee?

The ethical questions raised by these two cases are discussed below using Kitchener's model of ethical justification. However, the contemplation of professional ethics needs to extend far beyond the association with the dramatic issues of child abuse, battering, duty to warn, and exploitation of clients. The dramatic dilemmas captivate our interest because of their association with legal actions. Many therapists' version of ethics is to protect themselves by staying out of court. Case notes are written for a fictitious lawyer, judge, or jury rather than to inform the therapist or other service providers about the unabridged process of the therapy. Since the United States is a highly litigious society, fictitious lawyers can become an all-too-real presence. The expanded range of legal suits against therapists is reflected in the rapid escalation of professional liability rates. Thus, adherence to a professional code of ethics is self-protective. Supervisors need to enhance their supervisees' view of ethics beyond the drama of the courtroom and into the contemplation of everyday practice.

EVERYDAY ETHICAL DILEMMAS

A wife comes to an individual session and tells the therapist about an affair that she is having in a different city. She is convinced that the marital problem is completely her fault. She wants to deal with her intimacy and sexual problems without her husband attending any therapy sessions. What should the therapist do? What should the therapist do if the wife agrees to bring in her husband?

A family comes to therapy because of a 15-year-old's predelinquent activity. The mother is concerned about her daughter's choice of friends. However, the therapist notices that the 6-year-old son looks very depressed as he plays alone in the therapist's office. He is ignored during most of the hour. His mother seems to prefer her daughter, and his father, a traveling salesman, is distant in the interview. Should the therapist proceed with the mother's presenting problem or introduce concern for the welfare of her son?

A female homemaker has minimal power in the family. She has virtually no choices regarding the expenditure of money as well as most major decisions other than child care. The husband talks disdainfully to her. He frequently reminds her that he is the breadwinner and so she'd better do his bidding. She seems very passive-aggressive in her approach to his belittling remarks. Should the therapist introduce the issue of money or is it a private matter that should be determined by their values? Will the therapist's gender values disrupt the stability of their marriage?

During an intake session, the therapist discovers that the family recently ended a one-year therapy relationship with another therapist without terminating the therapeutic relationship. What should the therapist do about the previous therapist? Should he call the previous therapist, see the family without contacting the previous therapist, or request that the family appropriately terminate? Will the lack of feedback from the previous therapist hinder the current therapist's work with this case?

A family is going through a messy divorce and the mother (custodial parent) initiates therapy to deal with her eldest son's school problems. The mother refuses to come if her ex-husband comes to the session. The boys miss their father a great deal and he may be able to help with their school problems and other adjustment issues. Should the therapist see the father without the mother? Will this interfere with the therapeutic relationship with the single-parent family? What should the therapist do?

Similar questions confront therapists and supervisors almost every day. The choices about whom to see, what to talk about, whether to form a temporary alliance, when to request additional resources, etc., are decisions based upon theoretical orientation, values, and moral judgment. Often, such decisions are made on the spot with minimal time for contemplation. The supervisory setting, on the other hand, offers another pair of eyes to view common dilemmas. The external position of the supervisor provides a more removed perspective. Combining the supervisee's proximity and the supervisor's distance offers an added dimension in the review of reflexive ethical decisions.

For instance, in a live supervision session, an African American female client said that she was misunderstood by her classmates because of her different socioeconomic background. Although the client was an academically gifted graduate student, she felt impoverished and different. Perhaps in an effort to make the client more comfortable, the Caucasian female therapist avoided discussion of their racial and socioeconomic differences. Although the therapist espoused acceptance of diversity, avoiding race in the therapeutic dialogue created the same problem in therapy as the client experienced in school. That is, the client could not work through her feelings of inadequacy and difference. Upon the suggestion of the supervisor, the supervisee broached the issue of their racial difference The client readily acknowledged that she felt misunderstood. Consequently, she discussed the shame that she experienced in her childhood due to her family's poverty and chaotic structure. The client's riveting and emotional expression of her childhood feelings concomitantly validated the respect and emotional proximity that already existed between therapist and client. The ethical dilemma prior to the supervisee's frank conversation about racial differences was her concern not to affront the boundaries and esteem of her client. The conversation about racial differences, as well as the impoverishment and chaos of the client's background, heightened the client's discomfort. Should the therapist (and supervisor) have risked pushing the client to stretch her boundaries of emotional expression? This decision could have backfired if the client imploded and withdrew as a result of the therapist's candor.

Thus, quite simply, the risk of taking an ideological position regarding the importance of culture (oppression) on the development of the self must be guided by ethical principles that carefully consider the context of the individual, family, community, and culture. In this case, the incremental distance of the supervisor helped the supervisee shift to a proactive position of greater intimacy with less protection. Paradoxically, the ensuing relationship based on difference fostered more intimacy than the former relationship based on protection.

THE DANCE OF VALUES AND ETHICS

Is it ethical to look at someone in the eyes after he or she looks away? Perhaps the cultural or familial values prohibit prolonged eye contact. If a therapist pursues eye contact with a person who prefers to communicate without eyes, then the therapist establishes a relationship that demands client subservience to the therapist's value of eye contact. The client loses autonomy and the comfort of working within a familiar framework. Most supervisors would agree that such a supervisee would be therapeutically inappropriate and perhaps unethically prejudicial in the rigid dedication to the establishment of an eye-dominant environment. The supervisor would be wise to ask the supervisee about the rationale and utility of engaging in a power struggle over the eyes.

Although this example seems a bit far-fetched, ethics and values inevitably bump against one another. The resulting oscillation can instigate change. Ethics (or values) are not static principles. They evolve as the conscience and consciousness of social or professional organizations become alert to incorrect assumptions, unfair judgments, and harmful actions that create problematic circumstances. For instance, homosexuality was formerly considered as a behavioral malady. Therefore, well-intentioned therapists attempted psychological and social interventions to alter the inclination and "aberrant" sexual behaviors of homosexual clients. When the profession no longer considered homosexuality a diagnosable behavioral illness, professional codes of ethics were modified so that individuals of minority sexual orientations would not be subject to unfair, prejudicial, unreasonable, and nonsensical therapeutic interventions. The modification of an ethical principle demonstrates that the punctuation of ethics varies with the consensus of the conscience and consciousness of the profession, which is directed by the culture.

Although there is a great deal of controversy around some ethical principles, the effort to find a consensus for the welfare of the social order is a notable enterprise. Ethical principles are generally safer when discussed in a public forum than secretly followed with idiosyncratic rationalizations behind closed doors. This is not meant to deter contrarian opinions. Otherwise, the sexual preferences of homosexuals would still be under therapeutic pressure to conform to majority sexual practices. Rather, contrary views to ethical codes should be explicated and explored in supervision, collegial consultation, journals, and other professional forums.

> The dialogic process promotes a shared analysis of meanings, actions, existing conditions, and claims to truth and value. Such analysis expands counselor awareness of particular beliefs and values, clarifies contradictions, and helps reconcile the moral issues involved in the practical problems the counselor may face. (Tennyson & Strom, 1986, p. 301)

FEMINIST VALUES IN THERAPY?

An issue that has generated significant contention in the eighties and the nineties involves reckoning feminist values in the therapeutic context. Feminists argue that the prevailing culture favors, benefits, and empowers masculine values. Traditional gender stereotypes have kept women subservient to men. Women earn less money, have less governmental representation, have less career potential, and have greater responsibilities in the family system than men. Luepnitz (1988) traced the inequitable roots of masculine privilege to the historical roles in which women and children have been regarded as the property of their husbands and fathers. Therefore, in the face of a hierarchical marriage, can the therapist promote equity in the marriage by ignoring imbalances and working to resolve problems expediently? If a woman does not have a concern or problem with a lack of economic power or decision making in the family, should the therapist raise this as an issue? When do our values inform the therapeutic process or get in the way of therapy?

Some feminists have maintained an approach-avoidance relationship regarding the issue of the therapist's introduction of values. On one hand, Hare-Mustin (1978) and Margolin (1982) cautioned therapists about imposing their values onto clients. On the other hand, these same authors have advocated the adoption of feminist values in the therapeutic system. Wendorf and Wendorf (1985) noted these feminist therapists' contradiction about the role of values. Furthermore, they emphatically adopted the position of value neutrality. "As therapists, are we employed by clients to help solve their problems or to help liberate them? We believe that we are culturally sanctioned to be healers but not crusaders" (p. 451). Although they did not deliver a satisfactory retort to the argument that value neutrality reinforces the status quo of patriarchal inequity, they raised a basic and vital question about the integrity of the contract between the therapist and clients. As basic as the issue of therapeutic contract seems to be on the surface, it is a rather complex question in the therapy room. The resolution of problems and liberation of people is not an either/or issue. Relational and psychological wounds heal more satisfactorily through the promotion of equality and differentiation than by domination and deference.

The American Psychological Association *Guidelines for Therapy with Women* (1978) reinforce the notion that therapists should adopt positions that promote the rights and welfare of all clients. "The conduct of therapy should be free of constrictions based on gender defined roles, and the options explored between client and practitioner should be free of sex-role stereotypes" (p. 1122). This maxim clearly defines therapists' responsibility to open doors of possibility for both sexes. It should be noted, however, that this principle advocates that gender roles should be free of constrictions. This includes freedom to make choices that differ from the views of the therapist. The supervisor needs to help therapists walk the fine line between promotion of options and promotion of an ideology based on the therapist's value systems.

Problems arise when disadvantaged clients lack the ability to make choices in their best interests. Supervision provides a check and balance system that discerns the clients' ability to make free choices. For instance, "battered wife syndrome" presents an obvious example where the ability to choose is hampered by a life-threatening context. Ethical interventions in therapy with a battered wife should be far different than those with a woman who chooses to follow religious principles that endorse marital inequality. The supervisor needs to scrutinize the gender or other values that inherently direct therapeutic directions and choices. Such vigilance is necessary to prevent terrible injustices that have occurred through the ages in the name of the *correct* belief system. Through Socratic questioning of values by the supervisor, the supervisee can begin to develop an internalized monitor that tracks personal values and consequent professional choices. "The importance of differentiating between values and ethics lies in the following: Values are not always ethical" (Zygmond & Boorhem, 1989, p. 270).

Conflicting Needs of the Individuals in the System

Who is the client? Is the client the individual in the office? Or does the client include individuals in the family or other systems? On one level, this is a theoretical question. Nonetheless, the answer to this question imposes many ethical considerations. If the individual is the sole client, then the therapy would consider the choices that best promote the rights and welfare of the client. If the system is the client unit, then the therapy would consider the systemic impact on the rights and welfare of the relevant members of the system. An obvious example is the issue of child abuse. Laws have mandated that the child is the unit of consideration even though the child may not be in the consulting room. If a therapist learns of possible abuse or neglect from another family member, then the therapist is legally mandated to report suspicions to child protection agencies. What should the therapist do in cases that are not mandated by law?

For instance, if a spouse requests individual therapy to help her deal with the loneliness that she feels in her marriage, then how should the therapist handle the request? Most individual therapists would not hesitate in the formation of a therapeutic relationship that would focus on the best interests of the individual. On the other hand, Whitaker and Miller (1969) raised ethical concerns that individual therapy may increase the likelihood of divorce. This intuitive clinical judgment received empirical support in

Gurman and Kniskern's (1978) review, which cautioned against the deleterious effects of individual therapy on the marital relationship. In this view, the spouse should be literally, or at least figuratively, present in the therapy.

Hare-Mustin (1980) presented a different view of deleterious outcomes in her provocative paper, "Family Therapy May Be Dangerous for Your Health." Hare-Mustin disagreed with routinely involving the entire family in the clinical interview. She was concerned that the interests of power players in the family would be better served than those of less powerful members. The dialectical needs of individual members of a system demonstrates the increased ethical complexity in the therapeutic contract with multiple parties. The therapist must assume a posture and a position (passive, active, neutral, allied, etc.) amidst the conflict within the clients' house. The decisions of where and how to proceed in the house are difficult. Therapists may be confronted with secrets or fabrications in the different rooms of the house. This information could skew the therapist's behaviors, thereby limiting flexibility and ethical fairness to all parties.

Maintaining a dialectical balance between the needs of the individual and the other members in the system requires a fine sense of ethical responsibility. Attention needs to be paid to the unexpressed and often unseen voices in the therapy. The system must be considered when encountering the needs of the individual, and the needs of the individual require attention in the face of the other members of the system. The needs of the individual and the system do not present an inherent contradiction. Evolution requires the development of specific species within the context of the ecology. The individual and the system need to thrive in a process of coevolution. If individuals are exploited in order to maintain the system, then the therapist needs to structure the therapy in ways that protect and enhance the rights and welfare of all members. The flexible consideration of the unit of observation and treatment can offer increased options to our clients.

KITCHENER'S MODEL OF ETHICAL REASONING: META-ETHICS

Karen Kitchener's (1984) landmark paper adapted and expanded Beauchamp and Childress's principles of biomedical ethics to the fields of psychology, counseling, and student affairs (Kitchener, 1985, 1986). In addition, Zygmond and Boorhem (1989) adapted her ethical justification model to the field of family therapy. Kitchener's model has been widely employed because it teaches a method of ethical reasoning that goes far beyond the rationale of professional codes and various theoretical models. (A theoretical exception is Boszormenyi-Nagy and Krasner's [1986] contextual family therapy model, which is based on ethical principles.) In addition, Kitchener's model establishes a meta-ethical model that enables practitioners and supervisors to weigh and evaluate the consequences of clinical decisions. The model does not provide correct answers to ethical dilemmas, but furnishes a process that critically evaluates the complexities of decision making.

Kitchener's model distinguishes two approaches of ethical reasoning: the intuitive level and the critical-evaluative level. The critical-evaluative level subdivides into three ascending levels of distinctions: ethical rules (codes of ethics), ethical principles (autonomy, nonmaleficence, beneficence, fidelity, and justice), and ethical theory (universalizability and balancing). The model of ethical justification begins on the personal, intuitive level and moves up the various distinctions of the critical-evaluative level as increased abstract reasoning is necessary for ethical reasoning (see figure 5.1).

Figure 5.1: *Kitchener's model of ethical justification*

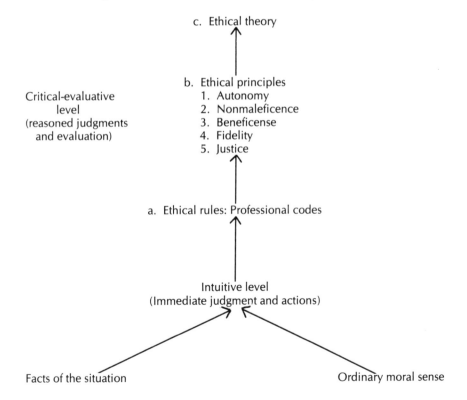

Intuitive Level

The intuitive level of ethical reasoning is an immediate, gut-level, prereflective response to the facts of an ethical situation. It is based on prior ethical knowledge and experiences. For example, lying to a client about a diagnosis or about a conversation with another family member would feel intuitively wrong to most clinicians. On the other hand, embellishing elements of a personal or clinical disclosure that includes useful information may make intuitive sense to some clinicians, while other clinicians may still have ethical objections. When uncertain, clinicians could either reject the embellishment and look for other ways to get their point across or use the critical evaluative levels to examine the consequences of the embellished story. For instance, embellishing a story of survival that parallels the clients' circumstances (Lankton & Lankton, 1983) may have positive consequences.

The intuitive level presents a useful front-line screening for determining ethical decisions. Kitchener (1984) contended that individuals' intuitive moral sense is generally a reliable method for determining moral actions. Professionals intuitively know that receiving expensive gifts from a supervisee muddies the supervisory waters. Most unethical actions happen when professionals bypass their intuition and provide rationales to offset their intuitive misgivings. "This gift is not too elaborate and it will not compromise my evaluative objectivity." However, intuitive moral sense does have its limitations. Complex moral dilemmas may be too novel or difficult to handle intuitively. In addition, supervisors may make mistakes based on their intuition. The gut level belief that a supervisee may be able to handle a difficult case without extensive supervision may result in compromising the client's welfare. Finally, the major difficulty with following one's intuitive, moral sense is that it precludes critical evaluation of ethical reasoning.

Critical-Evaluative Level

This level provides a schema involving three ascending levels of ethical and abstract reasoning. The ethical rules listed in the various professional codes emanate from ethical principles, which in turn emerge from ethical theory.

Ethical Rules

Ethical rules, found in professional codes of ethics, delineate guidelines for appropriate professional moral conduct. Since these guidelines represent the accepted level of professional conduct, they are of crucial importance to the supervisor and the practitioner. The codes cannot provide a guarantee against malpractice claims and judgments, but they can provide answers to moral dilemmas that may be obscure to beginning therapists. For instance, many supervisees do not know whether they can affirmatively respond to a client's request for services while the client is receiving similar services from another professional colleague. Are they obligated to report this information to the colleague or can they proceed with the client's proposal? Most codes agree that the professional should sensitively consider the therapeutic issues of the unique situation and act in the best interests of the client. The welfare of the client preempts collegial obligations.

Problems may arise with the use of professional codes. Although they mandate certain decisions (i.e., do not have sex with clients or supervisees), they do not have answers to all of the "gray" questions (can I invite my supervisee to stay alone with me in my house for the weekend to work on a professional project?). The codes cannot address all of the specific questions that require ethical justification. Usually, regulations represent a conservative interpretation of ethical conduct (Drane, 1982). In addition, since many professionals ascribe to several organizations that have different rules concerning ethical behavior, ethical dilemmas may involve selecting the least bad alternative in cases when regulations conflict. A classic example would entail forsaking confidentiality in order to provide protection against self-inflicted or interpersonal violence. Supervisors need to teach supervisees to understand the ethical principles that provide the foundation for the ethical rules.

Ethical Principles

As previously mentioned, Kitchener adapted Beauchamp and Childress's (1989) five ethical principles for the consideration of therapeutic ethical dilemmas. The principles of autonomy, nonmaleficence, beneficence, fidelity, and justice are fundamentally concerned with the rights and the welfare of the client. Since individual or group values may be bent by unethical, idiosyncratic decisions, these ethical principles should take precedence. If there is a conflict between the principles, then ethical theory is used to weigh the consequences of conflictual ethical principles.

Autonomy affirms the client's right to freedom of choice. The first requisite for autonomy is the client's ability to assume responsibility for his or her actions. (Obviously, in cases where the client is a minor, the guardian has responsibility for some treatment decisions.) Clients have the right to understand treatment approaches and bestow informed consent. For example, clients should approve conditions of therapy, such as working with a trainee who receives supervision or the trainee's videotaping of therapy sessions. The second requisite for autonomy is the willingness to respect other individuals' rights. The famous Tarasoff case clearly illustrates an abuse of autonomy. The boyfriend informed his psychiatrist that he planned to kill his girlfriend, Tatiana Tarasoff. The court of California (Tarasoff v. Regents of the University of California, 1974) found the psychiatrist guilty of professional negligence for neglecting his duty to warn the victim. In essence, the court found that a client loses his autonomy (right of confidentiality) when he threatens the autonomy of another individual.

Nonmaleficence is an old medical concept that protects the physical and psychological welfare of the client. The adage "Above all, do no harm" concisely establishes the doctrine that clients deserve to feel safe when they are in the hands of a clinician. If a supervisee is concerned about the welfare of a client, then a consultation session with the supervisor or other esteemed professional may be the most ethical course of action. Kitchener described the issue of *no harm* as an ambiguous one for therapists, because the therapeutic confrontation of repressed or denied memories is often followed by anxiety and pain. The temporary discomfort within an individual or system may foster a search for new ways to handle problematic circumstances. However, determining when psychological pain is good medicine is very difficult. The aforementioned case of an African American, academically gifted, economically disadvantaged client with a relatively affluent, Caucasian therapist confronted the limits of nonmaleficence when the supervisor asked them to process their racial differences. The directness and persistence of the supervisee helped the client voice her longstanding problem with feelings of inadequacy. Beauchamp and Childress (1989) suggest that, all other things being equal, the avoidance of harming clients is a stronger ethical obligation than the avoidance of benefiting them. In other words, if there is an equal decision between avoiding pain or avoiding gain, avoiding pain takes priority.

Beneficence means contributing to the health and welfare of our clients. Provocative and experiential therapists like Andolfi, Satir, and Whitaker take calculated risks when they feel reasonably sure that the discomfort of the experience will help individuals in the system experience increased choices. Therefore, experiential therapists use their clinical judgment to determine that the *gain* outweighs the *pain*. Similarly, a supervisor might believe that a detour into selected family-of-origin issues may be the most parsimonious intervention for the facilitation of a problematic clinical issue. Although this intervention could bring up painful subjects, the supervisee (according to the aforementioned principle of autonomy) could elect to participate in the family-of-origin detour. Therefore, supervisors and therapists have an ethical responsibility to utilize their clinical wisdom to intervene beneficently with problems rather than merely choosing nonmaleficent inactivity that results in persisting problems for our clients. Rigid and protracted problems often require strong interventions. Beauchamp and Childress (1989) affirm that ethical procedures must find the greatest imbalance of value over harm.

Fidelity involves promoting safety and trust in the therapeutic relationship. This principle requires that professionals maintain promises, respect confidences, act professionally, and remain loyal to the therapeutic contract. In the last section of this chapter, the ingredients of a supervision contract are specified. Explication and adherence to such contracts promote fidelity. Without fidelity, supervisory and therapeutic relationships suffer from mistrust and superficiality.

Justice comprises the concept of fairness and the doctrine of equal treatment. "Individuals must be treated as equals unless their differences justify different types of treatment" (Zygmond & Boorhem, 1989, p. 274). In the context of the family, married partners must be treated as equals, whereas children should be treated as unequals. The parents have the authority to dictate the rules of the home, but they do not have the authority to mistreat the child. The parent is responsible for maltreatment even if the child acts inappropriately. Parent culpability in child abuse has been legally established in all 50 states of the U.S.A. However, laws protecting the physical safety of spouses (a basic right of equality) have been enacted much more slowly and sporadically. The therapist must conduct therapy in a way that promotes the rights and welfare of each member in the system.

The supervisor's goal is to ensure that the therapist provides equal treatment. If the therapist's values or impairment get in the way of just treatment of certain family members, then the supervisor must intervene in order to insure therapeutic justice.

Ethical Theory

Ethical theory provides a framework for critically evaluating ethical decisions when ethical principles are in conflict. It allows clinicians to test the consequences of specific actions from a higher level of cognitive abstraction than ethical principles. Kitchener (1984) described two ethical theories: The first, *universalizability*, asks whether an ethical decision can generalize to all similar situations. Kitchener advised clinicians to place themselves or family members in the circumstance to see if they still agreed on a certain ethical decision. For example, an alcohol and drug counselor was unsure whether to continue treatment services with a client who had several drug-tainted urine screens. Many alcohol and drug agencies have a policy that "using" clients should not receive treatment because the practicing addict lacks the *autonomy* to comply and *benefit* from treatment services. In addition, *justice* is a concern because the client's slippage may corrupt other vulnerable members in the treatment program. However, the principles of *fidelity* and *nonmaleficence* raise concern for the client's well-being after termination of treatment. How should the supervisor respond to the alcohol and drug counselor? Following the concept of universalizability, the counselor may be reluctant to terminate the drug-abusing client. The supervisor may encourage the counselor to look for the least problematic option. For example, procedures could be developed for noncompliant clients. They could be removed from the treatment program yet periodically contacted by the agency. Criteria could be established for allowing them to resume treatment services. The ethical theory of universalizability encourages clinicians to be more flexible and less punitive in making treatment decisions.

Kitchener's second theory for dealing with conflicting ethical principle is called the *balancing principle*. "When . . . supervisees use the balancing principle, they weigh all possible benefits that their clinical decisions may produce against all possible costs. Thus, this procedure yields a clinical decision that produces the least amount of avoidable harm to all individuals involved" (Zygmond & Boorhem, 1989, p. 275). The application of the balancing principle to the aforementioned example represents difficult choices. Neither alternative is a good scenario. Continuing treatment that is not working may contaminate the treatment of compliant clients and discontinuing treatment may increase the desperation of the client. The balancing principle encourages supervisors and therapists to look for novel ways to handle difficult dilemmas. Thus, ethical quandaries instigate greater clinical creativity. In fact, many of the advances in the treatment process, such as sensitive gender considerations, have resulted from challenges to the ethics of accepted methodology.

APPLICATION OF KITCHENER'S MODEL TO OUR
TWO ETHICAL DILEMMAS

Kitchener's model of ethical justification can be applied to sort out the ethical decisions of the two cases presented earlier in the chapter. The first case, *Report or Not to Report?*, brought up the question of whether the supervisee should report a therapist/minister for sexually exploiting her client.

Since the supervisee was a social worker, we reviewed her code of ethics to see if there was a clear answer to her question. The NASW code of ethics unequivocally states, "The social worker should take action through appropriate channels against unethical conduct by any other member of the profession" (p. 9). However, further review of the code revealed, "The social worker's primary responsibility is to clients" (p. 5). Furthermore, the code stated, "The social worker should respect the privacy of clients and hold in confidence all information obtained in the course of professional service" (p. 6). Therefore, the code gives the message to both report and not to report.

The ethical principles of *fidelity* and *autonomy* would be compromised if the confidence were revealed against the client's will. Furthermore, the principle of *nonmaleficence* would dictate that the social worker avoid the risk that the disclosure would impair the therapeutic relationship and cause further psychological guilt and consternation to the client. On the other hand, the therapist may believe that the revelation would serve the client's best interests in the long run (*beneficence*) and provide *justice* because the offending professional had unequal power in the relationship. Therefore, the principles, like the code of ethics, do not indicate a clear-cut answer to the ethical dilemma.

Using the balancing principle of ethical theory, let us weigh the consequences of reporting the sexual exploitation. Fundamentally, the client deserves a therapeutic relationship that protects her rights to autonomy and trust. The previous therapist victimized her by abusing the dependent nature of the therapeutic relationship. The consequences that the client might feel betrayed by another professional weigh more heavily than the potential positive outcomes from the unilateral filing of the ethical grievance. Although the grievance procedure would serve to protect the potential victimization of other clients by the offending professional, the integrity of the client's autonomy and therapist fidelity are more important than pursuing professional justice. Except for legal statutes, the professional's first obligation is to protect the integrity of the privileged, confidential relationship. Therefore, the simple answer to the therapist's question is to defer reporting the ethical violation without the client's permission.

The complex answer concerns the further direction of the therapy. The therapist needs to help the client work through her feelings of victimization. Perhaps then the client will want to file a grievance. However, the client should make the decision on the basis of her values, since she is the one who has to live with the consequences.

The second case, *What Should the Therapeutic Contract Be?*, broached the issue of how to work with individuals in a family who have conflicting needs, plus the husband's difficulties with alcoholism and self-control. Despite the husband's episodic physical aggression and frequent drinking binges, the wife has chosen reconciliation rather than divorce. The issue of how to proceed effectively with their request for reconciliation presents a variety of theoretical and ethical concerns. Many women's shelters would diagnose the problem as "battered-wife syndrome" and question the ability of the wife to make autonomous decisions that are in her best interests. Therefore, most counselors in women's shelters endorse women support groups and/or individual therapy. Many alcohol and drug centers would prescribe alcohol treatment for the husband as a necessary first step. They would consider marital therapy only after a period of sobriety. Many marital and family therapists would work with the couple conjointly to deal with their presenting concerns (reconciliation). Ten clinicians of diverse orientations staffed and debated the issues of this case. The theoretical positions of the feminist, alcohol and drug counselor, and family therapist enabled them all to see different and relevant issues for the treatment of this couple. The staffing resembled the famous story of the three blind men and the elephant. Each blind man had a distinct view of the physical structure of the elephant. As will be shown from the deliberation of the case, the three distinct professional viewpoints converged into a comprehensive and ethical treatment plan.

The ethical codes do not prescribe how to proceed with the case. Since the husband has used his greater physical strength to combat his wife, her vocal equality had been undermined. Due to the wife's loss of personal authority in the violent episodes, her ability to make *autonomous* and *just* decisions was in doubt. In addition, the husband's drinking problem impaired his ability to make *autonomous* decisions. These factors would impel the therapist to take actions that protect both parties so that they can better handle the principles of *autonomy* and *justice*. Since both parties wanted to give the marriage another chance, the choice of refusing marital therapy seems to be antagonistic to the principles of *beneficence* and *fidelity*. However, the principle of *nonmaleficence* raises concern about the marital therapy because there is a possibility that raising conflictual issues in therapy could instigate further violence.

Considering the above deliberation, the supervisor and supervisee agreed to receive the referral from the university discipline office. The university representative stated that participation in marital therapy was necessary for the husband to be allowed back into university housing. However, the supervisor and supervisee felt that marital therapy would not be sufficient. They requested that the discipline office assign, monitor, and enforce the husband's alcohol abuse evaluation and potential treatment. Furthermore, an individual therapist contacted the wife, so that she would have a safe arena to process her fears and receive support for her own voice. The balancing principle helped in constructing these recommendations; we wanted to maximize the benefits of therapy while mitigating the potential for harm.

These cases demonstrate the utility of Kitchener's model in critically evaluating moral decisions. Ethical principles and theory can resolve complex, ethical dilemmas when the use of ethical codes and intuitive judgments fail to provide satisfactory answers. All too frequently, ethics have been used as a haughty maneuver by therapists for self-protection or to one-up professional colleagues. Ethical debate should actually be a humble undertaking by professionals in the quest of the best way to affirm the rights and welfare of our clients.

ETHICAL SUPERVISION BEGINS AT HOME

What we do is more important than what we say. Supervisors can best convey an intrinsic understanding of moral reasoning by modeling ethics in their approach to supervision, therapy, collegial relationships, public welfare, continuing education, and all other professional endeavors. Unfortunately, ethical standards and delineated responsibilities for the practice of supervision remain incomplete (Upchurch, 1985). The following guidelines will identify issues and responsibilities that should be considered in the practice of supervision. In addition, the ingredients of a supervision contract that outlines the responsibilities of the supervisor and supervisee is presented in figure 5.2.

Dual Relationships

The inherent inequity of the roles in supervision creates the possibility for exploitive dual relationships. In order to protect supervisees (as well as clients, employees, and students), most ethical codes warn supervisors (as well as therapists, employers, and teachers) about the perils of dual or multiple relationships. Although most codes admit that some dual relationships are unavoidable, the tone of the codes conveys a vague and ominous warning that these relationships are generally problematic and should be avoided. In most codes, the words dual (or multiple) and exploitive are usually in the same paragraph, often the same sentence. For instance, the AAMFT 1991 code states, "Therapists, therefore, make every effort to avoid dual relationships that could impair professional judgment or increase the risk of exploitation" (p. 3). Many supervisors and therapists respond to the warnings of exploitation, impropriety, or impaired judgment by completely avoiding dual relationships. Ryder and Hepworth (1990) have objected to AAMFT's goal of simplifying relationships through ethical injunctions rather than dealing with the issues of relationship complexity and exploitation. They propose that relational complexity can facilitate understanding and learning. Tomm (1992) has clarified the distinction between exploitive and dual.

> Exploitation and dual relationships are very different phenomena. To exploit is "to use selfishly for one's own ends" (Webster, 1989). In the context of a professional discipline it refers to taking advantage of one's professional relationship to use, or abuse, another person. . . .

Figure 5.2: *Supervision Contract*

Name of supervisor:
Name of supervisee:
Name of the site of supervision:

The following is an agreement between _____ and _____.

A. Service Requirements
  1. Work schedule:
  2. Caseload:
  3. Administrative responsibilities:

B. Supervision Requirements
  1. Time of supervision meetings:
  2. Delimitation of supervisory responsibilities:
  3. Handling of therapeutic emergencies:
  4. Out-of-office client or referral contacts:
  5. Confidentiality:
  6. Preparation for supervision:
  7. Knowledgeable willingness to abide by code of ethics:
  8. Content of supervision (see outline of maps of supervision in previous chapters):
  9. Modalities of supervision (could refer to section II of this book):
 10. Review of progress and evaluation of supervision:
 11. Grievance procedure:
 12. Timely response with supervision documentation and letters of recommendation:

I understand and agree to abide by each of the preceding obligations of the supervision contract.

_____Date_____
(Supervisee)

_____Date_____
(Supervisor)

A dual relationship is one in which there are two (or more) distinct kinds of relationship with the same person. . . . While dual relationships always introduce greater complexity, they are not inherently exploitive. (p. 11)

Supervision, in particular, has substantial relational complexity. The supervisor needs to learn quickly how to engage constructively in multiple relationships. At any moment in the week, my role as a supervisor may involve: intervening in a crisis, working side by side on a committee project, supervising my supervisee's supervision of another therapist, consulting on a case, working as a cotherapist, formally evaluating the progress of the supervisee, teaching or participating in seminars, exploring issues at the professional and personal interface, etc. The diversity of these roles can add to, rather than subtract from, the benefits of the supervisory experience. Supervisors need to learn how to wear and switch different hats according to the circumstances of the required role. For instance, the process of evaluation usually requires a more formal hat, whereas working on a personal/ professional interface issue requires hats that convey exploration and respect. The supervisor also needs to help the supervisee learn how to put on different hats. The supervisee's hats in the roles of a cotherapist, seminar leader, consultee, or case presenter are quite different. Different roles do not signify greater or lesser importance but, rather, different functions.

Nonetheless, the professional organizations' paranoia about dual relationships follows years of court cases that have found therapists and supervisors guilty of unduly using their influence to promote their own interests both sexually and financially. Beginning supervisors need greater role clarity about the boundaries of dual relationships than experienced supervisors who have had many years of developing clear boundaries. If a supervisee comes into a supervisor's office in tears, the experienced supervisor would not send him or her out in order to preserve a clear boundary in the supervision relationship. However, the experienced supervisor would know how to listen to and frame the emotional experience of the supervisee without formulating an ongoing therapeutic relationship.

Confidentiality

In supervision, confidentiality applies to two levels: the supervisee's clients and the supervisee. The confidentiality of the supervisee's clients must be upheld by the same standards as if they were the supervisor's clients. Furthermore, the supervisee's clients should consent to being discussed (videotaped, consulted, or "live" supervised) after having been informed about the identity of the supervisor. The process of receiving informed consent can be cumbersome for supervisees in the beginning of supervision. They may heighten clients' anxiety about the presence of the supervisor with such statements as, "Do you really want my supervisor to come in as a consultant?" Or they can simply present the fact, brief rationale, and advantages of supervision: "I am getting supervision from Dr. Russell Haber to facilitate my work with all of my cases. If I videotape our sessions, they will only be used for the purposes of supervision. I need you to sign this release acknowledging that you have been informed about my supervision. Do you have any questions?" As the supervisee becomes more comfortable with receiving supervision, the description of the process becomes simpler, friendlier, and more hopeful.

Similarly, the supervisor should simply state the limits of confidentiality to the supervisee. Quite often, the supervisor may be required to submit an evaluation of the student's work to a governing body, such as a school or licensing board. In addition, the supervisor may process supervision issues with other staff supervisors. In other situations, clinical supervision may become intertwined with the administrative supervision issues of job appraisal, raises, and assignment of duties and privileges. In any case, the uses of and communication about the process of supervision should be mentioned to the supervisee prior to beginning supervision. *To be forewarned is to be forearmed.* Finally, if the supervision process uncovers any personal issues of the supervisee (such as family-of-origin information), then the disclosure of such personal information should be treated by a different standard of confidentiality than the discussion of clinical skills and progress. Personal information that does not compromise client welfare should not be communicated without the consent of the supervisee. Clarifying issues of confidentiality increases the trust in the supervisory relationship.

Responsibility

The hierarchical nature of the supervisory relationship is never clearer than in cases of malpractice. "The psychotherapy supervisor assumes, in general, clinical responsibility much as if the patient was in his or her personal care" (Slovenko, 1980, p. 462). This is known as the doctrine of vicarious liability. For example, in the previously cited Tarasoff case, the supervisor of the psychiatrist, who maintained confidentiality despite a threat of murder, was also implicated in the finding of negligent failure to warn the prospective victim. The court held the supervisor liable for the improper judgments of the supervisee. Therefore, it behooves the supervisor to:

- carefully interview and select competent supervisees,
- delimit the areas of supervision,
- monitor the entire caseload of the supervisee on the job site,
- maintain a vested interest in the handling of difficult cases,
- be available, or make contingency plans, for emergency issues that arise,
- raise ethical and legal questions quite regularly,
- insure that the supervisee follows administrative office policies such as record keeping, release statements, case management, etc.,
- approve and cosign any communications or reports about clients that go outside the office,

- limit the supervisee's practice and caseload to areas of reasonable competence, and
- solicit additional expertise for clinical or supervisory problems that are intransigent or extend beyond the supervisor's expertise.

Appelbaum and Gutheil (1991) consider the two pillars of malpractice prevention to be *consultation* and *documentation*. Through consultative supervision (discussed in chapter 9), the supervisor can directly assess the clinical severity, appraise the capability of the therapeutic relationship to handle the problem, and intervene as necessary. Typically, consultations would include both the supervisee and the clients; they may also include other ancillary professionals or relevant members of the clients' social network (Haber, 1994d).

Record Keeping

Documentation, the second pillar of malpractice prevention, entails a written or videotaped record of the supervisory process. Although many supervisors maintain comprehensive records in their role as therapists, there is a tendency to keep less vigilant notes in their roles as supervisors. Since supervisors have vicarious liability, disregard of supervisory records is unwise. In addition, records could be useful in monitoring and informing the process and progress of supervision. Therefore, the following information could be considered for inclusion in the supervision records:

- Names of clients discussed
- Concerns of the supervisee
- Summary of supervisory interventions and recommendations (Is the focus on shifting position in the professional or client houses, augmenting one of the supervisory dimensions—ideology, use of self, methodology, or intuition-or managing an ethical issue?)
- Relational and process issues in the supervision relationship
- Future directions for clients' follow-up and/or supervisee development.

Even cursory notes can help contribute to the continuity and focus of supervision. Certainly, records can substantiate the process of evaluation and the handling of clinical or supervisory problems. They also provide running commentary on the supervision contract.

Evaluation

Evaluation is not the favorite topic of many supervisors. Many supervisors, like therapists, practice phenomenological approaches to supervision that unconditionally accept supervisees, promote positive regard, and facilitate professional growth and maturity. The supervisor intervenes in order to enhance awareness, augment skills and understanding, and circumvent clinical obstacles. If the supervisory interventions fail, where should the fault lie? Should the blame rest on the supervisor, supervisee, clients, the intervention, or the definition of the problem? A systemic perspective, which maximizes personal responsibility, would place blame on all of the above. Therefore, the supervisor, supervisee, clients, definition of the problem, and attempted solutions should all be subject to reevaluation. The recursive process of assessment, intervention, and reassessment helps the supervisor reach the bifurcated goals of the clients' and supervisee's development. Evaluation and reevaluation are the highway signs and mile markers on the road maps that indicate the progress of the journey. If the supervisee and clients do not get to their destinations, the supervisory team fails. Since the supervisor is the coach of the team, he or she must take the bulk of the responsibility. Some journeys are smooth and direct while others are rough and full of detours and destination changes.

The supervisor is like a player-coach. As a player, the supervisor is part of the journey. As a coach, the supervisor assumes a meta-position in order to observe and assemble the information needed to evaluate the progress of the journey. The supervisor should review the highway signs and mile markers throughout the journey rather than at the end of the road of supervision. Telling the supervisee that he or she has arrived at the wrong destination at the end of a 3,000 mile journey is not very helpful. Rather, a more effective evaluation is ongoing and recursive. The supervisory system of players, maps, and vehicles periodically needs to check, adjust, and recheck in order to ensure that the journey goes well and remains on course. For instance, a supervisor requested a consultation from me because the supervisee was not completing the requisite paperwork for supervision. The consultation explored the nature of the supervisee's resistance (which included a negative transferential relationship with the supervisor) and the supervisee's recommendations for the modification of the paperwork. Thus, the consultation provided a forum for the supervisor and supervisee to process and evaluate their journey. The consultation helped them make modifications that enabled them reach a mutually acceptable destination.

This example portrays the complexity of the supervisor's dual roles as the player-coach on the supervision team. The supervisor has ultimate authority and responsibility for the team, but also is a member of the team. The project of evaluation should sequentially clarify both the playing and the coaching roles. As the coach, the supervisor needs to give feedback to the supervisee (whether a rookie or seasoned player) about specific areas for modification and practice. In addition, the supervisee should hear details about what he or she does well, very well, and excellently. The identification and reliance on strengths can reinforce the skills and confidence needed to develop potential strengths. The ongoing evaluation process should be challenging; it should provide energy and focus for continued development. Evaluation, like psychological assessment, provides information that helps people consider the preferred path on the journey.

Many instruments have been developed for the formal evaluation of the supervisor and supervisee (see Powell's [1993] appendices for an excellent array of evaluation scales). These scales give a detailed view of the broad functions of the therapist, such as assessment and diagnostic skills, joining and relationship skills, case conceptualization abilities, interventions and techniques, and termination. They generate a great deal of information and provide a document that operationalizes and defines the supervisee's ability. The limitation of such scales is that they extend over an area broader than what could be covered in supervision meetings of one to two hours once a week that extends for brief to moderate periods of time (four to six months). Two-hour meetings for six months multiplies to 48 hours—a limited amount of time considering the wide range of responsibilities covered in supervision.

Selected "maps" from this book that could provide a framework for a personalized evaluation of the supervisee are:

- Position in the family and professional houses
- Individual growth areas (professional development, cultural, gender, and characterological)
- Therapeutic dimensions (ideology, methodology, use of self, and symbolic processes)
- Ethical issues

Although the territories of these maps overlap and provide an abounding amount of information, the supervisor and supervisee can give priority to a manageable number of goals and objectives. The following outline exemplifies objectives from each area. These objectives can drive the supervisory focus for both the weekly and the long-term journeys.

A. Family and professional house
    1. Family house: Include grandparental issues and resources in the definition and resolution of problems.
    2. Professional house: Involve more referral sources in the conceptualization of the problem and goals for therapy.

B. Individual areas
   1. Professional development: Develop strategies to leave cases in the office rather than bringing them home.
   2. Cultural: Use genograms to focus on culture differences in therapy.
   3. Gender: Practice doing some sessions from the opposite gender perspective.
   4. Characterological: Increase awareness of the effect of grandparents on therapeutic style and make necessary changes to increase effectiveness.
C. Supervisory dimensions
   1. Ideology (head): Read a book on aging and contemplate integration of the relevant concepts.
   2. Methodology (hands): Learn techniques to deal with issues about the resolution of death (gravesite work).
   3. Use of self (heart): Find appropriate ways to use disclosure of personal stories.
   4. Intuition (nose): Use metaphors to describe sessions in case notes.
D. Ethics
   1. Discuss dilemmas and the personal positions on the role of caretaking and autonomy for the aged that require familial assistance and the family caretakers.

Such objectives provide a working map in the supervision process. New routes and interesting landmarks will probably appear throughout the journey. It would be a mistake to be loyal to a predetermined trip plan if you discover the Grand Canyon is only ten miles out of the way. Although the supervisor and supervisee should mutually determine new goals, the supervisor has a wider and more experienced perspective. Therefore, the supervisor must be an active participant in the travel discussions from the back seat of the car. Choosing goals and objectives becomes a part of the supervision contract. The clearer the goals, the easier it will be to determine whether the supervisory team can reach the desired destinations.

The problem with the proposed evaluation (and the more general likert evaluation scales) is the lack of an operational definition of inadequate therapeutic behavior. Since the supervisor is responsible for the clinical work of the supervisee, the supervisor must give clear feedback about unacceptable therapeutic behaviors. Moreover, the evaluation process must have a contingency plan for impaired professionals. Suggesting personal therapy is analogous to requiring that an unsafe driver attend safe driving classes in order to preserve the right to have a driving license. Problems with an impaired supervisee require good documentation and discussions with appropriate professionals such as academic liaisons, consultants, or agency personnel.

As part of the evaluation process, the supervisor should be receptive to feedback from supervisees and potential changes. Besides, many supervisees are fantastic teachers. Immersion in a bilateral learning environment is one of the rewards of the supervisory process. For instance, my supervisees are currently helping me with my inept termination process. I am learning to say good-bye without evaluation papers or promises for future reunions. Therefore, challenges of my supervisees provide opportunities for me to expand my professional and personal options. The supervisor's appetite for learning provides a contagious stimulus for the supervisees, and vice versa.

Supervision Contract

The supervision contract enumerates the responsibilities of the supervisor and supervisee. Thus, the contract demystifies the supervision process by explicitly delineating maps, vehicles, and safety regulations. The supervisee should then be clear about obligations and expectations. Although the contract is a bilateral negotiable document, the supervisor may include some items that are nonnegotiable, such as supervision preparation, service requirements at the work site, and types of supervision. Early resolution of these issues provides the best basis for an acceptable contract. If the supervisee does not like the terms of the contract, then he or she could look for a better supervisory fit. For instance, I orally negotiated a supervision contract that included many misunderstandings about my style of supervision. After the supervisee settled into the placement at our agency, she adamantly resisted "live" supervision, ostensibly because of the intrusive nature of that method. I faced the dilemma of working in a manner that was disagreeable to the supervisee or myself. Furthermore, I had concerns about her work and felt that "live" supervision could be useful to her clients. This problem could have been avoided with a signed supervision contract in which the supervisee agreed to live supervision. Refusal to comply with the contract could have resulted in a grievance procedure, a way to intervene in the supervisory impasse.

The supervision contract in figure 5.2 is a significantly modified version of Williams's (1995, p. 24) model contract. As Williams suggests, the contract has "been made virtually 'empty' of content so that [it] might suit your own professional tradition. No doubt you will wish to add or subtract elements" (p. 23). Supervision in the context of private practice is quite different from on-site supervision at an agency. Each territory has a distinct balance between service, supervision, and administrative requirements and responsibilities. Therefore, view this contractual map as an overlay to the personal preferences and demands of your work environment.

Service Requirements

Supervision can be performed as a fee for service arrangement, part of one's job requirements, or part of a training requirement. The responsibilities that come with these three circumstances are quite different. It behooves the supervisor to unambiguously explain the expectations of the supervisee for receiving the service of supervision. The expectations may include receiving an hourly fee or seeing a specific number of clients. In either circumstance, administrative procedures (such as maintaining client records, complying with the administrative regulations of the agency, appropriate identification of credentials, abiding by client eligibility standards, conducting oneself in keeping with the professional style of the agency, etc.) should be defined. It is always better to do this at the beginning of the supervisory relationship rather than after a commitment by the supervisor, supervisee, and agency.

Supervision Requirements

1. *Time of supervision meetings.* A set schedule of supervision provides a structure that promotes accountability and trust in the supervisory relationship. Furthermore, the clarification of supervision hours indicates the possible number of hours for academic, licensure, or certification requirements.

2. *Delimitation of supervisory responsibilities.* Since supervision entails vicarious responsibility, the supervisor should specify the contexts of responsibility. For instance, a supervisor providing a one-hour-per-week meeting in a private practice would not be able to responsibly supervise a 30-hour-per-week caseload at a different setting. In addition, there may be two supervisors for a supervisee at some settings. The obligations of each supervisor should be specified so that the range of each supervisor's responsibility is clear.

3. *Handling of therapeutic emergencies.* Emergencies need to defined (suicidal, physical threat, physical or sexual abuse, drug abuse, etc.) and the policy of the handling of these types of cases specified. The supervisor needs to know about difficult and emergency clients. Furthermore, the supervisor should clarify a back-up procedure in case of unavailability.

4. *Out-of-office client or referral contacts.* The supervisor needs to know when the supervisee's work extends beyond the parameters of the office. In addition, the supervisor should approve and cosign reports and documents about the supervisee's clients.

5. *Confidentiality.* If the supervisor communicates about the supervision

process with agency or academic personnel, then these exceptions to confidentiality should be specified. Furthermore, the range of communication should include only the information needed to promote the interests of the supervisee, agency, or training program.

6. *Preparation for supervision.* Many supervisors require that supervisees maintain a log of cases that specify progress and problems. In addition, the supervisee may need to prepare clinical material (such as previewing videotapes) in order to maximize supervision time.

7. *Knowledgeable willingness to abide by code of ethics.* Both the supervisor and supervisee should abide by the ethical codes and principles.

8. *Content of supervision.* The content about the supervisee's development depends upon the constellation of maps outlined in the preceding section.

9. *Modalities of supervision.* The supervisor should disclose preferred vehicles of supervision (such as consultation, cotherapy, live supervision, live observation, videotaped review, case presentations, personal/professional interface exploration, etc.). Also, the supervisor's discussion of the range of personal exploration, rationale of supervisory methods, and theoretical orientation will help the supervisee make an informed decision regarding participation in the supervisory relationship.

10. *Review of progress and evaluation of supervisee and supervisor.* The supervisee should receive a copy of the instruments of evaluation (or individualized evaluation plan described in the previous section) during the contractual phase. Evaluation of the supervisee should include consideration of all of the elements of the supervision contract.

11. *Grievance procedure.* Grievances should be resolved as parsimoniously as possible. The first stage of a grievance process should always begin with a respectful, face-to-face discussion of the concern. If communications cannot resolve the grievance, then consider using of an outside consultant. The supervisee should also have opportunity for representation in order to maintain the balance needed to reach a fair decision.

12. *Timely response of supervision documents.* Since the supervisee has invested a great deal of time and energy complying with expectations of supervision, the supervisor must also professionally respond to the needs of the supervisee.

The disclosure of the supervision contract informs the supervisee of the expectations and requirements of the supervision process. Adherence to the contract will increase the chances the supervision will be both ethical and satisfactory.

CONCLUSION

Ethics require that the supervisor initially consider the rights and welfare of the client. Ethical deliberation of the goals of supervision must consider the goals of therapy. Further, the work of supervision must consider the future clients of the supervisee. Increasing the talent, compassion, reflexivity, and creativity of supervisees ensures that our profession will maintain proper standards of care in the future. However, the responsibility for cultivating effective professionals means that the supervisor must become comfortable with the role of the gatekeeper of the profession. Therefore, supervisory expectations and competencies should be addressed throughout the supervisory relationship. Finally, as outlined in the supervision contract, the supervisor must consider the rights of the supervisee and conduct supervision ethically.

Section Two

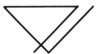

Vehicles for Supervision

6

Multimodal Approach
to Supervision

THE FIRST SECTION OF THIS BOOK presented a series of road maps to illustrate different pathways and terrain of the supervision process. These maps,
illustrated with supervisory examples, provided a guide to places to visit
along the supervisory journey. Nevertheless, the supervisory system needs
more than maps and travel stories to navigate the supervision process. The
supervisor and supervisee's commitment and willingness to traverse and
transcend clinical impediments provide the essential vehicles for movement.
As Lao Tsu (1954) poignantly observed, "The voyage of a thousand miles
begins with the first step."

Besides the willingness to walk through a discussion of clinical problems,
access to efficient vehicles can accelerate the progress along the supervision
journey. Therefore, this section will discuss the pragmatics of getting
around the supervision room using common supervision modalities (case
management, live supervision, consultation, apprentice supervision, and
professional/personal interface exploration) as well as options such as videotape review and experiential interventions. Selecting one modality precludes others, and we may agonize over "the road not taken." For instance,
live supervision limits the development of the supervisee to the issues raised
in the session with the clients. Some vehicles may fit the professional and

clinical demands of the supervisee while others may be somewhat superfluous.

The pressure and need for new vehicles emerge as maps become redrawn
to include different types of terrain. Thus, maps and vehicles intrinsically
influence one another. For example, enlarging the client system to include
family members called for the vehicle of live supervision in order to sort out
the complex needs of multiple family members. The vehicle of live supervision in turn helped stimulate the revision of the early maps of family therapy
to include principles of second cybernetics; that is, the one-way mirror
became a visual reminder that the mere presence of the supervisee significantly influences the clients. Isomorphically, the mere presence of the supervisor greatly influences the supervisee's work with the clients. Therefore,
the supervision of family therapy developed theories and approaches that
considered and utilized the impact of the therapist and the supervisor in the
family system. This example demonstrates the recursive nature of maps and
vehicles that essentially push for more creative explanations of the territory
and more interesting and efficient ways to supervise the work.

MANY WAYS TO GET TO ROME

The application of a multimodal approach in the supervision process uti-
lizes diverse vehicles:

- *Case management supervision* provides the most comprehensive transportation through the supervisee's caseload. Through the indirect channel of case discussion, videotaped review, or experiential interventions,
  case management offers a private arena in which to review the supervisee's work. The supervisor and supervisee can choose to focus on the
  specific issues of the case in relation to any of the maps (position in the
  houses, individual differences, supervisory dimensions, or ethics) described in the first section. Videotape review and experiential interventions augment case discussion. Since contact with the client is indirect,
  there is greater space and time than in other supervisory modalities to
  explore ideological (head) conceptualizations of clinical issues.

- *Live supervision* creates a context in which the action in the therapy
  room is observed as it happens. Interventions by the supervisor immediately affect the therapeutic system. Thus, the supervisor loses the safety
  and anonymity of being a Monday morning quarterback watching a
  videotape; the ability to comment makes him or her one of the players.
  Live supervision bolsters the use of the hands (methodology) because it
  provides a context that guides, supports, and challenges the therapist's
  interventions in the case. With more advanced supervisees, live supervi-

sion can also help amplify the therapist's heart (use of self) and nose (intuition and creativity).

- *Consultation*, facilitated in the presence of the therapist and the clients, provides a context that offers the supervisee tangible help in managing a clinical impasse. The consultant can modify the supervisee's position in the therapeutic system by offering a new perspective. Thus, the consultant creates discontinuity in the therapy process by building a bridge from the rigid functions in the impasse to new therapeutic possibilities. As a consultee, the supervisee has an inside position from which to observe the supervisor's flexible use of self with one's clients. Consultation offers an opportunity for the supervisee to witness and learn different applications of the nose, heart, and hands.

- *Apprentice cotherapy*, like consultation, offers the supervisee the opportunity to watch the supervisor work. Additionally, apprentice cotherapy provides the opportunity for the supervisee to work safely under the umbrella of the supervisor's expertise. Since the supervisor, as senior therapist, inherits responsibility for the session's outcome, the supervisee can codirect the therapy without the worry of causing harm. The partnership affords a safe arena to fully experience the use of self while noticing how gender, value, and cultural issues affect the therapeutic relationship. The supervisee has the freedom to become more vocal and active in the therapeutic process as he or she becomes comfortable.

PASSENGERS ARE MORE IMPORTANT THAN VEHICLES

During the termination session of a successful marital therapy, the female client asked my cotherapist (my spouse, Karen Cooper-Haber, Ph.D.) and me if we knew what impressed her the most in the therapy. In a brief moment, images of the therapy sped through my mind as though I were using the high-speed search function of a videotape player. I stopped to notice the metaphors, provocations, reframes, emotional cathartic experiences, structural realignments, empty chair dialogues, and a host of other techniques. Overcome with information from a 10-month therapy, I answered, "No, what?" She smiled and recounted the time that my spouse and I had an argument prior to the session and finished it in front of them before beginning the session. I had completely forgotten that scene. However, even if I had remembered it, the resolution of the argument between my spouse and me would not have made it to the top 25 most influential experiences on my list.

A similar fortuitous insight recently occurred. A person whom I supervised three years ago invited me to lunch to celebrate the completion of her Ph.D. degree. She asked the same question, "What do you think I remember the most from our supervisory relationship?" Again, I briefly searched through powerful live supervision sessions, family-of-origin conflicts with clinical implications, a consultation session, the work that we did to help her set clearer boundaries with clients, etc. She reported that *feeling respected* was the critical factor in our supervisory relationship. She described the following example of what she meant by respect. While I was her group supervisor and training director, she was assigned to receive individual supervision from a supervisor-in-training. The individual supervisor had comparable therapy skills as the supervisee and was a first-time supervisor. The supervisee felt that the supervisor could not offer her appropriate supervision. The supervisory impasse occurred when the exasperated supervisor attempted to establish her authority over the "resistant" supervisee. A symmetrical escalation of increasing control and resistant maneuvers quickly arose in the supervisory relationship. The supervisee brought the power struggle and lack of productivity to me for resolution. She requested reassignment to a different individual supervisor. The impasse in their relationship caused me great chagrin because I was both the group supervisor to the supervisee and the supervisor of supervision for the novice supervisor. Therefore, supporting either the supervisor or the supervisee would undermine my relationship with the other. I responded to the double bind by requesting that the supervisee train her novice supervisor to perform her role more adroitly. "You're just going to have to teach her how to be a better supervisor." My goals were to maintain the hierarchy of relationships, respect the concerns of both, and empower the supervisee to respond to her dilemma in a way that promoted self-care, responsibility, and altruism. She reported that my intervention conveyed respect for her feelings and confidence in her abilities to work through the impasse.

Both stories exemplify the power of the personal encounter in therapeutic or supervisory relationships. Each anecdote suggests that adherence to an internal decision was critical in conveying an important lesson to the client and the supervisee. In the case of the supervisee, she proved ready and able to accept the challenge to work out the problem with her supervisor-in-training. In other cases, I might have intervened directly by meeting with the supervisor and supervisee or even granted the request for transfer. I believe that my former supervisee experienced my concern for her welfare on a preverbal level when I refused her request for a transfer. If the former supervisee did not feel respected by me as a person and as a professional, then my refusal to comply with her transfer request would have felt like a punitive action. How can a supervisor enforce a boundary while conveying respect?

While there are no formulas or correct answers for what constitutes a respectful action, sensitivity to the emotional process of the other is a key ingredient. Respect depends upon the ethical juxtaposition of needs of all members in the system. The acid test is whether the internal responses of the supervisor's "I" can facilitate the supervisory role. If it does not, then the supervisor should forgo the impulses of the "I." Since the definition of an ethical juxtaposition of needs is in the eyes of the beholder, supervisors will invariably step on the toes of supervisees without conscious intention or awareness. Therefore, the supervisor should be alert to signals that convey all is not well. The supervisor should take the initiative to process issues in the supervisory relationship that are important for the maintenance of a respectful connection.

The hierarchical nature of supervision is paradoxical in that it works bests as an *I-thou* relationship. Although there is a power differential of roles, there must be profound respect for the personal worth of the supervisee. The supervisor needs to know how to work with both sides of the hierarchical-egalitarian coin. Like a parent, the supervisor should correct the behaviors and roles—not the personhood—of the supervisee. An ineffective supervisee is not a bad person but merely has difficulties adjusting to the role of therapist and supervisee. Similarly, if a supervisor fails to work effectively with a supervisee, it does not mean that the supervisor is a bad person but that he or she has merely missed the boat with the supervisee.

The esteem of the supervisee or supervisor-in-training needs attention and nourishment along with the development of professional skills. No vehicles will go far without fuel—respect, goodwill, preservation of dignity, willingness to deal with conflict, fairness, availability, reverence for unique gifts and perceptions, acknowledgment of strengths, willingness to take risks, confrontation of unproductive and problematic behaviors, regard for autonomy, consistency, maintenance of boundaries, fidelity, imagination, playfulness, integrity, congruence, and so on. The adherence to these qualities facilitates the basic ingredients for a successful supervisory journey: trust and vitality. Without these ingredients, the journey could become tentative, constrained, superficial, dishonest, tedious, and unproductive.

Whitaker (1989) was fond of saying that the therapy is in the person of the therapist. Similarly, supervision happens within the person of the supervisor. Maps and vehicles can help direct and facilitate the journey, but ultimately the supervisory journey depends upon the quality of the I-thou relationship between the driver and the passengers.

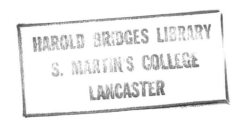

7

Case Management
Supervision

CASE MANAGEMENT SUPERVISION REFERS to an indirect approach to over-seeing the supervisee's caseload. Indirect supervision includes discussions about client dynamics, therapeutic process, the interfacing of the therapist's professional/personal dilemmas, and generic issues relevant to the refinement and development of professional skills. In addition to case discussions, case management supervision employs action procedures such as reviewing videotaped clinical interviews, role-play, and metaphorical work with figures, objects, and empty chair projections. In short, case management supervision includes various activities without the direct presence of clients.

The complexities and limitations of case management supervision are due to its foundation on double inferences. The supervisor must infer the relevant clinical and professional issues from the oral report of the supervisee. Similarly, the supervisee must extract and apply the message of the supervisory experience to the clinical situation. Since the supervisee is the common denominator in both contexts, the supervisor must attempt to clarify the supervisee's deductions of the clinical problems and the supervisory interventions. The distance between the inferences of the supervisor and the supervisee diminishes after the development of a common language in supervision. In addition, regular follow-ups of supervisory suggestions lessen the possibility of misconceptions. However, even with weekly follow-ups, the clarification of conjectures merely generates additional inferential hypotheses about the actual developments in the therapeutic system. Therefore, the supervisor must be cognizant of the limitations of *talking about* clients and therapy. Words can only present an abstraction of the actual experience.

Even a videotaped record of the session presents only a skewed and incomplete portion of the actual experience. Besides the obvious limitation of reviewing only selected and isolated segments of a session, the supervisor must infer the emotional tenor of the interview as well as other aspects of the session (such as facial expressions, eye contact, and smells) that are often inaccessible to the camera. In addition, the supervisor must deduce the flow of the session prior to and subsequent to the chosen videotaped excerpt. Therefore, even videotape, although to a lesser extent than case discussion, still requires double inferences.

Despite the supervisor's inability to directly experience the clinical interview and provide immediate feedback to the supervisee, case management supervision offers distinct advantages over direct supervision approaches. Since case management supervision does not have to attend to immediate clinical concerns, the privacy of the supervisory encounter can focus on issues relevant to the supervisee's clinical and professional growth. Since direct supervision approaches require a considerable amount of time with one case, they limit attention to a multitude of other relevant clinical concerns. In contrast, case management supervision efficiently reviews the judgments, decisions, and behaviors in many of the supervisee's cases. The ability to expand the focus to the entire caseload, as opposed to the amplification of a single case, provides the opportunity to compare and contrast the supervisee's work among various clinical concerns and clientele. Patterns of skill and comfort level with different clientele become evident. Exceptions to the supervisee's common level of clinical expertise guide supervisory explorations. For instance, if a supervisee has uncharacteristic joining problems with one of the spouses, then the focus of supervision could explore the supervisee's heart as opposed to his or her hands. "What happens with this particular couple that creates your discomfort and distance from the spouse? What would happen if you shifted your alliance in the relationship? What are your fears? Is your position in the marital relationship familiar to you?" On the other hand, if a supervisee struggles with the relevance and involvement of the grandparent floor in several client systems, then the supervisor needs to address supervisory intervention for the head and the hands. "What is the theoretical rationale for including the grandparents? Do you think their involvement would be useful at this stage? If so, how would you organize the invitation and structure their role in the therapy?" Thus, attention to the panorama of the supervisee's caseload informs the supervisor of germane issues in specific cases.

THE BREADTH AND DEPTH DILEMMA

Due to pragmatic time constraints, the supervisor and supervisee must prioritize the goals and objectives of the supervisory sessions. The dilemma in case management supervision is the selection of focus. Each case represents a complex and unique story. In addition, the supervisee's choices of position and role in the clients' house represent another intriguing story. One can easily become lost in the web of choices and experiences in each therapeutic story. However, the supervisory system must modulate concern for the entire caseload with the developmental needs of the supervisee in the allotted time for supervision. In other words, the goals of supervision are to provide supervisory support for the *breadth* of the caseload while expanding the *depth* of professional skills. Attention to both breadth and depth satisfy supervision's dual goals of clinical efficacy and professional development.

The experience of the supervisee and the severity of the clinical problem guide the focus of the supervisor. With a novice therapist, the supervisor needs to monitor the breadth of the caseload in order to protect the clients' welfare. Intermediate therapists, in time, can be trusted to identify appropriate clinical and professional concerns for supervision. Since the supervisor cannot comprehensively review each case, the supervisor needs to trust the supervisee's accuracy in reporting clinical problems that require supervisory attention. Trust is a two-way street. The degree of the supervisee's clinical transparency will depend upon the supervisor's ability to handle clinical problems effectively while attending to the esteem of the supervisee. A relationship based on trust and respect allows for the development of a supervision environment in which inadequacies, uncertainties, problems, questions, and personal interference with clinical problems can be explored safely and creatively.

The doctrine of vicarious liability holds the supervisor accountable for insuring a reasonable standard of client care. In turn, the supervisor must provide a reasonable standard of supervision for the supervisee. The standard of case management requires that the supervisor determine the supervisee's ability to handle the severity of the client problem, approve major treatment decisions such as referral or termination, deal with problematic and ethical decisions, and periodically monitor the progress of the case. The form in figure 7.1 has been used as a quick method for learning about the breadth of the supervisee's caseload. The supervisor and supervisee can

Figure 7.1: *Weekly case management form*

Please list all client sessions, telephone contacts, no shows, cancellations, and terminations; place * in concerns column for problematic cases.

Name(s) Date, Session #	Theme	Complaint/ Problem	Progress/Process	Concerns*

Supervisor's comments (Use reverse side as necessary.)

use the form to appropriately determine the cases or professional arenas that need greater depth exploration. It is purposefully succinct, so that six cases can be enumerated on each sheet. A longer version of this form has endured substantial resistance by supervisees who disliked paperwork. A compromise between breadth and depth, the form can be modified to accommodate personal and theoretical preferences.

The weekly case management form reminds the supervisee to reflect upon and track the developments of each case. This short form cannot substitute for a case note form, which details a more extensive description of the session; however, the case note form that most of my supervisees and I use is very similar (see figure 7.2).

There have been many occasions when the case note form has helped me as a therapist recover from being undifferentiated and lost in clinical interviews. For instance, the "Me" portion of the case note form asks one to describe the personal experience in the interview. Naming my experience (overzealous, bored, too parental, too aligned with one side of the family, etc.) helps free me to consider corrective actions. When I do not name my reality, I may remain stuck in unconscious coping mechanisms. Similarly, describing a hypothesis about the nature of the problem (why this problem with these people at this point in time) helps me to respect the important feelings and circumstances that have bred the problem. Even though a hypothesis about the problem is merely a conceptual construction from my head, the activity of generating a hypothesis about the dilemma of change helps me reconsider my relationship to the problem. Instead of echoing the clients' reality that the problem is "unconscious, irrational, and unnecessary," I develop a more respectful approach to working with the problem (Andolfi et al., 1983). In this way of working, the symptom functions as a pathway to the existential dilemmas of the client system.

Both the case note form and the case management form provide a writing activity that helps the clinician separate *from* the case in order to conceptualize *about* the case. Most supervisees report that they have found the forms to be both valuable and manageable training tools. The work with the forms (each entry takes as little as five minutes) becomes more than a report of the session. The forms reflect a theoretical orientation that organizes the multitude of information in a session. The essential aspect of the forms is that they become a mechanism and place to process sessions as if in the presence of a cotherapist, consultant, or supervisor. The forms advance the essential task of self-supervision, metaphorically linking the supervisee with the internalized supervisor.

Using the weekly case management form, the supervisor can request verbal amplification on specific cases or professional issues. The supervisor can choose to simply read the form, to briefly discuss nonproblematic cases,

Figure 7.2: *Case note form*

Theme: Session #:

Name(s) of person(s) present:

Date:

Complaint:

Summary:

Me:

Hypothesis and dilemmas:

Tasks, directives, or strategies:

or to discuss specific cases in depth. With perplexing therapeutic systems, the supervisor may discuss the need for live supervision, consultation, or videotaped review. In addition to specific case review, the supervisor could use the form to explore the supervisee's work with specific issues, such as strengths, feelings, or external resources, with the entire caseload. The following summary briefly and generically discusses each column on the case management form.

Name(s), Date, and Session #. Even though these facts convey straightforward information, they reveal the "architecture" of the therapeutic relationship (McCollum & Wetchler, 1995). Besides frequently having clinical significance, names indicate the members of the system who attend the session. The names of the absent people are as important as the ones who attend the session. Including absent family members and people who might be resources to the family is a topic often ignored by the supervisee. Therefore, names often reflect the therapist's relationship in the family and professional houses.

The date addresses the issue of the timing of the session. The plan for the next session illuminates the supervisee's decision regarding frequency of sessions. Many therapists develop habitual intervals between sessions irrespective of the clients' needs. Most therapists see their clients once every week or two. The supervisor can explore the impact of varying the session frequency depending upon the specific circumstances of the clients.

The session number impels the supervisor to consider the history and stage of the therapeutic relationship. Frequently, I have come up with ingenious plans for therapeutic interventions only to find out that the supervisee has already attempted a similar activity several sessions ago. The supervisor needs to respect the work that has already occurred in the therapeutic relationship. For instance, an aimless session that follows a very intense session may imply that clients are consolidating changes, whereas a prolonged impasse after significant changes may suggest that clients are approaching termination.

The session number also flags an initial session. Intakes require supervisory scrutiny regarding the type and severity of problem as well as the development of the therapeutic relationship. In addition, the supervisor should inquire about clients who cancel, do not show, or terminate. These occurrences may require a follow-up or indicate a problem with the supervisee's formation of a therapeutic relationship. For instance, I did a substantial amount of video and live supervision with a supervisee who had difficulty sustaining a relationship beyond the initial session. During supervision we found that he was too dogmatic with some of his clients and directionless with others. The live supervision guided him in the development of more focused and collaborative relationships with his clients.

Theme. The theme represents a title, metaphor, or other short description that encapsulates the essence of the session. The theme encourages the *nose* of the supervisee to synthesize a right-brain feel for the therapeutic story. In my supervisory role, the theme is the first category that catches my attention. For instance, one supervisee entitled a couples therapy session, "No wall to lean on." The title articulated the existential struggle of a couple's mutual emotional frailty. Each spouse was too distraught to support the other. The supervisee attempted to be the wall for the couple, but the escalation of at-risk behaviors proved that he could not be their bulwark. Therefore, the supervision explored the use of family-of-origin resources for each spouse. As the supervisor, I became the support beam for the supervisee. By leaning on the supervision process, the supervisee was able to take additional risks with the couple. Thus, the "wall" theme in this case provided a metaphor that sustained the supervisory and therapeutic process.

Complaint/Problem. The complaint or problem could be multifaceted, depending upon the number of clients in the session. Additionally, the supervisee's assessment of the problem may be different from the clients'. The definition of the problem varies according to the theoretical orientation of the supervisee. Whatever that theoretical orientation, the definition, assessment, and diagnosis of the presenting problem frame the ideology and methodology behind the goals of the therapy. The clients' complaint, hopefully, is not a static element and can change from session to session.

Progress/Process. This category identifies the ability of the therapeutic team to work together. The supervisee reviews the effect of therapeutic interventions on clinical problems and goals. In addition, the supervisee reflects on the process of the therapeutic relationship. Progress and process are the two central pillars of the therapeutic relationship; ignoring either weakens the foundation of the therapeutic encounter.

The focus on progress and process moves from the ideological rationalizations of the *head* to the phenomenological experience of the *hands, heart,* and *nose.* The supervisor inquires about what the hands did, how the heart felt, and what the nose imagined, and then reviews these supervisory dimensions in the context of the clients' and professional houses. The position and experience of the supervisee's place in the houses offer insight into the activity of the supervisee's hands, heart, and nose. The supervisor needs to ask obvious questions in order to investigate the interactions in the clinical interview. "What made you decide to confront the father and avoid provoking the mother's vague position? How did you feel about father's anger? Were you afraid that it could get out of control? What were your fantasies? Were any of your projections or introjections in the room? How did they affect your behavior in the interview? With hindsight, what would you do differently?" Although the supervision process engages the supervisee's head to make sense of the clinical decisions, the supervisor needs to keep the supervisee's feet in the phenomenological experience of the clinical interview. Increasing the knowledge and flexibility of the hands, heart, and nose can increase the likelihood of clinical progress through the augmentation of the therapeutic process.

Concerns. This flags the clinical apprehensions of the supervisee. In addition, items in this column raise questions about professional development. After the theme column introduces me to the case, my attention focuses on the concerns column in order to become alert to supervisory concerns and priorities. If the case raises a great deal of anxiety, the supervisee stars the concern so that the supervisor knows that it requires extra attention. Although ethical and crisis dilemmas may be noted, typical concerns also include countertransference reactions, confusion or discomfort with aspects of a session, client deterioration, or uncertainty about a future direction. Supervisees should be encouraged to make their concerns as specific as possible. Although some clinical problems generate minimal anxiety, most cases evoke some concerns and questions. The ability to raise legitimate concerns is a sign of a reflective and discerning supervisee. Some supervisees have minimal concerns or questions about their caseload, while other supervisees have major crises with most of their cases. Each extreme presents distinct supervisory problems. The handling of concerns and questions varies according to the unique constellation of the client, therapeutic, and supervisory systems.

Figure 7.3 shows an entry on the weekly case management form. The supervisee is a high-functioning therapist who is an experienced couples

Figure 7.3: *Case management form example*

Name(s) Date, Session #	Theme	Complaint/ Problem	Progress/Process	Concerns*
Joe & Jane Smith, 8/14, #3	Two mothers and a child	Jane is frustrated with Joe's neediness, depression, and stubbornness.	Took Joe's genogram, yet still feel annoyed with him. I am aligning with Jane in the attempt to fix Joe.	I worry about my annoyance with Joe. I have not established a therapeutic relationship with the couple.

therapist. I have developed a positive working alliance with her during the 10 months of our supervisory relationship. Although she connects better with females than males, she and I were both surprised by the strength of her negative reaction to Joe. Her concern about her annoyance with Joe suggested that a professional/personal interface intervention could best address her ambivalence in forming a therapeutic relationship with the couple. Thus, the supervision in this case involved expanding her use of self (heart) in order to increase her flexibility with and proximity to both the husband and the wife. I will return to this case in a later section on metaphorical objects.

The case management form is the flag, not the answer, for cases that raise concerns. The supervisor needs to use the form as a springboard for developing a supervisory structure that addresses the concerns of the case and the supervisee. Below I cover experiential supervisory methods that extend case and supervisee exploration beyond case discussion.

VIDEOTAPE SUPERVISION

Videotape supervision is a frequently used and highly rated supervisory modality (Romans, Boswell, Carlozzi, & Ferguson, 1995; Wetchler, Piercy, & Sprenkle, 1989). Despite its popularity, videotaped supervision is minimally described in the supervision literature (Breunlin, Karrer, McGuire, Rocco, & Cimmarusti, 1988). Videotaped review amplifies case discussion by providing a visual and auditory record of nonverbal and verbal communications that occur during a session. This record reduces the dissonance between the supervisee's report, the supervisor's imagination, and the actual session. The videotape organizes the reality of the supervisory system as it provides a common point of departure for the supervisory discussion. Furthermore, the remote control gives the supervisor and supervisee the options to pause, stop, slow-motion review, rewind, fast forward, search, and playback parts of the session according to the issues and the rhythm of the videotaped supervision.

Breunlin et al. (1988) have described videotape supervision as a "second cybernetic" process that attends to the internal (cognition and affect) and interactive experiences of the supervisee in the session. The videotape shows the interactional sequences of the interview, but does not reveal the supervisee's cognitive framework and affective experience. Videotape supervision exploits the mechanical luxury of freezing time in order to explore, clarify, and amplify internal experiences. Increasing awareness of and insight into the intrapsychic experience illuminates interpersonal interactions.

For example, a female supervisee described feeling physically vulnerable in her work with a male ex-convict. The videotape of the previous session portrayed her interactions with him as uncharacteristically terse and controlled. In several sequences, the client touched her on the arm (in a friendly yet intrusive manner), while the supervisee anxiously retreated from his verbal and nonverbal requests for greater emotional closeness. She never dealt directly with the client about her concerns around his physical proximity. Since the tape showed intrusive but not threatening behavior by the client (although the possibility of harm was never ruled out), I asked the supervisee if she had ever felt this vulnerable with other clients. The supervisee recounted a terrible incident in which she was assaulted and choked by a patient while working in an institution. In her memory she could still feel her former patient's hands around her neck and the resultant fear for her life. As she told this story, she realized that vestiges of this assault were present in the therapeutic relationship with her current client. After working on some of her unfinished feelings from the past assault, we looked at whether she could set appropriate boundaries with the ex-convict client while attending to his emotional concerns. It was mutually decided that live supervision would be necessary to ensure her comfort level so that she could better attend to the client's concerns.

This supervisory anecdote illustrates the mutual influence that occurs paraverbally between the supervisee and the client system. The affective and cognitive internal experiences of the supervisee influence the nature of the therapeutic interactions in the clinical interview. Similarly, clients' personalities and family configurations instigate the supervisee's internal reactions. Since videotape review aptly demonstrates the relationship of the supervisee's internal experience with concurrent therapeutic behaviors, the technology of videotape review fosters the consideration of the second cybernetic principle that the observer (supervisee) influences the process.

Breunlin et al. (1988) have connected the internal and interactive process of video supervision to three contexts: (1) the session itself as seen in the videotape record, (2) the supervisee's memories of the internal aspects of the session, and (3) the experience of the videotape supervision. These contexts also have temporal implications:

1. The review of the videotape therapy session is a present experience of a past event. Usually, the review of a videotape, by oneself or with a supervisor, brings forth new perspectives on the clients and the therapeutic interaction. One sees and hears oneself from the lens and microphone of the camcorder rather than from within one's body. The meta-perspective of videotape review enables multiple reviews of a sequence. Each review provides another chance to see more aspects of the session in the present.

2. The supervisee's memory of the internal aspects of the session represents

the supervisee's relationship with the past. After reviewing a videotaped clip, the supervisor's access to the pause button provides the opportunity to enter into the past and ponder memories of internal experiences. "What was your motivation to let this issue drop? What was your hypothesis about his request for more contact? Were your actions motivated by a theory? If so, what theory? How does that theory connect to this case? What was your connection to the client system? What were you feeling? Where did you think you were going when you asked him if he was angry with you? Do you think that significant people or experiences in your past influenced your decisions?" The supervisee's elaboration of the affective and cognitive memories provides an understanding of the supervisee's internal decisions during the interview. The knowledge and clarification of the world view of the supervisee make the supervisory process infinitely easier, more respectful, and relevant. Supervisory interventions can then more accurately approach the cutting edge of the supervisee's development.

3. The videotape supervision session can range through the past, present, and/or future. The remote control fosters a "time-machine" approach in videotape supervision. The supervisor could move from the present review of the tape to past personal experiences that organized the supervisee's position in the therapy session. The supervisor needs to selectively guide the personal encounter in the past and appropriately reset the clock in the time machine in order to reenter the supervisory encounter in the present. The goal of the time travel is to utilize learnings from personal encounters in the past to understand professional dilemmas in the present. The reconstructed encounter in the past could also stimulate new options in the present. Finally, the supervisor could reset the time machine to enter a future session with the client so that the supervisee could practice the application of the learnings of the past in a projected and constructed view of the future (Haber, in press a). The time machine approach provides a context for the supervisee to alter personal approaches to professional dilemmas.

The previous supervisory anecdote, about the physically vulnerable supervisee who had been choked by a former client, illustrates the use of the time machine in videotape supervision. Revisiting the traumatic choking experiences with new eyes and additional hands enabled the supervisee to work through several unfinished feelings of that experience. First, she felt emotionally supported through the remembrance of that experience and was therefore able to relive the emotions while feeling protected and supported. Second, although she admonished herself for being alone with the client, she received the message that it was not her fault. She was very young at the time of this incident and did not expect to be attacked in the line of duty. Third, a reconstructed version of the past enabled her to attend to her client's proclivity for intimidation and violence. In an empty chair dialogue, she clarified the boundaries with her client and solicited support from her colleagues at her former job. Thus, she envisioned a wall of protection in her work with her institutionalized client. This scene challenged her ominous, internalized message that she had to manage her vulnerability in overwhelming situations alone. Although there were inferences that this message had its roots in her childhood, the supervisee's past was not followed in the supervision experience. Setting the time machine to explore the existence of childhood traumas would have further muddled her boundaries and deprofessionalized her. Supervision would have unnecessarily crossed into the province of therapy because the intervention would have shifted from her professional dilemma with her current client to a therapeutic catharsis.

The reconstruction of the trauma created a "synthetic memory," that is, an alternative to the actual event, so that the supervisee could access the learnings of the more functional, synthetic memory, rather than the emotionally paralyzing, traumatic memory (Pesso & Wassenaar, 1991). This enabled her to have more options in intimidating relationships. In order to practice more differentiated ways of handling the intrusiveness of her client, the time machine was set to a future encounter.

The supervisee conducted an empty chair dialogue with her imagined client in order to explain her decision to assert appropriate boundaries. In this dialogue, she informed him not to touch her without requesting and receiving prior permission. In addition, she changed the pattern of dealing with her problems by herself by eliciting the aid of the supervisor for future live supervision sessions.

This example demonstrates how supervisory review of a videotaped session can lead to a detour into the interfacing of personal/professional issues. After watching the client touch the therapist, we did not go back to the tape. I usually hold the remote control and alternate between the play, pause, and stop buttons. Less frequently, I ask the supervisee to use the remote to control the focus of the supervisory attention. The issue of when and how long to stop the video player depends upon the nature of the supervision contract and the issues present in the therapeutic system.

Breunlin et al. (1988) suggested that goals for video supervision should be limited in scope, operationalized, achievable, and at the cutting edge of the supervisee's skills and abilities. Goals, which could be selected from any of the road maps that were described in the first section, give a needed focus for the selection and review of videotaped segments.

The supervisor should avoid watching a videotape as if viewing a television program without commercials. Whiffen (1982) has appropriately suggested that the attention span for reviewing a videotape is limited to approximately four minutes. After an extended period of time, the supervisor and supervisee can become passive observers in the supervision process. The supervisor must remember to interact with the three contexts of videotaped supervision: the review of the videotape, the affective and cognitive memories of the session, and the supervisory experience (which could include attention to the present encounter or relevant time travel to the past or future). The interactions with the multiple contexts in videotaped supervision provide for a very interesting and fruitful supervisory outcome.

Generally, after pressing the pause or stop button, the supervisee begins the supervisory discussion by reporting present and past impressions of the videotaped segment. The supervisee's description orients the supervisor to the rationale, concerns, questions, and coherence with desired goals. Then the supervisor can amplify, redirect, support, or challenge the supervisee's assumptions through questions, experiential activities, or comments. These supervisory interventions can use the videotaped segment to increase the supervisee's awareness, intentionality, and coherence in the use of the head, hands, heart, and nose in the therapeutic interview. Videotape supervision offers an ideal context to teach self-supervision. "Make believe you are supervising yourself behind a one-way mirror: What generates your concern about the interview? Why do you think the therapist intervenes in this manner? What suggestions would you make? How do you think the therapist and the family would respond to the suggested interventions?" Besides encouraging self-supervision skills, videotape supervision offers a concrete opportunity for the supervisor to comment on the specific strengths and skills of the supervisee. The value of reinforcement should not be overlooked in the zealous desire for further improvement, change, and growth. Like all supervision modalities, videotape supervision must balance challenging and supportive interventions and comments to the supervisee. "A teaspoon of honey helps the medicine go down."

In particular, the videotaped record provides a point of reference for the supervisee's professional development. In the beginning of supervision relationships, I ask supervisees to select five minutes of good therapy and five minutes of bad therapy and to comment about their self-evaluation. Thus, supervision begins by balancing strengths with weaknesses. Supervisees need to be taught to have a self-critical eye for improvement, as well as a self-appreciative eye for clinical successes; successful segments of videotaped interviews articulate and reinforce supervisees' competence.

EXPERIENTIAL WORK WITH METAPHORS AND
METAPHORICAL OBJECTS

In addition to rational discussions about cases, skills, and professional issues, case management supervision can become a metaphorical interplay
between the supervisor and supervisee. Metaphors and experiential procedures encourage an inferential and symbolic approach to professional problem-solving and development. The language of inference (Whitaker, 1989)
invites a joint expedition into the unconscious of the supervisory system.
Rational discourse gives way to parallel inferences based on metaphors,
associations, stories, or internal experiences. The metaphor or experiential
activity becomes the mutual pathway to discovering new angles about the
role of the supervisee in the client system. The metaphorical mind "wanders
through awarenesses, experiences, images, and all our tacit knowings like a
gentle predator as it searches for being. If there are gaps in experience or
knowledge, it hardly pauses but seeks an alternate route. If there is no valid
alternate route, the metaphoric mind invents one. For that is what it does
best . . . it invents" (Samples, 1976, p. 62).

Engaging the metaphorical mind is more than a mere trick of language
learned in grammar school. The generative capability of metaphor creates a
new and expanding form of consciousness (Jaynes, 1976). Metaphor moves
the supervisory system from a reliance on logical, sequential analysis to
consideration of the world of images and creative alternatives. The logical
mind is typically given more credence than the metaphorical mind because
it appears more trustworthy and reliable to the meaning of experience.
However, rational language is a much more abstract description of experience than symbolic language. Watzlawick, Bavelas, and Jackson (1967)
said that analogic (symbolic) communication has "its roots in far more
archaic periods of evolution and is, therefore, of much more general validity
than the relatively recent, and far more abstract, digital mode of verbal
communication" (p. 62). A picture is worth more than a thousand words.
A digital discussion of what happens in a therapy session is often quite
different from the analogic picture of the actual process.

A metaphorical experience creates a common ground for the supervisor
and supervisee. Symbolic phenomena provide a *point of reference (definition)* and *direction* for supervisory exploration and intervention. For instance, if the supervisee describes the therapeutic relationship with the husband as parental, then the familial metaphor conveys information about the
nature of the relationship with the couple. Continued work with this metaphor could provide more specific images about the type and style of parenting, compelling factors in the decision to parent, the husband's response to
the parenting, and the metaphorical relationship with the spouse. Rather

than interpreting the supervisee's images, the reverie with the metaphorical images elaborates the organization, expectations, fears, and hopes that constitutes the relational foundation. The contemplation of the images provides different vantage points that capture and restructure the nature of the therapeutic relationship. Thus, the supervisory utilization of the conjoint metaphorical mind illuminates a useful map of the supervisory.

The following steps apply to the therapeutic and supervisory use of metaphors (Haber, in press b):

1. *Interpersonal communications.* Observe the supervisee's description or videotape of digital and analogic interpersonal communications. Ask triadic and circular questions that uncover communication patterns (relational complementarity and symmetry), roles and rules of the client system, therapeutic system, and the social network. "What happens in the client system to make you take this position? What do you do when they take that position?"

2. *Intrapsychic experience.* Inquire about the supervisee's intrapsychic experience in the past with the clients and in the present discussion about the clients. "What's going on inside? What are you feeling? How does this compare to what you felt during the session?"

3. *Nodal parts.* Search for the nodal parts of the system. Look for the recurring patterns and interactional impasses in the confluence of the interpersonal/intrapsychic realities. "What message do you hear when you take this position? What prevents you from shifting your position in this scene? What were the feelings in the room before the impasse?"

4. *Metaphorical theme.* Introduce, elaborate, or cocreate a metaphorical theme. "How would you describe your position in the impasse? What would your familial role be? What scene, movie, or occupation best encapsulates your feeling of being stuck? Does the impasse with the clients feel familiar? When have you felt like this before?"

5. *Repetitious use of the metaphor.* The metaphor becomes a code to encapsulate an aspect of a personal and relational reality. The frequent use of the code reinforces the shorthand language of the metaphor and establishes the symbol as an integral element of the supervisory system.

6. *Interaction with the metaphor.* Since an experience with the metaphoric code is merely a representation of the impasse (not the actual impasse), the supervisee gains distance through the externalization of the problem. The metaphoric interaction typically mirrors the impasse. The subsequent sections on the empty chair and metaphoric figures exemplify metaphoric interactions.

7. *Intervention in the metaphoric interaction.* If the supervisee remains
   stuck in a habitual pattern with the metaphoric interaction, the supervisor can help generate new alternatives, leading to a new approach with
   the old metaphor or a different metaphor with increased options.

8. *Reinforcement of the transformed metaphor.* Similar to step 5, appreciation and recognition of the new metaphor strengthen the transformation
   of the supervisee.

9. *Enough is enough.* Metaphors can remain in the supervisory system as
   codes for impasse and transformation. However, the supervisor needs
   to recognize when metaphors are worn-out and allow new metaphorical
   pathways to emerge.

The metaphorical mind defines and invents reality. These steps should
be used as a backdrop (not a map) for the embellishment of the metaphorical mind. The next two sections on therapist use of the empty chair and of
metaphorical figures exemplify the work with metaphorical experiences.

The Empty Chair

The empty chair, popularized by Fritz Perls (1969), is a wonderful device
for exploring the supervisee's projections. Selected clients, members of the
supervisee's family, the supervisor, or other occupants of the family or
professional houses could metaphorically sit in the empty chair. In short,
the empty chair can represent anything from the minute aspect of a person
(for example, the seductive aspect of a client) to a large organization (psychiatric hospital). The projections that are encountered in the empty chair
can range as far as the limits of the imagination of the supervisor or supervisee.

Work with the empty chair is very fruitful when the supervisee experiences significant emotional charge, extreme ambivalence, confusion, or
passivity with regard to a person(s) or issue. Although the dialogue with the
empty chair is clearly a construction of the supervisee, the externalization of
issues helps the supervisee separate intrapsychic conflicts from projections
or introjections.

Typically, the supervisee first addresses the entity in the empty chair.
The supervisee should be coached to disclose nonrational, gut feelings
rather than socially appropriate dialogue. "Do not say what you ordinarily
say to the client; say what you are feeling in your gut." After the supervisee
comes to a natural stopping point, the supervisor asks him or her to shift to
the empty chair, become the entity addressed by the supervisee, and respond with the gut reaction to the supervisee's disclosure. This old-
fashioned gestalt technique dramatically increases the level of empathy and

understanding for the position of the client in the family and therapeutic systems. The empty chair induces the supervisee to see the self as therapist from the perspective of the client. In addition, the dialogue with the supervisee's projections enables him or her to experience a range of emotions and fantasies that are less readily available when he or she is performing the role of the therapist.

To illustrate the empty chair technique, I will refer to the supervision of the third therapy session described on the case management form in figure 7.3. The supervisee called the session "Two mothers and a child" because she felt like the husband, Joe, immediately became the project that needed attention. The wife, Jane, seemed exasperated with Joe's neediness, depression, and stubbornness. Thus, the supervisee, like Jane, took Joe on as the project. Joe is an "only" child whose father was murdered when Joe was five. His mother became depressed and alcoholic after his father's murder. Joe grew up in a context that provided poorly for his emotional needs. Despite Joe's pathetic story, the supervisee felt angry with him. She acted appropriately but internally resented his dependence.

Since I was curious about the extent of the supervisee's annoyance with Joe, I asked her to address him via the empty chair. She expressed anger with his whininess, indecisiveness, and dependence. She did not want to take over Jane's job as Joe's emotional caretaker. When the supervisee became Joe, he (she) talked about his unfulfilled needs of childhood and his inability to satisfy either Jane or his mother (who vied for his attention). The supervisee switched chairs several times and increasingly became more empathic with Joe's predicament. I asked her where she got the idea that she had to take care of Joe. She described her childhood role of being her father's emotional caretaker. We then had her father and mother symbolically enter the room; the supervisee told them about the burden of her emotional role in the family. When she assumed the position of her mother, she emphatically told her daughter (the supervisee) that it was not her job to take care of her father. Hearing/saying this message moved the supervisee to tears. She then spoke to her father (in the constructed version of the past) and told him that she would not be his emotional caretaker. Then the supervisee's attention returned to Joe. She told Joe that her job was not to be his mother but to help him develop his manhood. The supervisee switched into her father's chair and he became a consultant in her work with Joe. The father said that he would help her recognize Joe's dependency tricks and teach her how best to deal with them. Thus, the supervisee shifted her position with Joe and retained her father and mother as internal consultants in her work. Instead of repeating family dynamics, the supervisee used the introjects of her parents to adopt a more flexible and therapeutic position with an emotionally deprived man. Thus, the empty chairs became vehicles to transform the supervisee's internal position with Joe.

Some supervisees, like many clients, dislike speaking to empty chairs. The supervisor needs to be very flexible in the use of this approach. Classical compliance with the empty chair technique is not at all important; however, reckoning with interfering projections and introjections is. The empty chair technique merely represents a vehicle that helps the supervisee gain clarity about the impasse and potential directions for change.

Role-play

Role-play is an excellent alternative to the empty chair. Enacting a segment of a session or of a professional dilemma offers the supervisee the opportunity to demonstrate or observe the handling of an issue from different perspectives. If the supervisee lacks skills or ideas about how to handle a situation, then it may be helpful to have the supervisor role-play the therapist while the supervisee plays the client. The supervisor could model different ways to handle the impasse. If the supervisee is emotionally stuck in the therapeutic relationship, it may be better for the supervisor to role-play the client so that the supervisee can deal with the problem. In either case, the supervisor must consider the role or experience that best expands the supervisee's professional growth and clinical expertise. After the supervisee's rigidity is exposed in the role-play, he or she can practice a more flexible approach.

For instance, a mature but novice supervisee discussed her concern about her response to a direct question. In a conjoint interview, a partner in a lesbian relationship dealing with commitment problems asked the supervisee how she felt about the previous, initial session. The forthright supervisee responded that she felt tested and not fully trusted by the other partner. The "testy" woman accused the supervisee of being angry with her. The supervisee responded that she was not angry but had honestly answered the other woman's question. The session ended quickly thereafter without the couple's making an additional appointment. The supervision process began with my asking the supervisee to wonder about the client's question. "Did she really want to know your feelings about them or did she want to know whether they should proceed with their relationship, whether you minded working with lesbian couples, or whether you felt partial to one of their positions?" I role-played the questioning client and the supervisee played herself as the therapist. Her job was to understand the latent meaning behind my question. The supervisee was very literal in the role-play and concretely responded to questions without touching the feelings and insecurities that I had as the client. I stopped the role-play in order to process our experiences; we resumed after she received feedback as to how to proceed differently with the lesbian couple. During one of our pauses, we switched roles and I played the therapist and she played the client. As her version of the "resistant" client, she asked me whether she should continue counseling. She was surprised by the simplicity of my response, "Yes, I would like to continue a therapy relationship with both of you." I pointed out that I was responding to her need for hope and acceptance rather than tossing the question back to her ("What do you think?"). The role-play provided a safe arena for the supervisee to learn that seemingly obvious questions could have many different meanings and require different approaches.

Metaphorical Objects

> The metaphorical object, even more than the metaphor, presents many levels for changing connections. The clear visual and tactile presence accentuates the contrast between its literal, material meaning and its symbolic implications, creating confusion as to which level is relevant. (Angelo, 1983, p. 104)

The metaphorical object is a concretized metaphor, a sensory reminder of the *definition* of the therapist's position in the therapeutic drama and the *direction* of choice. The metaphorical object and the supervisee connect the two triangles of the supervisory system. The metaphorical object joins the supervisor and supervisee as a focus for definition and direction; likewise, it brings new possibilities into the relationship between the supervisee and the clients. Thus, the object metaphorically carries the supervisory feedback into the client system.

Metaphorical objects have different meanings depending upon the supervisory circumstances. For instance, one supervisee was told to take a favorite childhood toy to his next family session as a reminder to involve the young children of the family. An extremely intellectual supervisee was given a book to sit on when she felt too lofty in relationship to her clients. Amazingly, the clients neither commented nor questioned the supervisee about the use of the book; nevertheless, sitting on a hard book was enough to curtail the supervisee's pontifications. Another supervisee, who tended to muffle her voice with a professionally successful yet aloof father, put a bear on her shelf prior to the next session to remind her of her strong voice. Each of these metaphorical objects represented relational problems and solutions in the therapeutic relationship.

The key to visual supervision is having an object represent some other thing—whether a person, a role, a "state," or a relationship—leading to the possibility of seeing many elements interconnected in a system. (Williams, 1995, p. 173)

Artwork, sculptures, pictures, pantomime, improvisational theatrical techniques, puppets, or other symbols could also signify the supervisee's rigid and transformational responses to systemic patterns. Again, once the metaphorical object helps clarify the therapeutic impasse, the supervisor can suggest, guide, facilitate, or provoke new behaviors for handling clinical dilemmas.

All therapy rooms contain objects that can be metaphorical—tissues, books, lights, walls, or anything else that can have meaning. In other rooms toys, puppets, and symbolic figures can be intentionally assembled to elicit symbolic representations. Maurizio Andolfi, Carl Whitaker, and Lars Brok have been great models in their application of metaphorical figures. When they have lead workshops, their pockets usually contain a toy, puzzle, or figure. Such objects, at times, help the professional gain needed distance from clients and reflect on aspects of the self and the session. With several versatile objects, the supervisor or supervisee can reconfigure the objects into a better fit. "The essential elements are physical representation, movement, and the intellectual breathing space that is created by memory having an external 'parking lot,' where things can stay put while one thinks" (Williams, 1995, pp. 173–174).

The following supervisory anecdote demonstrates the use of figures in a supervision session concerning the couple described in figure 7.3 and further depicted in the empty chair enactment. After the empty chair experience, the supervisee reported that she was no longer frustrated and annoyed with Joe, but Joe's emotional enmeshment with his mother remained a focus of the marital therapy. The wife, Jane, was very angry with her fiancé, Joe, because of his close attachment to his mother. Jane felt that Joe's mother disapproved of their relationship because she did not want to lose Joe to another woman. Joe felt torn in the middle of the triangle between his mother and Jane and did not decisively support Jane, which exacerbated her frustration and insecurity. The supervisee spent most of the session clarifying Joe's emotional position between the two women.

In the supervisory session, I asked her to use figures to demonstrate the relationship between her and the couple. Even though she metaphorically described her position as maternal to Joe, the use of objects compelled her to present a three-dimensional view of the therapeutic relationship. She positioned herself between the couple, facing Joe with her back to Jane. While the figures reaffirmed the notion that Joe was the chief project, the configuration also made her uncomfortably aware that she did not face

Jane's issues. She realized at that moment that she was intimidated by Jane and much more comfortable in dealing with Joe's problems. She said that Jane had competitive and imperious characteristics that were similar to her older sister. I asked her to hold a figure that represented her sister in her hand as she continued her work with the figures. When I asked her if any other people belonged in this figural sculpture, she selected Joe's mother and grandfather.

Then I asked her how she would prefer to reposition herself in the symbolic sculpture. She moved the metaphorical object representing herself out of the middle of the couple and along the side, facing Jane, now turned away from Joe. She felt relieved to be in this new position. She did not feel overcome by Joe's pain and could also address the Jane's vulnerability. The object in her hand representing her sister encouraged her to find out more about Jane's pain and fear of abandonment. The supervisee planned to work with Jane's family of origin rather than remain glued to the problematic relationship with Joe and his mother. Incidentally, the supervisee said that this couple was very pertinent for her at this point in her life because she was working on developing a closer and more balanced relationship with both her older sister and her younger brother.

The supervisee used figures in the next therapy session with Joe and Jane. Jane placed her mother and sister facing each other by her side. When the supervisee asked Jane to put her father in the picture, the client began sobbing as she discussed her grief about her father's death five years earlier. She said that her father was an angel, floating around the scene but mostly hovering over her head. The supervisee now understood that part of Jane's fear and anger about Joe's relationship with his mother was her fear of losing another man. Thus, the supervisee became aware of Jane's need for support.

Working with metaphorical objects (in the supervision and therapy sessions) externalized the relational dynamics, enhancing the clarity of presentation and analysis of this case. The supervisory system was better able to define the supervisee's role in maintaining the pattern and to identify potentially fruitful directions for work with the couple. In addition, the use of metaphorical objects indirectly influenced the supervisee to use symbols in her work with this couple and others.

CONCLUSION

The case management supervisor wears many hats. As the name suggests, the first priority is to manage the supervisee's caseload. Secondly, the goal is to assist the supervisee in development of professional skills. In order to accomplish these aims, the case management supervisor provides *educative, administrative, consultative, facilitative, evaluative,* and *mentoring* responses to the supervisee:

- The educator teaches and guides the supervisee's development of professional expertise.
- The administrator responds to the legal, ethical, and procedural requirements of the job.
- The consultant addresses specific clinical dilemmas.
- The facilitator acknowledges the growing edges of the supervisee's professional skills and works with the personal interferences that obstruct development.
- The evaluator performs the gatekeeping role of the professional and judges the quality and professionalism of the supervisee's performance.
- The mentor allows a supervisory encounter that is less role-bound than the others. In the professional context of the supervision, mentoring enables the personhood of the supervisor to connect with the personhood of the supervisee.

These different roles need to be addressed in the contractual phase of the supervision so that the supervisee is clear about the different roles of the supervisor; this permits a relationship based on professional flexibility and respect. Although not as flashy as direct supervisory approaches, case management supervision promotes professional transparency between the supervisor and supervisee. The multitude of roles and mediums to expand the supervisee's repertoire fosters an enduring supervisory relationship in the mind of the supervisee.

8

Live Supervision

THIS CHAPTER IS THE FIRST OF THREE on the supervisor's direct involvement with the clients and the supervisee. Each of these direct supervisory approaches—live supervision, consultation, and apprentice cotherapy—enables the supervisor to perceive and experience the therapeutic system in the here and now, while retaining the potential to intervene in the therapist or client system. However, live supervision, unlike consultation and cotherapy, usually involves a one-way mirror that forms a physical boundary between the supervisory and therapeutic systems. Although the permeability of the mirror clearly engenders a partnership between the supervisor and the therapeutic system, this boundary offers the supervisee greater autonomy than cotherapy or consultation in conducting the therapeutic interview. The supervisor must choose when to permeate the boundary of the mirror, keeping in mind that the therapist's development of self-reliance must be juxtaposed with the supervisor's ability to help facilitate acquisition of therapeutic and supervisory goals. The partnership and immediacy of live supervision make it a very popular approach for supervisors (Mckenzie, Atkinson, Quinn, & Heath, 1986), supervisees (Liddle et al., 1988), and even clients (Kivlighan, Aangelone, & Swafford, 1991; Piercy, Sprenkle, & Constantine, 1986).

Lynn Hoffman (1981) stated that the act of watching clinical interviews from behind a mirror changed the course of therapy. "The advent of the one-way screen . . . was analogous to the discovery of the telescope. Seeing differently made it possible to think differently" (p. 3). Therefore, the mirror became more than a device of supervision; it also became a context that supported two realities of the therapeutic relationship (Berger & Dammann, 1982). The person inside the therapy room experienced and accommodated to the clients' emotional needs, while the person behind the mirror had a more abstract position from which to see the patterns of the family and therapeutic system. The one-way mirror (and subsequently camcorders) impelled the supervisor to include the therapist's behaviors in the consideration of supervisory interventions.

Problems arise when the views of supervisee and supervisor do not match. The supervisor must understand and accommodate to the supervisee's experience in the room, while the supervisee can benefit from the supervisor's meta-perspective. The integration of these two views accelerates the process of change. If the supervisor and supervisee work as a team, clients learn to appreciate their contributions to the therapeutic process.

Since the supervisor is clearly an immediate resource in the field of a live supervision arrangement, the supervisor cannot assume the position of a "Monday morning quarterback." More accurately, the supervisor is a player-coach with shared coresponsibility for the outcome of the session. For instance, if the supervisor tells the supervisee to begin with the stepparent and the child runs out of the office, then the supervisor cannot hide behind the anonymity of the mirror and refuse responsibility for the intervention by blaming the therapist's delivery. Similarly, if the supervisee does not handle a physical threat effectively, a passive, unintrusive supervisor would be responsible for the ensuing crisis. Therefore, live supervision presupposes a context of interconnections between the therapeutic and supervisory systems. The supervisor, supervisee, and clients are in the same field, mutually affecting one another. Live supervision, more than any other supervisory approach, demonstrates that the functions and boundaries of the supervisory system must respond to the therapeutic system.

Figure 8.1 illustrates the interlocking relationships between the supervisor, therapist (supervisee), and clients. Most obviously, the therapist (supervisee) is the common denominator between the supervisory and therapeutic systems. Therefore, the therapist is in danger of becoming triangulated between the demands of the supervisor and the clients. Thus, it is very important that the supervisor has a respectful, trustworthy, and knowledgeable alliance with the therapist before embarking on the project of live supervision. If there are misunderstandings and disputes in the supervisory system, then this will no doubt affect the therapeutic system. Clients might respond to problems in the supervisory system by aligning with the thera-

Figure 8.1: *The therapeutic and supervisory systems in live supervision*

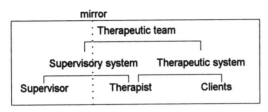

pist against the supervisor, refusing to participate in live supervision, withdrawing from therapy altogether, sacrificing their concerns in order to restore harmony in the supervisory relationship, or employing other ways to balance the excessive stress in the system. In this manner, clients respond to an incompatible supervisory relationship like children in a dysfunctional marriage. Their maneuvers attempt to absorb, divert, or mediate the tensions in the system (often to their own detriment and to that of the system). When the supervisory system works as a therapeutic team with the clients, all become collaborative partners in the therapeutic endeavor.

Forming a therapeutic team is easier said than done. Frequently, live supervision initially creates a great deal of stress because the mirror removes the anonymity of the therapeutic interview. The supervisee, exposed in front of the mirror, often feels inadequate and incompetent. The supervisee may become so concerned with the reflection in the mirror or so absorbed in a fantasy of a disappointed or disapproving supervisor that he or she stays remote from the clients. Each phone call seems proof of the supervisee's inadequacies and negative evaluation.

In a live supervision session with a supervisee interviewing a family for the first time, I made a couple phone calls to help expedite exploration of the family members who were not present at the interview. I had a good relationship with this supervisee and respected her work a great deal; further, I was enthusiastic about the way she handled her first family interview. After the session was over, she came to the other side of the mirror and burst into tears. She felt that she had disappointed me. My reaction to her work was not in sync with what she was feeling. Later, I learned that she never received much positive feedback from her father, despite valiant efforts to win his approval. This session taught me to respect the power of internalized self-reproach that comes with the territory of performing one's trade while an esteemed professional watches on the other side of the one-way mirror. Significant doses of reinforcement and positive affirmation are necessary concomitants to supervisory feedback and challenges.

Once supervisees get through the paranoia of professional observation, they usually become fond of the collaboration that comes with the mirror. The mirror on the wall moves from an instrument of incrimination to an augmented reflection that expedites professional and clinical change. Sometimes, in a difficult or stuck moment, the supervisee may look to the phone to bring in a different perspective. I even had one supervisee describe her malady as "phone dependence." Since overreliance on the phone undermines the supervisee's reliance on his or her resources, the supervisor needs to discriminate whether phone dependence relates to lack of information or to a deeper process replicated across multiple subsystems.

ISOMORPHISM IN THE LIVE SUPERVISION PROCESS

As figure 8.1 portrays, there are multiple systems in the field of live supervision. As discussed in chapter 2, interconnected systems have a tendency to replicate isomorphically. That is, while there are differences in content, the process or form of the systems can be uncannily similar. The supervisor must notice whether an impasse in the therapeutic system parallels a pattern in the supervisory system. If this is the case, the supervisor can deliberately choose a new way of acting in the supervisory system (Elizur, 1990). This "top down" intervention models a new mode of behavior that ripples through the process in the therapeutic system. The supervisor's change of "heart" does not guarantee change in the therapeutic system but it does open the door to new possibilities.

For instance, it is quite common for beginning supervisors to "oversupervise" by micromanaging the supervisee and the therapeutic process. This style of supervision leads to what has been called *robotization* of the supervisee. "Some degree of robotization is inevitable in live supervision, and, if it is a temporary process, there are times when it may be helpful and necessary, such as during early stages of training. But robotization is harmful when it is prolonged to the point at which it erodes trainees' confidence . . . " (Schwartz, Liddle, & Breunlin, 1988, p. 184). Further, it unwittingly models micromanagement to the supervisee, who may attempt to do the same with clients. Once the supervisor becomes aware of the isomorphism between the systems, he or she should intervene in a manner that changes the pattern. The supervisor might intervene directly by instructing the supervisee to be less intrusive in the client's process or more indirectly by changing his or her intervention style. For instance, the supervisor could change his or her part in the pattern of an overreactive system by intentionally talking more slowly, minimizing interruptions of a session, reinforcing the supervisee's resources to handle the situation, etc. The supervisor's differentiation changes the tempo in the supervisory system. As the supervisor becomes more unpredictable (e.g., the phone does not ring during a prolonged silence), the supervisee has the option and space to function more autonomously.

In a family therapy with a severely rebellious adolescent, the therapist became very frustrated with the father's lack of flexibility. Despite other rigid behaviors in the family, it seemed that the therapist's attention and energy were totally taken up in a battle of wills with the father. When, either prior to or during the session, I formulated a plan with the therapist to approach the family differently, it did not seem to be carried out by the therapist with any resonance. In other words, he would mimic the plan, but without carrying through using the family's feedback. I felt that he would respond to my direction, but would go only as far as my last sentence. Since he was a much better therapist than he was exhibiting, I felt very frustrated with him. Thus, the client system contained a frustrated father in relationship to his son; the therapeutic system had a frustrated therapist in relationship to the father; and the supervisory system included a frustrated supervisor in relationship to the supervisee.

In the post-session following live supervision, I became aware of the isomorphic pattern of the frustration between real and symbolic fathers and sons. I shifted my position by becoming a different type of father. I began by honestly discussing my respect for his work and my puzzle about his lack of spontaneity with this family. He told me that my valuing of him was very important and that he was afraid of disappointing me. He spoke about how he lived in his father's shadow and struggled to be his own person. He described his father as perfectionistic and critical. He still carried this image of his father around with him even though his father had mellowed with age. I asked him what his father would say now about the interview if he were supervising him. He said that his father would tell him that he was okay and to trust himself and everything would work out fine. By the end of the post-session, the supervisee felt accepted by both me and his internalized image of his father. In the following session, he had a much more relaxed, self-accepting, and family-accepting demeanor. In particular, he had a softer and easier relationship with the client father. Thus, my vocalized acceptance of the supervisee set in motion greater self- and other acceptance, which rippled through the system.

Despite the intentions of the supervisor, the one-way mirror often creates a context that challenges a supervisee's level of confidence, competence, and self-acceptance. If the supervisor is aware of a negative transferential or countertransferential relationship in the supervisory system, then the supervisor needs to rectify the projections in the level of the supervisory system. Since live supervision involves the supervisee's intersection in the supervisory and therapeutic systems, a shift in the supervisee's heart in one system will be carried into the other system. Therefore, the supervisor must keep one eye on his or her heart while pondering live supervision interventions for the head and the hands of the supervisee. A supervisee who feels supported by the supervisor (or who intrinsically has high self-esteem) is proportionately able to tolerate greater challenges in the live supervision context. The following live supervision interventions must be read with sensitivity to the appropriate percentages of support and challenge.

PHASES OF THE LIVE SUPERVISION PROCESS

Live supervision logically includes pre-session, session, and post-session phases. The pre- and post-session phases, which generally include only the supervisory system, provide an opportunity for the exploration and clarification of the head and the heart of the supervisee, as well as arenas in which to address the interface of the training and clinical goals. The live session itself is not an appropriate context for lengthy elaboration of the professional or personal quandaries of the supervisee; rather, the live session focuses on how the supervisee is or could be using the hands (in conjunction with the nose, heart, and head) to connect, assess, or intervene in the therapeutic system.

Pre-session

The length of the pre-session phase depends upon the temporal constraints of the work context, the supervisee's level of expertise, the unique demands and complexity of issues in the client system and/or the supervisee, and the level of compatibility between the supervisee and supervisor. In most cases, 15 minutes is saved for the pre-session. I have found that this is adequate time to review the previous and current developments of the case, connect with the supervisee's recent thinking and current clinical and professional goals, and add any cursory remarks (which could also include remarks by other team members or observers, if available).

The brevity of time compels a focused dialogue that does not provide too much information or stimulation for an already expectant supervisee. It would be easy to overload a supervisee with too many options and contingency plans. Although it is beneficial for a supervisee to begin the session with a general plan for approaching the professional or client houses, the plan in the pre-session cannot predict recent developments in the client system; therefore, it may turn out to be irrelevant. A flexible plan will help orient the supervisor to the supervisee's goals, which serve as a common reference point. Nevertheless, the supervisee and supervisor have to learn the art of responding to the ambiguity and spontaneity inherent in human systems. A detailed plan of operations can precook the session without respecting the integrity of the basic ingredients. The supervisory or therapeutic plan that does not fit the context of the session will be useless and/or destructive to the therapeutic team.

An anecdote can highlight the folly of predicting client reactions to planned therapeutic interventions. A very strong father challenged the supervisee to prescribe a plan to deal with a longstanding enuretic condition of his 12-year-old son. He complained that all of the medical and behavioral doctors had been useless in helping his son deal with this embarrassing condition. The supervisee did not know how to respond to this direct and earnest request of the father. If he gave nothing, the father would be disappointed and become even more resistant to the counseling process. However, he did not have an answer to father's question. Out of the direct line of the fire, I had the luxury of emotional distance, which enabled me to muse on a strange intuition for an intervention.

I called the supervisee out of the room and told him that the enuresis was the boy's way of coping with his anxiety and that he needed the support of both of his separated parents to handle his bedwetting. Since the doctors had not come up with a solution, the parents would have to be the ones to handle the boy's problem. The separated mother and father were asked to have the boy sleep in their beds in their respective homes. This sleeping arrangement would be a way to give him support and help him cope with his enuresis. It was explained that several accidents might happen before they resolved the problem, but that they should persist with this procedure until the problem was corrected. The father was outraged that he might end up in a puddle of urine, but was willing to do this for his son. On some level, I felt that he enjoyed a family resolution to the problem rather than a medical solution. The son and mother had no objections to the procedure.

In the pre-session of the next interview, the supervision group believed that the directive probably would not work. In order to prepare for the failure of the directive to ameliorate the enuresis, the supervisee role-played two situations: one in which the family was noncompliant with the request, and the other in which the prescribed ritual failed to ameliorate the enuresis. The supervisee was well-coached to handle the family feedback in both of these scenarios. In fact, the family reported that there were no bedwetting accidents, to the astonishment of the therapist and the supervision team. The supervisee was completely unprepared to deal with the success of the intervention. He struggled to answer the family's questions, such as how long to continue the parent-child sleeping operation, and ultimately congratulated them and said they obviously knew best. Thus, despite the most careful and best-intended pre-sessions, the supervisor has to impart the lessons of therapeutic spontaneity.

Session

In a rigid system, the therapist is vulnerable to succumbing to the tensions of the client system by reflexive, inflexible responses that maintain rigidified dysfunctional patterns (Andolfi & Menghi, 1982; Snyders, 1986). Thus, the solution becomes part of the problem (Watzlawick, Weakland, & Fisch, 1974). For instance, a warring couple may induce the therapist to play the role of a judge or mediator in order to handle their tensions. If the therapist regularly enacts a mediative function in the therapeutic system, then the predictability of his or her behaviors preempts the necessity for the couple to learn the skills of problem resolution or differentiation from the origins of their emotional reactions. Instead of providing a permanent mediative resolution, the therapist's fixed role limits the discovery of resources in the couple by fostering overreliance on the therapist. Ideally, the meta-position of the supervisor enables him or her to see the rigidity of functions in the client system and to support the individuation process of the therapist by advocating greater unpredictability of functions.

Similarly, the supervisor must avoid developing a rigid role in relationship to the supervisee. Supervisory overfunctioning will invariably lead to supervisee underfunctioning. The supervisor must be careful to introduce novelty in the therapeutic system rather than producing predictable noise that has minimal impact. This danger is of particular concern in rigid therapeutic systems that have a high level of tension.

Liddle and Schwartz (1983) have developed a fascinating and comprehensive taxonomy to guide decisions about whether and how to intervene in live supervision.

The following questions direct the supervisor to use greater restraint and discrimination during live supervision:

- *Urgency.* What will be the consequences if the intervention is not delivered?
- *Probability of unprompted actions.* How likely is it that the supervisee will make the intervention on his or her own if the supervisor uses restraint and waits a bit longer?
- *Probability of successful implementation.* Will the supervisee be able to implement a particular intervention at this time?
- *Dependence and differentiation.* Will the supervisory intervention create

undue dependence on the part of the supervisee? (Liddle & Schwartz, 1983)

The supervisor must consider the juxtaposition of goals and relationship issues in the client system, therapeutic system, and supervisory system. Since the first priority is to protect the clients and ensure that no harm befalls them because of treatment, live supervision offers an appropriate setting to deal with clinical and ethical quandaries. However, the overall goal for the supervisor is not to demonstrate clinical expertise and guile, but to work in a context that can respect the "good enough" aspects of the supervisee and expand those attributes as necessary. Since the supervisee's body is with the client system on the other side of the mirror, the supervisor has to respect the integrity of the supervisee's head, heart, hands, and nose. The supervisor should not produce generic interventions, but should fit the supervisory directive to the physical capabilities of the supervisee. "The supervisor must ask himself or herself, not, 'How can I help these clients?' but, 'How can I change this therapist so that the therapist can help these clients?'" (Mead, 1990, p. 97).

Through the years, I have become much slower and parsimonious with live supervision interventions. However, I still actively intervene with problematic clinical circumstances, beginning supervisees who desire/need structure and support, more advanced supervisees who are shifting to a different level of expertise, or supervisees who are struggling with professional/personal interface issues. These situations, depending upon various clinical and supervisory scenarios, require varying levels and classes of live supervision interventions such as the following:

- *Directive:* " Follow this direction and see where it goes."
- *Supportive:* "I like your work with this issue."
- *Declarative:* "Please give this message to the family from me."
- *Interrogative:* "What do you think about so and so? Do you think this will be a worthwhile direction?"
- *Explorative:* "What's going on inside with you when this happened?" or "How can your nose work and shift to a metaphorical level?"
- *Reflective:* "I feel lonely in this situation."
- *Intensive:* "Only you can help them handle the pain that they are feeling!"

Beginning supervisees prefer clear concrete, brief, and supportive directives, whereas intermediate and advanced supervisees prefer questions, reflections, and good-natured challenges. Advanced supervisees prefer greater autonomy in the supervision process and can do more with less intervention.

The levels of interventions can be delivered in many forms. Since live supervision is a multisystemic context, the supervisor can choose to intervene with the supervisee, members of the client system, or both together in order to employ the subsystem that will most readily facilitate the process.

Post-session

The exclusion of the client system in the post-session provides the latitude to sharpen the focus on the professional development of the supervisee. Since the supervisee is shifting contexts from participating in the clients' story to rejoining the supervisory story, the supervisor should help ease the transition by providing brief positive feedback, humor, a smile, or any other message that conveys acceptance of the personhood of the supervisee. Especially in the context where a supervisee receives feedback, suggestions, and challenges, the personhood must be respected, honored, and appreciated. The supervisor must be mindful that the typical supervisee is well-meaning and performs to the best of his or her ability in the time, place, and relational circumstances of live supervision. After all, if our supervisees were perfect professionals, then supervisors would be superfluous.

Usually, the supervisee begins debriefing the interview by discussing his or her experience, the rationale for the approach taken, the range of realization of client and professional goals, and reaction to the supervisory directives. Similar to the goal setting in the pre-session, the supervisee's post-session remarks orient the supervisor to his or her growing edges. In addition, the supervisee's explanation of what happened provides a common language for exploration of new edges. Finally, the supervisee responds to the question about what he or she wants from the post-session. Thus, the supervisee's position and questions begin to be articulated.

Of course, the supervisee continues to discuss his or her experience and introduce new questions throughout the post-session. But at least the supervisor has a foot in the door inside the supervisee's experience. What the supervisor does from that vantage point depends upon the issues presented in the session, the head, heart, hands, nose of the supervisee, and the same body parts of the supervisor, both as a therapist and as a supervisor. The supervisor does not need to be overly organized by the supervisee's reality, but he or she does need to link his or her meta-perspective with the supervisee's experience. The supervisor's goal is to present to the supervisee new information that will foster new approaches.

Figure 8.2 presents a live supervision form that has been helpful in organizing and recording the germane issues in each phase of the live supervision

Figure 8.2: *Live supervision form*

Theme:

Persons present:

Date:

Pre-session

   (a) Client's presenting and current problem(s):

   (b) Therapist's questions/problems about clients:

   (c) Therapist focus on skill development:

Session

   (a) Summary:

   (b) Therapist and therapeutic relationship:

   (c) Supervisory interventions:

   (d) Supervisor and supervisory relationship:

Post-session

   (a) Client's goals, developmental issues:

   (b) Therapist's goals, developmental issues:

   (c) Supervisor's goals, developmental issues:

   (d) Tasks:

process. The form focuses on the dual issues of clinical and professional goals in the therapeutic team.

METHODS OF INTERVENTION
DURING LIVE SUPERVISION

Once the supervisor makes the decision to intervene in the session, the context of live supervision affords multiple spatial arrangements for conveying messages to the therapeutic system. A mirror and an intercom present concrete metaphors of a boundary separating the two rooms and a potential dyadic linkage between the supervisor and one of the members of the therapeutic system. In addition, the mirror concretely represents a reflection of the therapeutic relationship that is seen by the supervisor on the other side of the mirror. The unseen but felt presence of the supervisor offers members of the therapeutic system a responsible party to monitor their reflection and provide resources to help them through times of stagnation, uncertainty, and excessive anxiety.

Live supervision can also occur without the accoutrements of a mirror and intercom. Prior to using these technological luxuries, I organized the room so that there was a space for the therapeutic system, with me sitting physically out of the circle; an empty chair amidst the therapeutic system replaced the intercom. When I felt it necessary to make a supervisory (or I should say, consultative) comment, I occupied the empty chair and spoke to the supervisee in earshot of the client system. In that way, I simultaneously communicated with the clients while presenting a new perspective for the supervisee.

The privilege of being physically apart from and apart of the therapeutic system not only ratifies that the supervisor a part of the therapeutic team but also makes it clear to all that the supervisor can affect the supervisee's (therapist's) and client system's behavior through a direct intervention. This idea frees the supervisor to judiciously vary supervisory interventions in any of the units of the therapeutic team, including the supervisor, supervisee, and any of the client members. "The supervisor must decide and then connect at any given moment with the individual who can have the greatest impact on the therapeutic relationship" (Andolfi, Ellenwood, & Wendt, 1993).

For instance, after being unable to get the supervisee to attend to the grief issues in the session, via the intercom I asked one of the children to ask the other family members if they were ready to let the therapist hear about the emotional impact of the loss. The question, delivered by this caring and concerned child, simultaneously challenged the family and the therapist to be braver in facing the issue of emotional loss. The intervention resulted in the supervisee's helping the family sort out the impact of their grief. Thus, live supervision offers other ways to influence clinical and supervisory issues than just giving directives to the therapist.

Andolfi (Andolfi et al., 1993; Andolfi & Menghi, 1982) has developed two different schematic models for demonstrating the flexibility of spatial arrangements in live supervision. Here I elaborate his use of different formations in the therapeutic team to advance the supervisee's clinical and professional development.

Phone Intervention from
Supervisor to the Therapist

The intercom is the most parsimonious method of conveying information from the supervisor to the therapist (see figure 8.3). The intercom is an audible and physical metaphor of the supervisor's ability or potentiality to convey information. The phone call interrupts the flow of the session and forces the therapist to switch gears and attend to the supervisor rather than the client system. The discontinuity of the phone call can be a useful intervention if a therapist is too enmeshed, predictable, or role-bound in a therapeutic system. The intercom compels the client system to recognize that the therapist has one foot out of their system and belongs to a system with a professional purpose. Since the phone call disturbs the homeostasis of the therapeutic system, some of the client members (and some therapists) may object. The therapist must learn how to live in the triad of the therapeutic team and the supervisor must recognize the impact of the therapist's participation in this triad.

If a supervisor believes that the client or therapeutic system can benefit from a provocation of its predictable roles and patterns, he or she may offer many types of suggestions to produce greater unpredictability. The supervisor can ask the therapist to redirect the family, increase intensity, disclose personal feelings such as hopelessness, reframe the stuckness, introduce a metaphor, prescribe a ritual, or try a number of other interventions. The therapist can choose different ways of presenting the supervisor's ideas or provocations, assimilating the information and presenting it as his or her

Figure 8.3: *Supervisor-therapist linkage on the intercom*

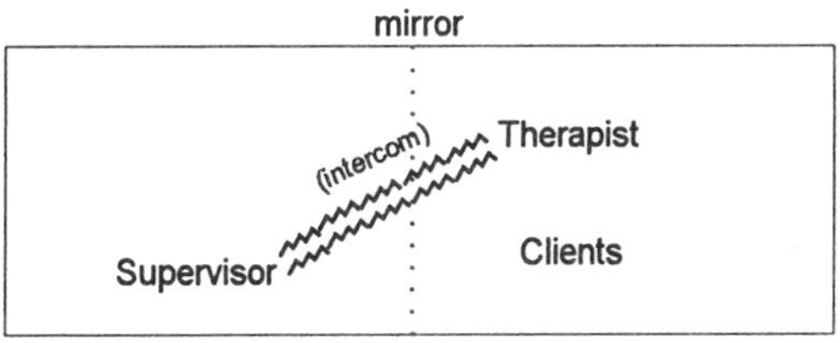

own or disowning it and presenting it as the property of the supervisor. Furthermore, the therapist can disagree with the supervisor's perception, thereby establishing a supervisory debate that supports the clients' ability to change. For instance, a supervisee was dealing with a volatile leaving-home process of an 18-year-old daughter. The parents felt that she was irrational and dependent on her girlfriend (ex-lover). The girl was equally vehement about her ability to function independently. The therapist did not broach the sexual orientation differences between the daughter and the parents because she was afraid of violating the trust of the daughter. After a phone call, the therapist told the family that the supervisor said that the family could not work through the normal grief of a separation process because the daughter and parents had a different sexual orientation. The therapist took a more optimistic view. The intervention prepared those in the therapeutic system to talk more openly about emotional feelings around the daughter's lesbianism.

There are certain precautions to take when using the phone that will help the therapist attend to the message of the supervisor while still feeling empowered and connected to the client system. Most of these suggestions originate from the research of Lorraine Wright (1986).

1. *Beware of intrusiveness.* Ideally, the supervisor should not call the therapist for at least the first 10 minutes of the interview. The temporal space gives the message that the therapist will run the session as opposed to the supervisor coordinating the development of the session from behind the mirror.

2. *Limit the number of phone calls.* Wright suggested that calls should not typically exceed more than five per session. Again, too much phone contact diminishes the autonomy of the therapist. Beginning supervisees may benefit from more frequent interventions by the supervisor, while advanced supervisees do not usually extensive guidance.

3. *Include positive reinforcement.* Supervisees like to hear what they do well. Especially during the first phone-in, they need to hear what they are doing well, so that they do not become too self-critical and doubting. Therefore, specific comments about their performance ("I liked the way you introduced the impact of father's separation from the home") can create more willingness to incorporate advice from the supervisor ("Find out how they could ask him in a way that he would want to come").

4. *Vary complexity to the supervisee.* A beginning therapist needs more concrete directives, while an advanced therapist can handle self-revealing questions or global directives. For instance, in an impasse a beginning supervisee may be given an idea or a frame from a supervisor

(head or hand information), whereas an experienced therapist may be asked to talk about feelings or fantasies about what is happening in the room (heart and nose).

5. *Limit the amount of information.* When the supervisee is in the presence of the client system, brief phone calls are less distracting and easier to assimilate than longer ones. Although Wright suggests limiting phone calls to 25 seconds, this timeframe may be too limited when brief explanations are needed to complement suggested interventions. Nevertheless, the scope of the information needs to be confined to one or perhaps two ideas.

6. *Veto power.* Supervisees should be informed, prior to the live supervision session, that they can refuse to carry out supervisory directives that do not make clinical or ethical sense. If a supervisee's head and heart are antagonistic to the directive, his or her hands will be unsteady, uncertain, and unconvincing in the delivery of the supervisory suggestion. Therefore, the supervisor should consider other alternatives for dealing with conflicting views of the supervisee. As mentioned in the example of the supervisory debate, the supervisee can give a supervisory directive without owning it and can even disagree with the supervisor's perspective. However, since supervisors are ultimately responsible for the outcome of clinical decisions, they can overrule the supervisee's veto in dire clinical circumstances.

Phone Calls from the Supervisor to Members of the Client System

As previously mentioned, not all supervisory intercom interventions need to go through the therapist. The supervisor can sometimes effectively change the therapeutic system and facilitate professional growth in the therapist through dialogue with members of the client system (see figure 8.4). The decision to speak with a client member acknowledges the obvious, that the clients are vital resources in the system and are in an ideal position to

Figure 8.4: *Supervisor-client linkage on the intercom*

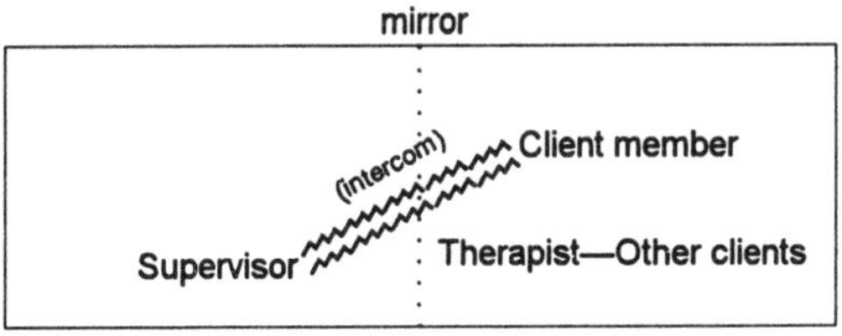

collaborate with the treatment process. Furthermore, the judicious inclusion of a client member into the supervisory system builds self- and systemic esteem as it signifies that the supervisor needs help from one of their own. Often the sensitivity, power, and desperation of the identified patient enable him or her to take greater chances than other members in the therapeutic system (including the therapist) (Ridgely, 1994a). In addition, the temporary relationship to the supervisor enlists the identified patient as an ally to the change process, releasing him or her from the role of the barrier that absorbs much of the tensions and energy in the client system. However, any member in the client system can provide useful information or support in the process of change.

In a session that involved an intractable deadlock between a teenager and the parents, the younger teenage daughter, ignored by the parents and the therapist, pretended to be asleep. The supervisor phoned in and asked the therapist to hand the phone to the girl. The supervisor "woke" her by asking her to speak about her dreams and to engage each of the family members in a discussion of their personal dreams. Her diversion enabled the family temporarily to escape an unproductive pattern and become more personal. It also showed her value to the therapist as well as to the process, even when she was sleeping. The post-session addressed the therapist's ability to bypass the head and hands when they are ineffective by incorporating the resources of the nose.

Midway in the therapy with a single mother, older sister, and 12-year-old boy struggling with attention-deficit and conduct disorder problems, an experienced therapist listed his goal as being able to maintain appropriate authority in the family session. He discussed the parallel process of the client family and his family-of-origin, as well as his similar coping mechanism of fading into the background. Despite some phone interruptions, he lost his executive ability in the session as he passively observed the boy's excessively noisy play in the room while the mother and sister talked about the problems that he was causing in the home and at school. With some frustration, I asked to speak with the boy, but he refused to be bothered with the supervisor. Feeling rejected, I asked to speak with his sister behind the one-way mirror; she readily responded to my request. I gave her a fishing rope and asked her to take the rope into the therapy room and, without talking, to tie up the therapist. Being a good sport, she went ahead with this unusual task. The therapist immediately got the metaphor and disclosed his feelings of being tied up in the therapy session. The boy untied him and became part of the process. This intervention demonstrates how temporary enlistment of a client into the supervisory system can further the goals of both the therapy and the supervision.

The Therapist Leaves the Therapy
Room to Join the Supervisor

If a phone call creates discontinuity, then the therapist leaving the room to join the supervisor serves as an even more dramatic break in the action (see figure 8.5). The separation creates anticipation in the client system about the reformed position of the therapist. In addition, the separation allows the therapist to leave the emotions of the clients to join the professional arena of the supervisor. The "call-out" could be initiated by either the supervisor or the therapist; however, it is rare for a therapist to take the initiative to separate from the client system. For better or for worse, the therapist's desire to stay with the client system usually precludes temporary withdrawal from the impasse. Nonetheless, separation may allow enhanced closeness. One cannot separate if one has not joined, and one cannot join unless one is separate. The ability sequentially to separate and join is vital for the flexibility and freshness of the therapist. Therapeutic impasse frequently results in an undifferentiated therapist who is neither joined with nor separated from the client system.

Phone-ins are optimal for minor tactical adjustments or when the supervisor and therapist share a similar mind-set. Call-outs, on the other hand, are more useful for major strategic redirections or when more extensive discussion is needed to sort out communication difficulties or important disagreements between the therapist and supervisor. The previous example involving the father's demand for a solution to his son's longstanding enuresis shows the benefits of a face-to-face collaboration between the therapist and supervisor.

Some approaches regularly schedule a break for the collaboration of the therapist and supervisor (Pirrotta & Cecchin, 1988), which becomes accepted by the clients as a regular treatment procedure. While effective, such procedures introduce the supervisor as a regular part of the treatment process. The differential use of live supervision offers greater flexibility to the supervisor, who can pass the lessons of increased flexibility on to the therapist

Figure 8.5: *Therapist joins the supervisor*

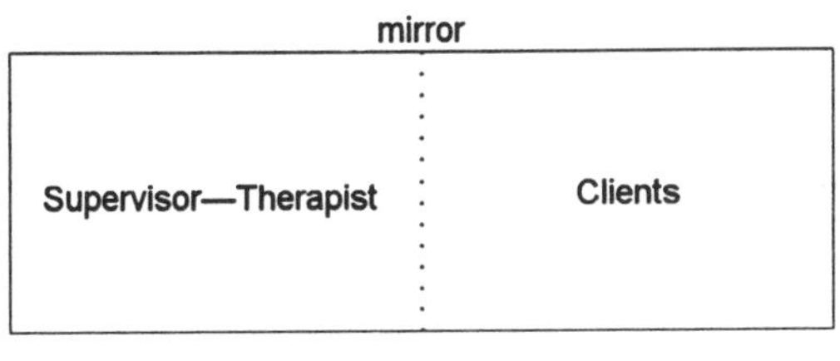

and the clients. The supervisor must be mindful to balance flexibility with parsimony; otherwise the supervisor may become a predictable fixture of the treatment process and undermine the autonomy of the therapist.

Client Leaves the Therapy Room
to Join the Supervisor

The supervisor can ask a client or client subsystem to come behind the one-way mirror to further clinical or supervisory developments (see figure 8.6). This procedure has been used by structural family therapists (e.g., Minuchin & Fishman, 1981) in order to establish boundaries around subsystems. Behind the mirror clients see the system from the meta-perspective of the supervisor, while clients inside the therapy room experience their separateness. This intervention offers the therapist an opportunity to work with a different composition of the client system, while the supervisor exchanges information with those behind the mirror.

An only-child family, referred by a high-school guidance counselor because of the son's multiple school suspensions for aggressive behavior, successfully found ways to handle the school problems. As the behavioral problem diminished, the parents disagreed about the way to run the home. The marital quarrel frequently resulted in arguments between the adolescent and his mother. As supervisor I asked the teenager to come behind the one-way mirror so that the therapist could work with the marital subsystem. Behind the mirror, I congratulated the adolescent on his diligent work in handling the family's tensions and expressed confidence that the therapist could handle his parents' problems. The adolescent enjoyed the perspective of the mirror and commented about the quality of supervisory suggestions to the therapist with regard to handling his parents' concerns. This formerly aggressive adolescent was incredibly perceptive about the nuances of his parents' communications. I allowed him to call the therapist in order to translate some of the nonverbals. The parents good-naturedly admitted to the emotional competence and sensitivity of their son. Although he and I had so much fun behind the mirror that we hated to separate, I sent him back

Figure 8.6: *Client joins the supervisor*

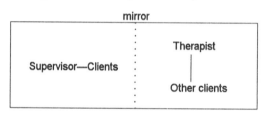

to rejoin the therapeutic system. At the next session, he wanted to rejoin the supervisor; however, in a phone call to him I suggested that he could handle his parents' problems without fighting or physical separation. This example illustrates that inviting a client or subsystem behind the mirror offers a different perspective, but it should be only a temporary intervention.

The Supervisor Joins the Therapeutic System

At certain times, the supervisor may come from behind the mirror to join the therapeutic system. The appearance of the supervisor generates an informed mini-consultation. It is informed because the supervisor is privy to the system's rigidified patterns, and it is temporary because the goal is to make a shift in order to hand the therapy back to the therapist. The supervisor unbalances rigid patterns in the therapeutic system by engaging the therapist or the client members (figure 8.7) in a dialogue that produces new information. A mini-consultation is a rather direct path of supervisory intervention, since the supervisor works with the entire system rather than with segments of it. Since the supervisor can affect the direction of the session more fully from inside the room, this procedure may cause a supervisory dilemma. It is important to ask:

- If the supervisor comes inside the room, how does this affect the autonomy of the supervisee?
- Can the supervisor use less intrusive procedures to change the therapeutic system?
- Under what conditions should the supervisor come into the session to promote more effective treatment?
- What are or should be the boundaries of the therapeutic system?
- How will a "walk-in" intervention affect the relationship between the supervisor and the supervisee?
- How will it affect the supervisee's view of his or her professionalism?

Figure 8.7: *Supervisor joins the therapeutic system*

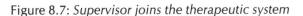
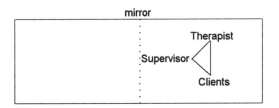

Walk-ins should be a procedure of last resort. As a beginning supervisor, I remember the excitement, intensity, and expectation of knocking on the therapy room door, uncovering new territory in the session, planting some seeds for the future, and then leaving the room before the germination process took hold. It was easier to supervise by doing the driving than by respecting, using, and augmenting the skills of the supervisee from the back seat of the car.

Despite these reservations, I would not abandon mini-consultations as one of the supervisor's vehicles. During a mini-consultation, the supervisor can demonstrate a different approach of working with clinical dilemmas and provide an in vivo learning experience for the supervisee. The supervisee can sit back and watch the supervisor perform his or her preferred intervention rather than attempt to decode supervisory messages over the intercom. Besides viewing the implementation of the supervisor's strategy, the supervisee will determine the impact of the intervention. Such observational learning provides a model for the supervisee to adaptively emulate when faced with similar clinical challenges. Supervisees have frequently commented that mini-consultations have taught them to be more flexible and creative in times of therapeutic impasse.

CONCLUSION

Live supervision is a dynamic endeavor that joins the supervisor and therapist in a therapeutic team. Thus, the triad of clients-therapist-supervisor is much more interactive in live supervision than in indirect supervisory approaches. The supervisor must monitor the subsystems of the therapeutic team and construe interventions as appropriate. Furthermore, the closeness of live supervision to the actual therapy provides an ideal environment in which to infiltrate the mind and body of the supervisee. The supervisor no longer has to imagine what the supervisee does in certain clinical circumstances, but can observe and modify his or her interventions. The impact of live supervision is very intense, so much so that the experience of live supervision stays with the supervisee long after the session(s).

The next chapter covers the use of consultation as a supervisory vehicle. I prefer the role of an invited consultant for a session and a follow-up than the role of a walk-in consultant during live supervision because the contractual parameters are clearer. A solicited consultant is invited to make comments and interventions that benefit a troubled therapeutic system. On the other hand, a walk-in supervisor, who is an unannounced guest, works in the presumptuous position of defining and repairing relational problems without a clear contract. Therefore, the supervisor in this role must carefully perceive and accommodate to the receptivity of the therapeutic system to his or her benevolent intrusion.

9

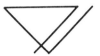

Consultation as a
Supervisory Intervention

WYNNE, MCDANIEL, AND WEBER (1986) defined consultation as a "process in which a *consultee* seeks assistance from a *consultant* in order to identify or clarify a *concern* or problem and *to consider the options* [emphasis added] available for problem resolution (p. 8). The definition implies that consultation is a supportive relationship similar to a supervisory arrangement, but with two important differences. First, the consultative relationship temporarily focuses on empowering the therapy versus being an ongoing, supervisory encounter. Second, the consultant offers *options for consideration*, not directions and imperatives.

Due to the supervisor's clinical, administrative, and legal responsibilities, meta-perspective, and advanced level of clinical experience, the supervisory role resembles that of a coach to the supervisee. On the other hand, in a consultative relationship, the consultant's role resembles that of a solicited advisor. The advisor is invited by the therapist or clients because he or she possesses the skills to help the therapeutic system function more adequately. The range and depth of the invitation depend upon the need and trust level of the consultee. It is important to differentiate the position of the coach to that of an advisor. An advisor provides information, guidance, and feedback as options or perspectives for consideration as opposed to directives.

Whereas the supervisee must answer to the coach, the consultee can retains responsibility for the direction of the therapy.

When a supervisor is invited to be a consultant, the juxtaposition of roles creates an identity issue for both the supervisor and supervisee. Is the supervisory, consultative relationship like that of a coach and player or advisor and client?

Despite role hierarchy, in actuality are the supervisor's suggestions or directives anything more than advice? Except in live supervision, the supervisor loses control of his or her input as soon as the supervisee closes the door to the therapy room. This feeling of powerlessness is similar to parenting an adolescent. A parent can feel good about the common understanding developed through dialogue (hopefully not by lecture) and can even implore the child to complete tasks. But, once the child walks out the door, the parent loses the guarantee of the child's complicity to directives or mutual agreements. The parent can only hope that the child will heed advice or, at least, learn from mistakes without inordinate pain. Appropriate autonomy operatively facilitates development. Therefore, in the supervisory encounter, the role of *advisor* actually may be more realistic than the role of *coach*, except in cases that present clinical or ethical impasses. The consultant exerts influence through the resonance and intensity of the interview rather than through hierarchical authority.

The planned entrance into the sanctity of the therapeutic relationship requires a spirit of collegiality and respect between the supervisor and supervisee. The alternative ("I can do therapy better than you") forsakes the previous and future work of the therapist and client system. Therefore, besides being a guest to the therapeutic system, the supervisor as consultant is an *ally* to the supervisee's professional and clinical development.

The consultant should always respect and consider the position of the supervisee in the therapeutic system and the resources and limitations of the treatment context, supervisee, clients, and relevant ecosystems. The goal of the consultation is to uncover ideas that increase the supervisee's clinical flexibility and adroitness. A seemingly powerful consultation does not guarantee a beneficial effect. Minuchin (1986), a recognized master consultant, warned about the dire consequences of producing interesting consultations without considering the treatment context.

> The families, the therapists, and I were satisfied with the consultations. But, when I did a follow-up a few years later, I learned that in a significant number of my consultations, I had failed to understand the context of therapist and family. In effect, I had constructed and then proceeded to consult an ideal family in therapy with an ideal therapist, divorced from the social context. . . . I now try to include a feedback

procedure in my consultation; never again can I be that blissfully ignorant. (p. xii)

In this regard, the supervisory relationship provides an ideal context for consultations because the supervisor's ongoing presence allows ample opportunities to reinforce or recalibrate the consultative intervention to fit the ensuing clinical developments. The supervisor can check the supervisee's direction in future supervision sessions. Furthermore, depending upon the clinical circumstances, the consultant could attend a follow-up session. Thus, rather than providing a one-shot intervention, the sustained involvement of the supervisor intertwines the magical intuitions and mundane suggestions of the consultation with the head, hands, heart, and nose of the supervisee. The shared act of consultation in the supervisory relationship usually results in increased vigor, investment, and collaboration in the aftercare of the clients.

Since the supervisor is already a *coach* and *ally* of the supervisee, why is it beneficial for him or her to be invited as a *consultant*? The previous chapter on live supervision describes the impromptu walk-in consultation as a method that quickly and intensely redirects the therapeutic system by bringing in a different perspective. The intrusion of an impromptu visit demands caution due to the lack of contractual clarity between the supervisor and therapeutic system. Is the supervisor wanted or unwanted, boss or advisor? A contemplated and predetermined request for a consultation shifts the responsibility for the entrance of the consultant to the therapist and clients. Once the therapeutic system initiates the request for a consultation, then the supervisor merely responds to the invitation rather than adopting the role of intruder into their system.

Frequently, the role of the consultant is more confusing for the professional than it is for the clients. The public usually welcomes a "second opinion" because it gives them the security and peace of mind that professionals are collaborating for their good. However, some therapists resist seeking consultations because of a need to protect themselves from the embarrassment of admitting that they need help with a clinical problem. There are too many therapists who feel that they should solely bear the burden of responsibility for resolving clinical and therapeutic dilemmas. However, remember that the most important responsibility of the therapist's is to "do no harm." Therefore, the second opinion should be a vital alternative to steadfastly working alone to resolve intractable problems. After all, if I were undergoing a complex surgical procedure, I would certainly appreciate a surgeon who had the integrity, foresight, and conscientiousness to request a second opinion. Consultation for mental health problems such as problematic relationships, compulsions, or mood disorders should receive no less vigilant attention by mental health practitioners than our medical counterparts.

The American Psychological Association (1992) has advised psychologists to consider receiving and giving consultations in clinically appropriate situations. "Psychologists arrange for appropriate consultations and referrals based principally on the best interests of their patients or clients. . . . When indicated . . . psychologists cooperate with other professionals in order to serve their patients or clients effectively and appropriately" (section 1.20). Mental health professionals seem more amenable to employing a consultation when the therapeutic encounter is unproductive and unresponsive. Besides insuring more prudent client care, consultation is one of the best ways to protect oneself from legal liability (Slovenko, 1980). Thus, consultation should be one of the optional vehicles in the supervisory garage. The more problematic the case, the more involved the supervisor should be with the supervision. Case discussion, video supervision, live supervision, and consultation incrementally involve closer participation of the supervisor with the case.

Since the benefits of consultation seem straightforward and obvious, why has this procedure not been more fully promoted by academic institutions, insurance companies, most theoretical orientations, and many practitioners? I believe that the answer to this question lies in the historical emphasis on transferential and confidential aspects of the therapeutic relationship. Psychoanalytic and many subsequent therapeutic approaches have promoted the notion that the therapeutic alliance, in and of itself, provides a corrective clinical solution to earlier deficits. On the other hand, systemic approaches have advocated the inclusion of the clients' problematic ecosystem as a resource and ally to the treatment process. Therefore, systemic approaches encourage a permeable therapeutic arena that works with and through the clients' external resources. The therapist does not replace resources of the clients' system but helps the system to use resources more adequately so that they can handle problems and developmental passages without depending upon professionals. In this regard, consultation parallels therapy, since the consultant's preeminent goal is to intervene in a manner that empowers the therapeutic system to better handle its problems and relational concerns. The effective consultation, like successful therapy, creates a context that operates successfully with appropriate autonomy.

ROLE OF THE CONSULTANT
IN THERAPEUTIC IMPASSE

The most common scenario for a consultation is when therapy becomes stuck and unproductive. Whitaker (1982b) succinctly described the therapeutic impasse as an "unhappy bilateral symmetrical dance." In an impasse, the choreography between therapist and clients is predictable, stagnant, and role-bound. Each member of the therapeutic system functions rigidly in relationship to the others. For instance, a therapist may willingly and necessarily take the role of instilling hope for a very depressed client. If the hopeless-hopeful complementarity between therapist and client enduringly and rigidly defines most of their relational encounters, then the optimism of the therapist may be of limited benefit. The therapist's position of hopefulness could coincide with the client's lack of impetus to collaborate in life-enhancing activities or increased dependency on the therapist for keeping hope alive in his or her life. The supervisee's request for a consultation can help reverse the responsibility dilemma by bringing in an "expert" who can augment the choreography so that the supervisee and clients learn new steps in their dance toward differentiation and intimacy. In this sense, the consultant can use his or her position in the *responsibility* chain of command to encourage therapist and client to each assume an appropriate percentage of responsibility for both problem and resolution. The supervisee's willingness to confront his or her omnipotence by asking for help offers an important lesson for the client system.

It is much easier to be an expert with another person's puzzles than with our own. Similarly, choreography is much more easily observed from the perspective of the outsider than from those within the dance. The choreographer accurately and globally perceives patterns, rhythm, and collateral movements, whereas the dancers are more mindful of their specific movements as well as passion in the dance. By witnessing, critiquing, and rearranging the individual and collective movements, the choreographer helps the dancers realize the joint goal of motoric actualization of emotional expression.

Similarly, the consultant helps the therapeutic system achieve fuller expression and relational flexibility. The therapist has the difficult task of being a change agent from within the therapeutic system. If the therapist is too *in* or *out* of the client system, it can be disconcerting for both therapist and clients. If left unchecked, an existential conflict arises in which the therapist cannot sequentially *be* and *belong* in the client system. This existential dilemma frequently results in defensive approaches that avoid facing frustration, aloneness, or failure. The therapist's rigidity could result in an "overbounded or underbounded" position, where the therapist is either kept within a predictable role inside the family system (overbounded) or kept outside the clients' emotional experience (underbounded) (Connell, Whitaker, Keith, & Connell, 1990).

Consultation induces a search for a new script with expanded roles in the therapeutic encounter. The very act of recruiting a consultant to augment the status quo induces discontinuity. Clients and therapists expect that the consultant will introduce new experiences, ideas, meanings, and directions. Even if the consultant echoes the opinions and directions of the therapist, the punctuation of the therapeutic system by the consultant brings new life, hope, and legitimacy with the chosen direction. The words and actions of the consultant live in the memory of the participants long after the session. Thus, the consultation provides a reference point for the therapeutic journey.

PHASES OF THE CONSULTATIVE ENCOUNTER

The first phase (see figure 9.1) subdivides into two common therapeutic impasses referred to earlier as *underbounded* and *overbounded*. In Phase 1-A, the underbounded predicament, the therapist is too far away from the emotional experience of the clients to make a significant impact (as noted by the line dividing the family and therapy). This impasse could occur in the beginning of therapy, a new phase of therapy, or in client systems that simultaneously request help and fear change. These systems earnestly want the problems to go away, but either fear change or do not know how to live differently. Thus, the identified patient or problem relentlessly remains as the predominant transactional link and focus. The therapist's peripheral position assumes less power and attention in the therapy than does the identified patient or problem. The clients blame the problem as the root of all evils rather than reflecting on or addressing other stressful dilemmas or changing their manner of coping with the problem. The consultant is needed to help the therapeutic system renegotiate a more productive contract, one that increases the clients' trust in the therapist to handle their subjective motivations and catastrophic fears. Thus, the consultant assists the therapist in becoming more central, relational, and aware of clients' fears of differentiation and intimacy.

Phase 1-B, the overbounded quandary, represents a more typical impasse in which the therapist becomes an introjected member in the therapeutic system. The therapeutic process becomes repetitious, as the therapist's rigid, role-defined position allows limited maneuverability. Thus, the therapist is frozen in the dialectic of *belonging* to the system rather than *being* a differentiated presence. This impasse could happen when the therapist becomes too responsible for the outcome of the identified problem, forms a stable alliance with one of the clients, or engages in other stereotypical complementary or symmetrical behaviors. For instance, the therapist could chronically defer (complementary behavior) or argue (symmetrical) with contentious clients. Rather than facilitating change, the therapist becomes the stable intermediary between the problem and the clients. In this case, a

Figure 9.1: *Progression of the consultative process**

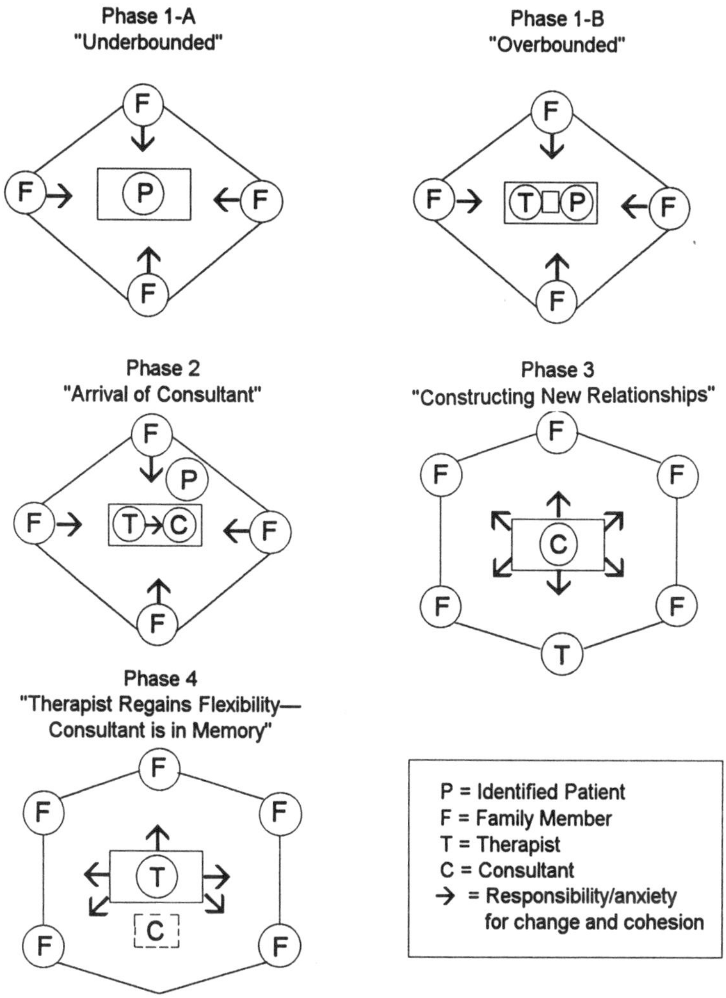

Phase 1-A
"Underbounded"

Phase 1-B
"Overbounded"

Phase 2
"Arrival of Consultant"

Phase 3
"Constructing New Relationships"

Phase 4
"Therapist Regains Flexibility—
Consultant is in Memory"

P = Identified Patient
F = Family Member
T = Therapist
C = Consultant
→ = Responsibility/anxiety
      for change and cohesion

*From Haber, R., 1994d. Reprinted with permission.

consultant is needed to help the therapist find more flexible ways to approach the clients and their problem.

The consultation begins when the therapist ponders the idea of inviting a
professional or nonprofessional resource to help with the therapy. During
such moments, the therapist begins to develop the idea of how such a
resource could benefit the therapeutic system. An internal dialogue could

proceed as follows: "If a consultant were here, I would feel more free to talk about my parentified fears for the adolescent. I would be less concerned about my objectivity and more in touch with my emotional reality. But I think my clients must be aware of my subjective feelings anyway or, at least, will be receptive to my concern." Thus, the very act of contemplating the inclusion of the consultant frees the therapist and other client members to consider alternatives in the therapeutic endeavor.

Prior to inviting a professional consultant, the therapist usually informs the clients that he or she wants a consultant to assist the therapy. The therapist should discuss this matter to the satisfaction of the clients, but should avoid either a deferent, permission-seeking manner or a forceful, coercive approach. Forcing a consultation would be as unproductive as maintaining rigid positions in the therapeutic endeavor. The conversation should build the hope and expectation that the consultant can help the therapy become clearer and more effective in its purpose and process. Client resistance should be explored versus being accepted or negated. "What do you think will happen in the consultation? Do you think my role will change for the worse? What changes concern you the most?" The information elicited from such a dialogue could provide useful information about the fear of change. The therapist could also agree with the clients' proposal to forego the consultation. "Maybe you are right. Perhaps we can make changes without the consultant. We can review our progress within a month and see at that time whether the consultant could be useful."

Phase 2, the arrival of the consultant, physically manifests a triangle between the consultant, therapist, and clients. Typically, the consultant begins by joining the system through the therapist. This maneuver allows the clients to listen to the therapist's presentation of his or her conceptualization of their problems, resources, relationships, accomplishments and limitations of therapy, and personal feelings about them. The consultation provides a context that enables the therapist to be more personal and transparent to the clients. Usually, the therapist's transparency strengthens the therapist-client relationship. In addition, the therapist explains his or her perception of the impasse and goals for the consultation. The link with the therapist reaffirms the notion that the consultant's job is to borrow the clients for the session and then return them to the therapist at its conclusion. As can be seen in figure 9.1, the identified patient or problem loses its centrality as the therapist introduces the consultant to the process of the therapy. After hearing from the therapist, the consultant asks the clients to respond to the therapist's perspective and answer similar questions. "What brought you to therapy? How is it going? What do you want to happen?"

Phase 3, constructing new relationships, begins with the centrality of the consultant. As depicted, the presenting problem and therapist have become

decentralized so that the consultant can unearth new information and neglected relationships. Since the consultant has a temporary relationship to
the problematic impasse, he or she is usually freer than the therapist to
think the unthinkable and say the unsayable. Therefore, the consultant can
engage the impasse without replicating the previous role of the therapist.
Whitaker (1986) used to compare the therapist to an anesthesiologist and
the consultant to a surgeon. The caring relationship of the therapist provided the anesthetic so that the consultant could perform the necessary
surgery. Thus, the surgical consultant escapes the stranglehold of the impasse by exploring, exposing, and intervening in the underbelly of fearful
motivations, unrevealed territory, or new directions.

For instance, a therapist requested a consultation because three previous
counselors at the clinic had been unable to engage his client in therapy. The
counselors liked the client but were miffed when she terminated without
saying good-bye. The client's pattern of termination was to "no show,"
disappear, and then request counseling from a different counselor. My
supervisee and I, with the client's prior knowledge, invited the three previous counselors to the consultation session. In chronological order, according to the inception of the counseling relationship, the client and each
previous counselor discussed the merits and limitations of the particular
therapy and therapeutic relationship. In addition, each pair ended their
conversation with a conscious good-bye. By the end of the third good-bye,
the client tearfully described how she had never learned to say good-bye
because she suffered many abrupt losses and cut-offs in her family. Therefore, unannounced departures were her modus operandi. The consultation
helped her say good-bye to her therapists and opened up her need to say
symbolic good-byes to people she had left or lost in the past. Instead of
being wary about being another therapist casualty of the client, the current
therapist became much clearer about the client dynamics and the work that
she needed to do in therapy. The consultation helped resolve the impasse
depicted in phase 1-A by increasing the intimacy and aspirations of the
therapeutic relationship.

Phase 4, marked by the therapist's regaining flexibility, ends the consultation the way it began—through the therapist. The consultant talks about
his or her experience during the consultation and summarizes reactions to
the therapist's and clients' questions. In addition, the consultant may provide suggestions for future directions, challenges to the therapist or clients,
questions to the therapist, and metaphorical images. As the consultant addresses the therapist, he or she is also speaking to the clients. Since the
consultant is in a temporary position, he or she can take a stronger position
on the possibility of change than the therapist. For instance, in a family
therapy consultation with a recovering alcohol-abusing father, the consul-

tant explored specific experiences that surrounded father's former alcohol abuse. In addition, the consultant asked the family members and therapist about how they would handle father's slipping off the wagon. The consultant brought alcoholism into the room, whereas the family and therapist skirted the issue. The consultant warned the family and therapist that alcoholism might return because the issues of loneliness, anger, and denial still festered in the family. The father was defensive about the exposure but agreed that the family members needed to talk about their traumas and fears about his alcoholism. In subsequent sessions, the therapist took a more active position in exposing the process and concerns of the alcoholism recovery as well as bringing up other issues surrounded by profound dejection, secrets, and denial. The therapist, who was still working with this family one year later, helped members turn to each other for support rather than escape in destructive ways.

Phase 4 in figure 9.1 shows a system in which the therapist is free to work with many tensions in the family rather than rigidly adhere to a prescribed role. Having seen the consultant assume a flexible and focused position in the therapeutic system, the therapist can occupy a similar position when it is therapeutically appropriate. An important role of the consultant is to validate the previous and potential work of the therapist and clients, thereby reinforcing the responsibilities of the clients and therapist in the therapeutic endeavor. The primary goal of the consultation is to leave the therapeutic system feeling enhanced and challenged to meet its goals. Although the consultant physically exits the system, the challenges, images, questions, and relational positions live inside the memory of the system as a ghostly presence. When the therapist or clients revert to preconsultation relational rigidity, the memory of the consultant's position reminds the members to take the risks necessary for greater differentiation and intimacy.

In approximately 100 consultations, I have never had a client or client system request a transfer from their therapist to me shortly after the consultation. I believe that two factors contribute to this interesting statistic. First, since the consultation produces stress in order to help the system change, clients eagerly embrace returning to the privacy and familiarity of the relationship with their therapist. It is to be hoped that the therapeutic system uses the postconsultation phase to reinforce and digest perspectives and options that enhance greater role-flexibility. Secondly, if the consultant is clear that his or her role is to enhance the therapeutic relationship and not to replace it, then therapist and clients inherit the challenge to become more flexible and "response-able" in their respective roles in the therapeutic and client systems. Optimally, they feel more responsible and empowered to make necessary changes rather than look for someone else to take the responsibility. If they do not succeed in making these changes, perhaps a second consult should occur, especially prior to considering referral or termination.

Unique Aspects of Consultation in the Supervisory Moment

As the ghostly presence of the consultant lives in the memory of the therapeutic system after the consultation, the physical presence of the consultant remains present in the supervisory system. Therefore, consultation in the supervisory context preempts the need of the consultant to say a permanent good-bye. The supervisor, however, needs to learn how to readapt to the indirect role of supervisor rather than the more direct and intrusive role of consultant. In other words, the supervisor needs to learn to get off the playing field and onto the sidelines so that the supervisee can autonomously implement the game plan of the consultation. The thrill of being on the playing field may be hard to relinquish if the supervisor prefers the role of player to that of coach. One dilemma of consultative supervision involves the supervisee's ability to handle the supervisor's change of focus. In addition, the supervisor may become so adamantly attached to an approach that he or she neglects building upon the supervisee's preferences and capacities. The supervisor must return to the decentralized role of coach by working through the body of the supervisee rather than expecting the player to mimic his or her style, tactics, and moves.

Generally, it is preferable for the supervisor to follow consultations through case management supervision. The indirect involvement of this format provides maximum autonomy for the therapeutic system to digest the consultative intervention, while still permitting the supervisor to recalibrate the consultative intent according to the developing circumstances of the case. Consultation is an intervention that lubricates the therapeutic process so that it may move forward more smoothly and effectively. Although the consultant usually provides a map of future possibilities, rarely is this map precisely followed. It is preferable for the supervisor and supervisee to see the consultation as a useful, prolonged time-out in the therapy rather than the solution to all of its problems. Case management supervision provides the opportunity to reassess the role of the therapist in mini time-outs, so that the therapy can stay on track.

The following excerpts from a consultative supervision depict its power to shift the focus of therapy. The consultant made an emotional connection between past and present issues in the family that persisted through the therapy. However, there was no need for the consultant to maintain a direct presence in the therapy because the therapist aptly integrated and built upon the consultation intervention; therefore, the supervisor merely followed the progression of the therapy through weekly case management supervision sessions.

The supervisee requested consultation in order to help her resolve an enduring dialectical problem of control and rebelliousness between a mother and 16-year-old daughter. The daughter's significantly escalating social and academic "at-risk" behaviors resulted in diminished trust and increased punishment by the mother. Mother's determination to control the daughter heightened the daughter's rebellious rejection of mother's authority, which resulted in mother becoming more controlling, and so on. The therapist became trapped in the helpless position of witness and referee to this problem. The rest of the family included the father, who was stationed overseas in the military, and the younger brother, who safely observed the parent-adolescent struggle from the sidelines. My initial goal as consultant was to build an alliance between the mother and daughter by finding common ground, as well as to provide a new focus and role for the therapist. During previous supervisory meetings, I had learned that a longstanding cut-off existed between mother and her parents. Although the supervisee hypothesized that the mother-daughter struggle connected to the pain from the cut-off, in therapy she responded primarily to the behavioral crises in the nuclear family. Therefore, I looked for the opportunity to link the present parent-adolescent struggle with parallel generational problems.

I tied a rope, signifying their intense reactivity, around mother's and daughter's waists. The rope introduced a point of reference, an umbilical cord, plus some humor into the previously tense relationship. The challenge to the umbilical connection between mother and daughter was not done as a masculine effort to encourage "appropriate" mother-daughter separateness. The rope challenged the primitive quality of their connection and introduced possibilities for establishing new understandings of the mother-daughter relationship. In this spirit, my task was to help them find their version of a better mother-daughter fit, rather than act like a father who would tell the women how to behave.

BROTHER   I don't think mom wants to get rid of the umbilical cord until the problems get worked out and Jamie wants to get rid of the umbilical cord right now.

CONSULTANT   But does your sister want to get the problem worked out?

BROTHER   She does, but not the way mom wants to.

MOTHER   It would probably make everything a whole lot easier for me to swallow her . . . I see her as doing things that I do not approve of to show me that she is a separate person.

The brother's initial statement demonstrates his acceptance of the meaning of the metaphorical object. The mother then amplifies the metaphor by introducing the idea of swallowing. My association to the swallowing metaphor was that mother wanted her daughter to be in the safety of her belly. My questions moved mother to expand the concept of safety to that of hunger.

CONSULTANT   Where does that hunger come from that makes you want to swallow her? Tell your daughter about your hunger, about where it comes from.

MOTHER   I guess partly from my mother. [looks toward therapist and consultant]

CONSULTANT   Tell your daughter.

MOTHER   [to daughter] I want to love you, I want you to love me even more. I got my part done, but I don't see your part coming through.

CONSULTANT   Tell her about the swallowing, because that is more than loving, that's ingesting.

MOTHER   I have never really thought about it until you brought it up [silence]. I have never combined the thought of my mother and daughter before.

CONSULTANT   This is the place to work those things out. [to the daughter] Look at your mom, and if she starts swallowing you, give me a signal and I'll help pull you out.

As mother is on the verge of identifying a symbolic and emotional experience from her past that affects her present relationship with her daughter, it is important for her daughter to join her in a relationship based on a new perspective. Although the mother frequently returns to the desire to protect her daughter from her current problems, the mother's affect signals interest in pursuing links between past and present generations.

MOTHER   [to daughter] Do you think I am swallowing you?

DAUGHTER   Sometimes.

MOTHER   This part of your life [referring to daughter's blatant sexual promiscuity], I would love to take over . . .

CONSULTANT   Talk to your daughter about how your mom is involved in the swallowing process.

MOTHER   [to daughter] I don't understand why we don't see my parents. I'm afraid that we are not welcome there.

DAUGHTER   Why aren't we welcome there?

MOTHER   Because they threw us out. We were asked to leave [pause] my parents' house!

DAUGHTER   Why?

MOTHER   I don't know why. For nine years I don't know why. I need Kleenex, guys. [In despair, she bangs her fist on the arm of the chair and begins to cry.] I have no idea why. But, until they say something I don't feel like we are welcome back at their house or wherever they are . . . I don't want that to happen to us.

CONSULTANT   [to daughter] Do you think that when you behave badly that your mother still recognizes you as her daughter? [Consultant links the parental rejection and adolescent rebellion, hopefully reducing the desperation and fear of the mother-daughter differences.]

DAUGHTER   Yes.

CONSULTANT   That's important!

Mother and daughter removed the rope and spontaneously hugged. Thus, they were no longer tied together, nor did they have to play "cops and robbers" as a way of manifesting their connection. The consultation ended in a discussion with the therapist about the need for the entire family to sort out the unfinished issues of the cut-off. It was hoped that facing the pain of the cut-off would help mother and daughter find better ways of being close to each other than repetitive control and rebellious interactions. Both needed to learn the lessons of individuation, although mother's job was much more difficult because she had to learn to individuate in the context of rejection.

Postconsultation supervision sessions continued to support the therapist's focus on mother's cut-off and daughter's concern for her mother, rather than letting the therapy slip back into the safer territory of parent-teenager, control-rebellion issues. The daughter's flagrant behavioral problems became reframed as a way to prevent age-appropriate differentiation from her mother because of her mother's need for emotional proximity with her daughter. The therapist initiated a letter-writing intervention in which each family member wrote a letter to mother's parents describing his or her personal feelings and thoughts about the impact that the cut-off had on the family. The supervisee brought the letters to supervision with the question of whether she should encourage the mother to contact her parents. It was decided that the mother should be in charge of that decision. The mother finally contacted her parents, with the support of her family, and was again disappointed by their aloofness. Nonetheless, mother's lack of parental support became a point of convergence with her daughter, as they became allies in dealing with the pain of the cut-off. The therapist helped them work together on the developmental issues of respecting each other's opinions and decisions. During this period, the daughter changed schools and made marked changes in her choice of peers and destructive and dangerous behaviors. Since the therapy progressed very well after the consultation, minimal guidance was needed to sustain the movement of the family. The therapist insightfully discussed countertransferential issues of adolescent tumult in her previous relationships with her mother and daughter. The supervision employed those decathected relationships as internal consultants for her work with the family.

On other occasions, clinical and professional development goals following a consultation warrant direct rather than indirect supervisory approaches. Vehicles of direct supervision (live supervision, cotherapy, and consultation) should be considered when therapeutic problems, ethical dilemmas, or significant countertransference problems persist after a consultation. Thus, increasing directness and frequency of supervisory contact should correlate with heightened rigidity and complexity of the case.

Besides consultation for therapeutic impasse, supervisory consultations serve other purposes. The following five categories demonstrate other situations that can benefit from supervisory consultations.

Consultation at the Beginning of Therapy

The experience of being in a room alone with clients can be intimidating, especially for beginning trainees. A consultation in the first or second session helps to ease the process of defining problems, establishing goals for therapy, and beginning to address the relational concerns in the therapeutic system. Whitaker (1986) said that consultations in the second session increase the intimacy and focus of the therapeutic relationship. In addition, clients and therapist realize that the consultant is a resource for them if therapy becomes unproductive and needs another point of view. The early presence of the consultant makes extending a future invitation less formidable. The encounter in a consultation provides the supervisor with more realistic information, images, and understanding of the clients, which can facilitate the relevancy and accuracy of supervision.

Consultation to Expand the Client System

Carl Whitaker frequently advised therapists to add resources to systems that are not working—from the professional side, clients' side, or both. The act of inviting a supervisory consultant changes the therapeutic system by adding a professional resource. It also disposes the therapeutic system to consider inviting resources from the clients' side of the ledger. The consultant, by virtue of the expertise and perceived objectivity associated with the role, gives added weight to the importance of recruiting additional resources from the social network system. Expanding the system helps the therapist and clients learn to lean on other resources rather than accept the delusion that the therapeutic relationship can understand, meet, and satisfy all of the clients' needs.

For instance, a therapist providing individual psychotherapy for a college student with bulimia and academic problems requested a consultation because of the tenacity of both problems. The ensuing consultation explored the way the client's sister's accidental automobile death affected her family. The client asserted that her family avoided directly discussing the death but used other methods to cope with their grief. Father buried himself in his work while her mother took in several foster children. The parents dealt with the client's feelings of vulnerability and neglect by indulging her with material things and overlooking her misbehaviors. For example, although the client dropped many classes and half-heartedly attended school, her parents stoically continued to pay for her education. Since the death of her sister tragically arrested the emotional development of each of the family members, the consultant suggested that the family, as a group, needed time to sort out their feelings and needs in relationship to the older sister's death. The client, who initially did not want her parents involved, finally agreed to bring her parents for one session. Thus, the inquiry and position of the consultant paved the way for the family interview. The therapist requested the consultant's presence in the family meeting because she worried that loyalty to her client would get in the way of the interview with her parents. The family bravely faced painful issues about the death and consequent coping mechanisms. The parents asked if they could continue coming to sessions in order to know how to help their daughter better deal with her problems. Therefore, the consultant, therapist, parents, and original client worked out a format of concurrent therapies: individual therapy with the therapist and family sessions with both consultant and therapist. This format enabled the original client to work on developmental issues in the privacy of an individual relationship while working on the unresolved family issues with her parents. Hence, the consultation expanded the individual therapy to a family consultation and then expanded the family consultation to include family therapy.

Gender and Other "Touristic" Consultations

Libby Ridgely (in her section on gendered supervision in chapter 3) discussed the advantages of becoming a cultural and gender "tourist" when dealing with clients of different culture or sex. Recruiting a consultant with a different orientation is like hiring a travel guide to explore nuances of the territory. I have found that my consultation forays into female supervisees' therapies have provided a gender check from a male perspective. For example, in a couples therapy consultation, I noticed that the therapist worked almost exclusively with the wife's presenting problems. Therefore, I added balance in the therapy by exposing the husband's contribution to the couple's problems. The therapist was startled that she did not even know anything about the husband's side of the genogram. Although the husband admitted that he kept the therapist at bay, he felt that he needed to be more open in order to work on the relationship with his wife. A similar situation of gender approach and avoidance occurred with a male supervisee who protected the wife in family therapy while frequently pressing the husband to be more open and less rigid. The consultative intervention explored whether it was safe for the wife to be less passive and more transparent in the family. As Ridgely has stated, gender is an organizing process in families, therapies, and supervisions. Therefore, it behooves supervisors to consult with an eye on gender issues.

My wife, Karen Cooper-Haber, has given me many consultations over the years. She has an excellent ability to help me be less responsible and more relational. I needed some help after having had a dream that my client, whom I had seen in therapy for two years, was going to kill my family when I was away on a trip. My client routinely became very fearful, anxious, and distraught when I traveled because she was afraid that I would abandon her, as had happened in most of her significant relationships. As a general rule, dreams about being killed by one's clients are a good indicator for a consult. Since my wife was in the plot of the dream, she seemed to be an obvious consultant. After listening to my fears about my client's inability to handle my plans for travel, Karen began by affirming the client's positive feeling towards me. She had the client and me draw pictures that illustrated the essence of our relationship. The consult normalized my clients' feelings of transferential vulnerability and helped me overcome my fears of the mutual transferences. The next day, the client delivered a bouquet of flowers for Karen and me. More importantly, she did not disintegrate during my trip and successfully terminated a couple of months after the consultation. I credit Karen's guidance through the transference as a major contributor to the satisfactory outcome of the therapy.

Consultation as an Evaluation and Preventive Check-up

Consultation has been used to evaluate the progress of therapy (Jutoran, 1994) and as a preventive check-up (Rubinstein-Nebarro, 1994). Evaluative and preventive consultations should be seen not as a critique of the therapist but a process intervention for the good of the therapy. If a supervisor is working with a sensitive or demoralized supervisee, it may be useful to begin with a consultation of a successful case. A benign, positive approach may help illuminate the strengths of the supervisee, so that he or she becomes more secure as a professional. The consultation may focus mostly on what has worked for the clients and the therapist and reframe unmet needs as part of the normal development of a therapeutic relationship. Bolstering confidence is especially important in consultation because it is easy for the supervisee to incriminate him or herself for being less effective and perceptive than the consultant.

More typically, consultation check-ups provide a pause in which the therapist and the clients can realistically and nondefensively review the process and progress of therapy. This pause can help the therapist adjust his or her position and approach in the client and professional houses. In addition, the consultant can amplify problems, concerns, and unmet goals in the relationship. As an external resource, the consultant encourages the therapist and clients to describe their relationship from both the inside (how it feels) and the outside (what it looks like). The consultant can consequently infiltrate the experiences, projections, and transferential aspects interfering with therapy. By discussing and experiencing the therapeutic relationship, the consultant can learn a great deal about the supervisee's work.

Consultation to Reverse the Hierarchy

Since consultations teach discontinuous, meta-level, expeditious, and high-impact interventive skills, it is useful to allow competent supervisees to assume the expert role of the consultant. The role forces them to look at therapy from the more distant and immediate eyes of a consultant rather than the warmer and more predictable eyes of a therapist. Furthermore, the supervisor's request for a consultation from a supervisee affirms the supervisor's trust in and respect for the supervisee's abilities. It also verifies that senior therapists also get stuck and welcome assistance. Supervisors need to model fallibility as well as dedication to learn from *mistakes* ("corrective actions for *miss-takes*," Guinan, 1977). Since elevating the supervisee to the meta-role may be confusing, the supervisor needs to be very clear before and during the session about his or her desire to receive assistance from the supervisee. I have always found it useful to watch my supervisees work with my clients. It gives me the opportunity to watch their choice of inquiry and interventions; plus, the position of consultee allows me sufficient distance to observe clients' responses to the consultant. Thus, my supervisees' consultations live in my head long after the consultation.

CONCLUSION

Consultation provides the opportunity for the supervisor to experience and participate in the supervisee's therapeutic world. Since the supervisee frequently has a large investment in his or her clinical relationships and professional image, the invitation to consult is a distinct privilege. In order to perform the role of supervisory consultation, the supervisor should modulate respect with acumen. If the supervisor becomes too deferential, then he or she loses the wisdom and perspective of the distinguished outsider. On the other hand, if the supervisor is disrespectful and pompous, then the members of the therapeutic system will probably hold their breath and close their minds until they get rid of the intruder. The consultant, like the effective therapist and supervisor, has to find the optimum balance between challenge and support.

Consultation is an effective medium for the supervisor and supervisee to learn more about each other's work. The images formulated in the consultation can amplify and augment the supervisory relationship. Three of my supervisees succinctly illuminated the uniqueness of the role of consultation in the training moment (Simons, Liggett, & Purvis, 1994) with the following:

> It is certainly true that ordinary supervision has the potential to provide a trainee with a more meta level of looking at his or her therapeutic process. However, consultation presents a meta-view of the process in a more graphic and dramatic form. The message is unfurled before the trainee's eyes—in the room with the clients and in the moment of therapy. The inherent drama and immediacy of consultation is what makes it such a memorable and effective training procedure. (p. 258)

10

Apprentice Cotherapy: Working Side by Side with a Supervisor

by Shirley Kirby

COTHERAPY IS DESCRIBED BY Roller and Nelson (1991) as "a special practice of psychotherapy in which two or more therapists treat one or more patients in group, family or couple, or individual psychotherapy at the same time and in the same place" (p. 11). While cotherapy describes the vehicle of supervision outlined here, a supervisee working within a hierarchical supervisory relationship is not truly engaged in cotherapy. The different level of responsibility, degree of experience, position in the work context, relationship with the clients, and the nature of the supervision contract create a unique cotherapy arrangement. Although cotherapy greatly influenced my development, style, and coherency as a psychotherapist, I struggled with the *co* in cotherapy. Discussing this, Libby Ridgely, Russell Haber, and I decided that cotherapy with a supervisor and supervisee represents an apprenticeship rather than a relationship of professional equality. Since an apprentice is a person who works for another in order to

Shirley Kirby, Ph.D., is a clinical psychologist in private practice. Shirley is a renaissance learner who has worked as a physician assistant, pediatric and family nurse practitioner, and hospice worker. She has taught me a great deal about illness, death, and dying, and the joys and love of life from the perspective of a lively grandmother.

learn a trade, apprenticeship connotes an experiential form of development. In addition, Cooper-Haber (Haber & Cooper-Haber, 1988) has noted that cotherapy benefits both clients and therapists when there are different levels of training, experience, style, gender, and other personal characteristics.

PERSPECTIVES ON APPRENTICE COTHERAPY

Apprentice cotherapy provides an opportunity for the supervisor and supervisee to view each other differently, to become more in touch with each other's personhood, to briefly see each other as colleagues, to provide the supervisor with an opportunity to teach both directly and indirectly, and to model the importance of timing and the implementation of an intervention or a coherent treatment plan. It nourishes the professional growth of both the supervisor and the supervisee as they combine their energies and resources for the therapeutic endeavor. It is an effective vehicle for facilitating the supervisee's integration of a coherent therapeutic approach. The supervisee uses the template of the therapeutic process to clarify similarities to and differences from the supervisor's therapeutic approach and style. The apprentice cotherapist can question or disagree with the senior cotherapist in a manner that advances the goals of the client. The apprentice's process of differentiation is a byproduct of the therapy, not the goal; nevertheless, apprentice cotherapy advances the ultimate supervisory goal of moving from an apprentice relationship to a true collegial one. Cotherapy with former supervisees is a marvelous opportunity for the supervisor to enjoy, learn, and relish the fruits of one's labor.

DEVELOPING THE MAP
OF APPRENTICE COTHERAPY

The expectations (or nonexpectations) of both the supervisee and the supervisor need to be addressed. In the case of my most recent apprentice cotherapy relationship in a private practice, the mutual expectations included teaming and brainstorming. I also looked forward to the chance to observe and feel a seasoned senior clinician at work and to participate in difficult cases without carrying the bulk of the responsibility for therapy outcome. It was a time for experiential learning.

Apprentice cotherapy is a very individualized arrangement. At times, a very "green" apprentice may simply want to participate nonverbally in the therapeutic encounter—especially in the beginning stage. If expectations are not verbalized, the apprentice's privileged experience of observing and feeling the therapeutic process may quickly revert to feelings of shame or embarrassment for not doing enough. For example, one supervisee confided that she felt extremely inadequate during a cotherapy session with a supervisor. She stated that she could not think of one word to say and so she was completely silent during the entire session. She felt that the client family and the supervisor must have thought that she was a "complete jerk." When she and her supervisor processed the session later, he expressed appreciation for the extra pair of eyes, ears, and hands in the room. Her temporary shame and embarrassment were alleviated when her behavior was normalized and validated. The supervisor's sensitivity to the supervisee's feelings is very important. In the case just mentioned, the supervisor felt that he had been very clear about his expectations—he did not have any. The supervisee was to say as little or as much as she felt was appropriate; however, she heard a critical father in her silence. This case demonstrates that time before and after the session must be allocated to process feelings and explore the supervisee's and supervisor's places in the personal and professional houses.

Cooper-Haber (Haber & Cooper-Haber, 1988) has stated that, in the first phase of apprenticeship, a novice cotherapist may have feelings similar to those of a client—vulnerable, scared, and even picked on. In one of my first opportunities to do apprentice therapy, I certainly identified with her remarks. During an intake session with a dysfunctioning couple, my supervisor asked me whether I thought their relationship would survive. I felt very vulnerable and anxious as I tried to come up with the answer that I thought he wanted. (Eventually, I learned that there were no right or wrong answers; he was able to work therapeutically with whatever I gave him.)

LESSONS LEARNED IN APPRENTICE COTHERAPY

The apprentice position provides a unique opportunity to develop one's capacity for nonverbal communication, to experience and utilize the power of "visual intercourse" with the client, to become comfortable with the power and value of silence. After all, the apprentice cotherapist not only is placed in a privileged position (meta to the process of a senior cotherapist) but also can both transmit and observe forms of nonverbal communication. Beginning supervisees often work too hard and give too much of themselves without taking into full account the importance of the client's ability to understand their perspective (Whitaker, 1982a). The apprentice experience creates an opportunity to observe the client's unspoken experience and resources.

After approximately three sessions with my supervisor cotherapist and a distressed couple, I had established a warm, nonverbal connection with the more silent female client. During the scheduling process for the next session, the client requested that it be canceled because I was not able to be present. This powerful connection was established almost entirely with a series of nonverbal communications that included eye movements, physical proximity, hand movements, and nods. My heart connection with the female not only helped her feel understood, but it also gave more freedom for my supervisor to work intensely with the male partner as he realized that the female partner felt nonverbally connected with me.

In addition to nonverbal communications, the supervisee has the opportunity to form hypotheses about the therapeutic theme and intervention strategies while the supervisor is working them out. These hypotheses may either validate the supervisor's impressions or differ from them. Either way, there is a basis for enrichment of the collaborative supervisory experience.

The apprentice is able to experience the importance of assumptions and perspectives and the effect they have on the therapy system. Apprentice cotherapy provides a place for the supervisee to determine, study, and experience how the senior cotherapist unravels clients' truths by offering a new perspective that may be quite different from the apprentice's and the clients' views. For example, in a marital therapy session, my supervisor offered his perspective on a husband's affair. The wife felt violated by the affair and the husband denied its importance. His denial reinforced the discomfort of his wife. ("If it meant nothing, what prevents him from having an affair again?") My supervisor argued that the husband's penis was disconnected from his heart; the problem was simply a misbehaving penis. The humor of the metaphor brought a smile to the faces of both clients. The supervisor then differentiated the wife's strong connection between her vagina and her heart. The coupling of the two perspectives shifted the impact of the affair from the genitals to the heart. The husband addressed his heart feelings to his wife and his wife showed the damage to her heart. This shift from the genitalia to the heart was an important change that provided hope for both the clients and the cotherapy team. As a result of this experience, I learned that provocation and humor can be used effectively when dealing with affairs, but that it must be used with sensitivity and appropriate timing.

Apprenticeship cotherapy not only provides an opportunity for the supervisee to experience the work of the supervisor but also offers the supervisee a chance to initiate and/or modify metaphors and perspectives. The following illustration demonstrates the interplay of my own use of self-disclosure and metaphor with the therapeutic and supervisory systems.

Bernice and Ted were being seen in therapy because of conflicts in their relationship. Bernice was upset because Ted was withholding information and showed very little affect. Ted was bothered about Bernice's constant anger with him. When the supervisee nodded in agreement with Bernice, the supervisor commented on the connection. The supervisee stated that she sometimes referred to her own husband as a "computer" because of his unemotional stance and described how she moved from anger to understanding in their relationship. The supervisor, who appreciated the metaphor (computer), built on the image as a way to clarify and challenge the couple's problem. As the supervisor observed that Ted's controlled affect appeared to be part of his "hard disk" (ingrained) and explored ways that software could be inserted, the couple moved closer to understanding each other. This effective collaborative intervention added to the connection of the apprentice team as they experienced the conjoint power of their cotherapy relationship. These moments illustrate the value of the apprentice and the flattening of the mythical hierarchy.

As an apprentice, my perspectives on the role of therapist have been modified, since I have been exposed to a set of attitudes as well as a set of techniques. (The supervisor's feeling life is exposed along with his professional role.) In one session with a couple on the verge of a divorce, the supervisor immediately placed responsibility for therapy outcome onto the couple because of his vulnerable feelings about hopelessness. In an intake interview that began with a bitter argument, he stated that it was important for him as a therapist to have some hope for the therapy and challenged the couple to give him hope. He willingly and appropriately exposed his feelings of hopelessness with the presentation of their complaint. From this dialogue, I both learned a new way to tap into the healthy perspectives of the couple and also experienced the humanness and limitations of even a senior therapist. Not only did this case help me to disregard feelings of omnipotence, but it also showed me that even a "hopeless" case may be treatable.

In another apprentice cotherapy session, I watched as the family of an anorexic female abruptly and prematurely ended therapy. This experience of a premature termination in a cotherapy relationship with an expert helped to modulate my feelings of inadequacy. The experience of cotherapy with a seasoned therapist is much different from watching an edited videotape of an expert, since apprentice cotherapy demonstrates the trials and tribulations of clinical work along with the expert modeling. Through apprentice cotherapy, I have learned to decrease internalization of feelings of both inadequacy and omnipotence.

Since supervisees are frequently observed and evaluated, the opportunity to be an observer and even an evaluator of sorts can be quite refreshing. Often shame, inadequacy, doubt, confusion, and uncertainty are attached to being "one down" in the learning process. I have innate respect for a supervisor who places him- or herself in the observed position. As mentioned earlier, mutual vulnerability and the experience of sharing a therapeutic disappointment with a supervisor model healthy resolution of shame.

Reflection on the therapy process may provide clues as to how the cothera-pists could have dealt differently with the therapeutic problem. In addition, the supervisor can model the acceptance of self when the therapy resulted in a poor outcome. Apprentice cotherapy teaches the supervisee to learn from mistakes rather than to become "burned out" by them. Najavits and Strupp (1994) suggest that more effective therapists rate themselves as making more mistakes than their less effective counterparts. "The relation between a therapist's willingness to reflect on and critique [his or her] own work and [his or her] subsequent effectiveness with the client corroborates Skoveholt and Ronnestad's (1992) findings that continuous professional reflection aids therapist development of competence" (Holloway & Neufeldt, 1995, p. 209). Apprentice cotherapy provides an ongoing source for reflection from two perspectives.

The opportunity for intense exposure to an experienced therapist is en-hanced by the supervisor's ability to take more risks when he or she has a cotherapist in the room. My supervisor frequently tells me that my presence helps him be more congruent with himself. Since mutual trust and respect exist between us, he can be more provocative, disclosing, metaphorical, or confused in the therapeutic process because I can attend to necessary developments. Thus, the apprentice provides a safety net for the supervisor and the clients.

CAUTIONS REGARDING APPRENTICE COTHERAPY

The cotherapy relationship gives the supervisor more incentive to act in a manner consistent with his or her convictions, rather than to conform inappropriately to client expectations. Inherent in this additional incentive to perform more competently, however, is the danger of possible grand-standing. Grandstanding could involve the supervisor showing off (at the client's expense) for the benefit of the supervisee. The supervisee may also grandstand by competing with the supervisor. The ethical goals for the apprentice cotherapy are the development of a respectful, professional rela-tionship between the cotherapists for the expressed desire of furthering the welfare of the clients and educating the supervisee. Apprentice cotherapy is an inappropriate context for the supervisor or supervisee to be striving for self-aggrandizing "points" within the context of therapy. I have found that the inherent hierarchy in apprentice cotherapy generally mitigates competi-tion, since it demands that a common language be presented to the clients. Although, that is usually the language of the supervisor, it is affected by the personhood and skill of the apprentice.

A supervisor can easily and respectfully redirect an apprentice when he or she feels that it may be useful to the client(s). The supervisor is always responsible for the therapy and the supervisory relationship is secondary to the therapeutic relationship. In one case of couples therapy, a beginning apprentice began to lead the session in a direction that went against the supervisor's intent to unbalance the position of one of the spouses. The supervisor felt that the supervisee's shift to the other spouse would neutralize the unbalancing intervention. Therefore, the supervisor redirected the language of the therapy. He was able to accomplish this by asking the apprentice a question in a manner that respected her lead and questioned a shift: "Do you think that the session has been too emotionally upsetting for the husband since it has been the wife who has always been the one to wear the emotions for the couple?" The apprentice cotherapist good-naturedly admitted that her personal anxiety probably motivated her protectiveness of the husband. In this case, the supervisor used the different viewpoints to advance a dialogue in front of the couple that illuminated their resistance to making an emotional shift.

Generally, mutual vulnerability appears to promote trust and flexibility in apprentice cotherapy, but the need to build a team of player-coach invites caution and planning. If the player does not like the coach, then he or she can (and should) switch teams. This can be accomplished by discussing the matter privately, pulling in a consultant, or using whatever means are necessary. Team building is most easily accomplished when there is mutual regard, respect, liking, dedication to clients, and similar world view and values. Napier and Whitaker (1973) maintain that therapists' basic disrespect for each other is the most serious difficulty in cotherapy. Where there is a large ideological and/or theoretical difference within the apprenticeship hierarchy, there may be less honesty regarding disagreement with a supervisor. Napier and Whitaker suggest that differing theoretical orientations often provide a rich foundation for trouble, especially when conceptual positions are polarized (e.g., authoritarian versus laissez-faire approaches). Problems may also arise due to personal idiosyncrasies, gender, and life-cycle positions. Napier and Whitaker view intellectual disagreement as less troublesome than personality conflict. Pre- and post-session processing and talking about the parenting process are helpful methods of working out these conflicts in order to keep clients out of the conflict.

APPRENTICE COTHERAPY POSITIONS

Apprentice cotherapy offers more possibilities for intervention in the treatment process than solo therapy. Most obviously, the hands, heart, head, and nose are multiplied by two. Four hands working together can accomplish more tasks and operations than two hands. More subtly, the two therapists are more than the sum of their parts (four hands, two hearts, etc.). They represent a relationship—a system. Thus, the system of the cotherapy team works with the client system. The system of a cotherapy team can play simultaneous "stereo" positions and roles, whereas the solo therapist is limited to sequential "mono" shifts. Haber and Cooper-Haber (1988) identified eight cotherapy positions with couples: parallel gender alignment, cross-gender alignment, unbalancing, meta-position alignment, therapist as patient, gossip "in" and gossip "out," the mirror model, and therapeutic debate. All of these have been implemented in my apprentice cotherapy experience at one time or another. Figures 10.1–10.8 (Haber & Cooper-Haber, 1988) portray these different positions, which can be modified when working with families, groups, or individuals. Whatever the treatment context, a team of therapists has more therapy options than an individual therapist.

Parallel Gender Alignment

In parallel gender alignment, the supervisee and supervisor connect with the same gender person while working with a traditional couple or family. This linkage between genders provides for the safest and most natural alliance. There is usually immediate acceptance, safety, and understanding. This natural (and nonverbal) connection was demonstrated earlier in this chapter with the story of Bernice and Ted. In another case, a supervisor was working with a couple and considered the case a "failed couples therapy." He suggested that the wife work individually with a female apprentice while he worked individually with the husband. The new dynamics lowered the spouses' reactivity to one another and increased individual responsibility for their contribution to the marital impasse. One year later, couples therapy with the apprenticeship team resumed as an adjunct to their individual work. For this couple, same gender connection provided safety for further exploration and eventual reconciliation.

Cross Gender Alignment

Cross gender alignment occurs when the male therapist aligns with the female client and vice versa. This connection creates a rich arena in which

Figure 10.1: *Parallel gender alignment*

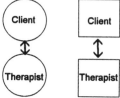

Figure 10.2: *Cross gender alignment*

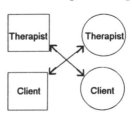

to deal with sexual and cross gender parenting issues. I have experienced cross gender alignment quite often in apprentice cotherapy but usually only after my supervisor has made an alignment switch. It has not been a natural alignment for me. The implications of my atypically aligning primarily with a male came to my supervisor's attention in the case of Dorene and John. They came to therapy because of a longstanding conflict that had resulted in an absence of any sexual contact. Dorene whined and John was passive. During post-session exploration, I was able to relate my alignment with John to an unconscious negative emotional response to whining women. This new information about myself came to light via a visit to the middle and upper floors of my personal house. After I became aware of the source of my connection to John, I felt more personally connected with Dorene. The work with this couple helped me align more quickly with other men.

Unbalanced Alignment

An unbalanced therapeutic alignment is a temporary yet powerful cotherapy relationship, in which both therapists form an alliance with one client in order to facilitate change. For example, in one case a husband did not want to deal with intimacy and sexuality. He would only bring in issues about the children. When the therapists aligned with the wife, there was added pressure on him to deal with marital issues. Unbalancing was also helpful in the case of Dorene and John. When my supervisor and I aligned with Dorene, John became less passive in their marriage. He felt the need to

Figure 10.3: *Unbalanced alignment*

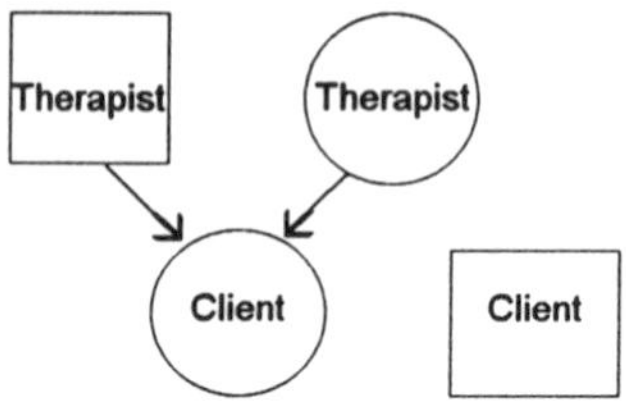

Figure 10.4: *Meta-position alignment*

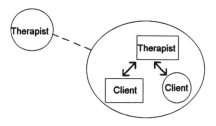

take action when his power in the relationship was neutralized by the therapists' aligning with Dorene.

Meta-position Alignment

Meta-position alignment often occurs naturally in apprentice cotherapy.
Since the supervisor therapist frequently leads the direction of the session,
the apprentice observes from a meta-position. These positions flexibly reverse according to comfort, energy, creativity, and personality alliances
with the clients. In one instance, a male supervisor was involved in a rather
combative encounter with a male client when the female apprentice in the
meta-position commented on the client's feelings of inadequacy. This comment helped the supervisor understand and affirm the client rather than
continue the power struggle. Although the apprentice was silent during
most of the session, her brief contribution was very powerful and enlightened the course of the therapy. The meta-position enables the "outside"
cotherapist to notice patterns of the relationship from a totally different
perspective. In the meta-position the nose has the space and privacy to
creatively and intuitively wander through different images.

Therapist as Patient

Therapist as patient models self-disclosure. This position usually touches
personally relevant issues for the couple or family, although there is a

Figure 10.5: *Therapist as patient*

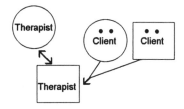

departure from the therapy per se as one therapist attends to the other. A clinical vignette that portrays this position involved a male therapist who asked his cotherapist (wife) for a hug as a way to help him with the loneliness that he felt during a family interview. A teenager in the family commented that one minute and 20 seconds should be deducted from the bill because he timed the hug. When the male therapist indicated that it was part of the therapy, his cotherapist offered to hug the boy for one minute and 20 seconds. When one therapist attends to another therapist, it may touch the clients' personal issues. In this case, the therapist's need for closeness and the hug connected with the loneliness and longing in the family. I have occasionally focused on strong feelings expressed by my cotherapist supervisor in session. Our interaction, at such times, has provided permission for clients to take increased risks in dealing with their feelings.

Mirror/Model Position

In the mirror/model position, the cotherapists can either mirror behaviors of the clients or model another way to deal with problems. For example, in a marital therapy session, I mirrored the quiet, demure manner of the female client while my supervisor modeled a more verbally dominant position. When I began challenging my supervisor's direction, he was very receptive to my suggestions. As we escaped rigid role definitions, we modeled a respectful way for the wife to disagree and for the husband to share the task of decision-making. Typically, we do not strategically plan cotherapy positions such as mirroring or modeling in advance; however, cotherapy teams should notice whether their patterns replicate or complement the couple or family and look for opportunities to model new possibilities.

Gossip Positions

"Gossip in" (inside the therapy room) is a common cotherapy position in which the cotherapists discuss aspects of the therapy in the presence of the

Figure 10.6: *Mirror/model: (a) parallel, mirroring relationship between cotherapists and clients, and (b) a non-parallel, modeling relationship*

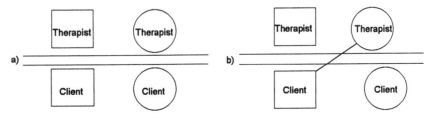

Figure 10.7: *Gossip positions: (a) inside, and (b) outside the therapy room*

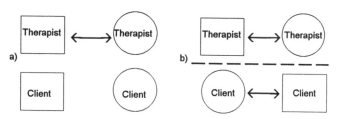

clients. (In a session the male cotherapist spoke to the female cotherapist: "I worry about the husband's loneliness." The female cotherapist responded: "Do you think his propensity for loneliness interferes with the wife's willingness to be more focused on her own life rather than be preoccupied with her jealousy?") Such discussion reveals the therapists' thoughts, feelings, motivation, and insight about the clients and the therapy to the clients, who are usually very curious about the therapists' inner world. The discussion between the therapists is thus a triadic way of talking to the clients.

"Gossip out" occurs when the therapists are outside of the room when they talk about the clients.This position usually occurs in pre- and post-session conversations. When gossip is shared with the clients, they wonder about our real responses to their plight. "You must think we are crazy." "No, we thought you were just having trouble saying good-bye to your parents." It is a way of staffing the case outside of the client's presence where the team can bounce ideas off each other.

Therapeutic Debate

Therapeutic debate is similar to gossip but it is more prolonged, as each therapist voices a different view of an issue. Frequently, one therapist voices the reason for keeping things the same while the other argues for change (Haber & Cooper-Haber, 1987). In the case of one family, the supervisor

Figure 10.8: *Therapeutic debate*

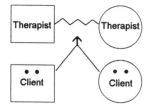

took the position that the family members were too angry to work together. I disagreed; I felt they could work out their problems. Another time, with Bernice and Ted, I felt that their marriage appeared to be hopeless while my supervisor was more optimistic about their chances to resolve their problems. Ted was greatly motivated by my verbalized perception that the relationship might be hopeless; that is, he was startled into exploring ways that he could make the relationship better. Thus, the therapeutic debate produces a stereophonic message that plays both sides of the clients' dialectical issues. Gossip and debate interventions generally occur spontaneously, rather than as part of a preplanned strategic approach.

These eight positions are not prescriptions for apprentice cotherapy; they are descriptors of therapeutic alignments. As my apprentice cotherapy relationship (with the author) has matured, our positions have become much more flexible. We often ask ourselves where we are in the family house and why. These thoughts may reaffirm our position or point to alternate alignments. The positions have helped us to be sensitive to "me," "us," and the role of the apprentice cotherapy.

CONCLUSION

Apprentice cotherapy has been my most satisfactory supervisory vehicle. As a beginning apprentice, I found that the meta-position of apprentice cotherapy was very comfortable. From that position, I clearly observed my supervisor's work and integrated what fit for me. At the same time, there was ample opportunity for me to understand and integrate my own personhood into my role as a therapist. Few responsibilities and clear expectations kept my anxiety level low.

Issues around gender and sex unique to my personal history have become clearer in the process. Apprentice cotherapy with another female is quite a different experience from cotherapy with a male. Consistently, with a male I tend to be quieter, more passive. I have connected that phenomenon to a subtle rule learned in my family-of-origin that men are entitled to the predominant role. Since the entitlement dilemma is not a problem for me when working with a female, I am able to participate more actively and more quickly.

One of my first experiences in apprentice cotherapy involved working with a female supervisor in group therapy.We devoted adequate time to process the group dynamics. In addition, she was attentive to my goals, opinions, theoretical growth, hypotheses, and personal development. Mutual respect was paramount, and that respect was conveyed to the group. Her expectations were spelled out in a clear and concise manner. At that time, I was not aware of the specific rules outlined by Roller and Nelson (1991) regarding an apprentice team, but in retrospect I realize that she had adhered to every one of them. These rules for supervisors are as follows:

1. Establish a learning contract that clearly distinguishes this training experience from cotherapy.
2. Provide a theoretical model of how cotherapy teams evolve.
3. Encourage questions, especially naive ones and those that challenge your own theories and practices.
4. Express congruence. Be frank about what you know and what you don't know.
5. Formulate questions yourself and communicate your sense of curiosity.
6. Anticipate the student's questions and dilemmas.
7. Acknowledge and support the student's growing sense of beginning competence.
8. Eschew one-upmanship and unnecessary competition.
9. Share with your student your own fears in the present and those you felt as a trainee.
10. Observe and listen to the student closely, and generously acknowledge what you learn from him or her. (p. 42)

Attention to these rules provided the groundwork for understanding how to use an apprentice cotherapy relationship.

My most meaningful apprentice relationship has been with a male supervisor. In our apprenticeship (both in and out of the therapy room), he is nondirective, supportive, and respectful. Although his primary motive for initiating our cotherapy relationship was my professional growth, he generally presents a case from the perspective that my presence will be helpful to both clients and to him. Clients are always notified prior to my joining him as a cotherapist. I am introduced in a respectful manner and I have always had the option of continuing in the therapeutic relationship as a cotherapist. Once I have committed myself to the cotherapy position, I have always wanted to continue. Our relationship has shifted from an apprenticeship to a collegial relationship. He is frank regarding his own anxieties and concerns. There have been times when he has expressed his feelings of inadequacy. For example, he has requested my participation to obtain a female perspective when he felt unable to sustain a therapeutic alliance with an entire family, when he felt limited or biased in the rooms or floors of the family's house, and when he simply perceived a problem to be especially difficult. Unlike my earlier apprentice experience, we have not established many formal or informal rules and we do not have a rigid schedule regarding processing time. There is much more flexibility in our contract. I believe that the team works because of the genuine liking and trust we have for each other. Virginia Satir said that people connect because of similarities and grow because of their differences. Some of our similarities are dedication to the therapy, a desire for continued learning, respect for ourselves and others, and flexibility. In addition, we both have a full and rewarding personal life. Our differences include (but are not limited to) age, sex, religion, culture, and previous life experience. These differences have enhanced the quality of our cotherapy relationship.

Apprentice cotherapy has allowed me to experience and expand my ability to visit different floors of the family house and to be more effective when I make those visits. I feel that I have been able to help my supervisor connect better with the top floor, while he has helped me navigate through the middle floor. Sometimes he has escorted me to the middle floor by metaphor or other verbal interventions, but I have also chosen to venture to the middle floor through my own initiative. During a therapy session with Bernice and Ted, I once (at my supervisor's request) played the role of Bernice in an interaction with Ted as he discussed an incident involving a conversation between Bernice and another man. Although I was taking the role of Bernice, I reacted from my own personhood and experience. When Ted observed that my reaction was different from Bernice's and his own, he was able to consider the possibility that Bernice's conversation may not have indicated a desire to have an affair. The experience helped me sort out the differences between universal and unique aspects of motivation for the same behavior (flirting). I was able to risk spontaneity in the interaction because I was being monitored by the supervisor. Through this experience, I learned that my personal value system influences my perceptions of the expectations of persons and that I (like Ted) may display a blaming attitude when my expectations are not realized.

I have learned to be less rigid and stereotypical in both my theoretical and personal viewpoints. My observations and my relationship with my supervisor have helped me gain confidence in my professional life. My personal style of therapy has been influenced by this relationship — so much so that in a cotherapy session he commented (with humor), "Who do you think you are — me?" I did not realize that I was emulating his style. However, through my apprenticeship with him, I have integrated aspects of his style and approach into a comfortable integration of my own work. As Carl Whitaker said, "Nothing that is worth knowing can be taught. It has to be learned" (1989, p. 50).

References

Allen, G., Szollos, S., & Williams, B. (1986). Doctoral students comparative evaluation of best and worst psychotherapy supervision. *Professional Psychology: Research and Practice, 17*, 91–99.

American Association for Marriage and Family Therapy. (1993). *Code of ethics.* Washington, DC: AAMFT.

American Psychological Association. (1978). Guidelines for therapy with women. *American Psychologist, 30*, 1122–1123.

American Psychological Association. (1992). *Code of ethics.* Washington, DC: APA.

Andolfi, M. (1994). The child as consultant. In M. Andolfi & R. Haber (Eds.), *Please help me with this family: Using consultants as resources in family therapy.* New York: Brunner/Mazel.

Andolfi, M., Angelo, C., Menghi, P., & Nicolo-Corigliano, A.M. (1983). *Behind the family mask.* New York: Brunner/Mazel.

Andolfi, M., Ellenwood, A.E., & Wendt, R.N. (1993). The creation of the fourth planet: Beginning therapists and supervisors inducing change in families. *American Journal of Family Therapy, 21*, 301–311.

Andolfi, M., & Haber, R. (Eds.) (1994). *Please help me with this family: Using consultants as resources in family therapy.* New York: Brunner/Mazel.

Andolfi, M., & Menghi, P. (1982). Provocative supervision. In R. Whiffen & J. Byng-Hall (Eds.), *Family therapy supervision: Recent developments in practice.* New York: Grune & Stratton.

Angelo, C. (1983). The use of the metaphorical object in family therapy. *American Journal of Family Therapy, 9*, 69–78.

Aponte, H.J. (1985). The negotiation of values in therapy. *Family Process, 24,* 323–338.

Appelbaum, P.S., & Gutheil, T.G. (1991). *Clinical handbook of psychiatry and the law* (2nd ed.). Baltimore: Williams & Wilkins.

Atkinson, B.J. (1993). Hierarchy: The imbalance of risk. *Family Process, 32,* 167–170.

Bateson, G. (1972). *Steps to an ecology of the mind.* New York: Ballantine Books.

Beauchamp, T.G., & Childress, J.F. (1989). *Principles of biomedical ethics* (3rd ed.). New York: Oxford University Press.

Berger, M., & Dammann, C. (1982). Live supervision as context, treatment, and training. *Family Process, 21,* 337–344.

Bernard, J.M. (1994). Multicultural supervision: A reaction to Leong and Wagner, Cook, Priest, and Fukuyama. *Counselor Education and Supervision, 34,* 159–171.

Boss, P.G. (1987). The role of intuition in family research: Three issues of ethics. *Contemporary Family Therapy, 9,* 146–159.

Boszormenyi-Nagy, I., & Krasner, B. (1986). *Between give and take: A clinical guide to contextual therapy.* New York: Brunner/Mazel.

Bowen, M. (1978). *Family therapy in clinical practice.* New York: Jason Aronson.

Breunlin, D.C., Karrer, B.M., McGuire, D.E., & Cimmarusti, R.A. (1988). Cybernetics of videotape supervision. In H.A. Liddle, D.C. Breunlin, & R.C. Schwartz (Eds.), *Handbook of family therapy training and supervision.* New York: Guilford.

Brofenbrenner, U. (1989). Ecological systems theory. In R. Vasta (Ed.), *Annals of child development.* Greenwich, CT: JAI.

Charney, I.W. (1986). What do therapist worry about: A tool for experiential supervision. *Clinical Supervisor, 4,* 17–28.

Cleghorn, J.M., & Levin, S. (1973). Training family therapists by setting learning objectives. *American Journal of Orthopsychiatry, 43,* 439–446.

Connell, G.M., Whitaker, C.A., Garfield, R., & Connell, L. (1990). The process of in-therapy consultation: A symbolic-experiential perspective. *Journal of Strategic and Systemic Therapies, 9,* 32–38.

Cook, D.A. (1994). Racial identity in supervision. *Counselor Education and Supervision, 34,* 132–139.

Doehrman, M. (1976). Parallel process in supervision and psychotherapy. *Bulletin of the Menninger Clinic, 40,* 9–104.

Drane, J.F. (1982). Ethics and psychotherapy: A philosophical perspective. In M. Rosenbaum (Ed.), *Ethics and values in psychotherapy.* New York: Free Press.

Elizur, Y. (1990). "Stuckness" in live supervision: Expanding the therapist's style. *Journal of Family Therapy, 12,* 267–280.

Elizur, Y. (1993). Ecosystems training Conjoining supervision and organizational development. *Family Process, 32,* 185–201.

Ellis, M.V., & Douce, L.A. (1994). Group supervision of novice clinical supervisors: Eight recurring issues. *Journal of Counseling and Development, 72,* 520–525.

Falicov, C.J. (1988). Learning to think culturally. In H.A. Liddle, D.C. Breunlin, & R.C. Schwartz (Eds.), *Handbook of family therapy training and supervision.* New York: Guilford.

Figley, C.R., & Nelson, T.S. (1989). Basic family therapy skills, I: Conceptualization and initial findings. *Journal of Marriage and Family Therapy, 15,* 349–365.

Figley, C.R., & Nelson, T.S. (1990). Basic family therapy skills, II: Structural family therapy. *Journal of Marriage and Family Therapy, 16*, 349–365.

Franz, M.L. von. (1971). The inferior function. In M.L. von Franz & J. Hillman (Eds.), *Lectures on Jung's typology*. Zurich, Switzerland: Spring Publications.

Friedlander, M.L., Siegel, S.M., & Brenock, K. (1989). Parallel process in counseling and supervision: A case study. *Journal of Counseling Psychology, 36*, 149–157.

Friedman, E. (1991). Bowen theory and therapy. In A. Gurman & D. Kniskern (Eds.), *The handbook of family therapy* (Vol. II). New York: Brunner/Mazel.

Gilligan, C. (1982). *In a different voice*. Cambridge, MA: Harvard University Press.

Goldberg, P. (1983). *The intuitive edge: Understanding intuition and applying it in everyday life*. Los Angeles: Jeremy Tercher.

Goldner, V. (1985). Feminism and family therapy. *Family Process, 21*, 21–41.

Goldner, V. (1988). Gender and generation: Normative and covert hierarchies. *Family Process, 27*, 17–31.

Goldner, V. (1993). Power and hierarchy: Let's talk about it. *Family Process, 32*, 157–162.

Gray, J. (1994). *Men are from Mars, women are from Venus*. New York: Harper-Collins.

Guest, P., & Beutler, L. (1988). Impact of psychotherapy supervision on therapist orientation and values. *Journal of Consulting and Clinical Psychology, 56*, 653–658.

Gurman, A.S., & Kniskern, D.P. (1978). Deterioration in marital and family therapy: Empirical, clinical and conceptual issues. *Family Process, 17*, 3–20.

Haber, R. (1978a). *The evaluation of Gestalt warm-up exercises by individuals according to their Jungian typology*. Unpublished doctoral dissertation, University of South Carolina.

Haber, R. (1978b). A synopsis and synthesis of the theories and techniques of Carl Gustav Jung and Frederick Salomon Perls. *The Gestalt Journal, 1*, 104–119.

Haber, R. (1979). What they never told me about counseling in graduate school. *Personnel and Guidance Journal, 61*, 204–205.

Haber, R. (1980). Different strokes for different folks: Jung's typology and structured exercises. *Group and Organizational Studies, 5*, 13–121.

Haber, R. (1981). A foreigner's view. *Terapia Familiare, 10*, 151–153.

Haber, R. (1983). Family therapy: Italian style. *Family Therapy Networker, 7*, 42–43.

Haber, R. (1984). Parental permissiveness. In R. Corsini (Ed.), *Encyclopedia of psychology*. New York: Wiley.

Haber, R. (1987). Friends in family therapy: Use of a neglected resource. *Family Process, 26*, 269–281.

Haber, R. (1990a). Handicap versus handy-capable: Training systemic therapists in the use of self. *Family Process, 29*, 375–384.

Haber, R. (1990b). Social network members as lay consultants. *Journal of Strategic and Systemic Therapies, 9*, 21–31.

Haber, R. (1994a). Response-ability: Therapist's 'I' and role. *Journal of Family Therapy, 16*, 269–284.

Haber, R. (1994b). Harnessing the 'I' and role: Process and progress. *Journal of Family Therapy, 16*, 293–294.

Haber, R. (1994c). With a little help from my friends. In M. Andolfi & R. Haber

(Eds.), *Please help me with this family: Using consultants as resources in family therapy* (pp. 112–131). New York: Brunner/Mazel.

Haber, R. (1994d). An overview of therapeutic consultation. In M. Andolfi & R. Haber (Eds.), *Please help me with this family: Using consultants as resources in family therapy* (pp. 3–32). New York: Brunner/Mazel.

Haber, R. (In press a). Reconstructing abusive stories. In M. Andolfi & M. De Nichilo (Eds.), *Feeling and systems.*

Haber, R. (In press b). Therapy with the right brain: Therapeutic use of metaphor. In J. Banmen (Ed.), *Virginia Satir: System and impact.*

Haber, R., & Cooper, K.D. (1980). A review of the research of the Jungian typology. *Journal of Counseling and Psychotherapy, 3*, 39–51.

Haber, R., & Cooper-Haber, K. (1988). Use of selves in cotherapy. South Carolina Association for Marital and Family Therapy Teleconference, Columbia, SC.

Haber, R., & Cooper-Haber, K. (1987). Paradox and orthodox: A cotherapy approach. *Journal of Strategic and Systemic Therapies, 6*, 41–50.

Haley, J. (1976). *Problem-solving therapy.* San Francisco: Jossey-Bass.

Haley, J. (1988). Reflections on supervision. In H.A. Liddle, D.C. Breunlin, & R.C. Schwartz (Eds.), *Handbook of family therapy training and supervision.* New York: Guilford.

Hare-Mustin, R.T. (1978). A feminist approach to family therapy. *Family Process, 17*, 181–194.

Hare-Mustin, R.T. (1980). Family therapy may be dangerous for your health. *Professional Psychology, 11*, 935–938.

Ho, M.K. (1987). *Family therapy with ethnic minorities.* Newbury Park, CA: Sage.

Hoffman, L. (1981). *Foundations of family therapy.* New York: Basic.

Hogan, R.A. (1964). Issues and approaches in supervision. *Psychotherapy: Theory, Research and Practice, 1*, 139–141.

Holloway, E.L., & Neufeldt, S.A. (1995). Supervision: Its contributions to treatment efficacy. *Journal of Consulting and Clinical Psychology, 63*, 207–213.

Hunt, D.E. (1971). *Matching models in education: The coordination of teaching methods with student characteristics.* Toronto: Ontario Institute for Studies in Education.

Jacobi, J. (1962). *The psychology of C.G. Jung.* New Haven, CT: Yale University Press.

Jaynes, J. (1976). *The origin of consciousness in the breakdown of the bicameral mind.* Boston: Houghton Mifflin.

Jung, C.G. (1968). *Analytical psychology: Its theory and practice.* New York: Random House.

Jung, C.G. (1976). *Psychological types (Collected works, Volume 6).* Princeton, NJ: Princeton University Press.

Jutoran, S.B. (1994). Consultation as evalutation of therapy. In M. Andolfi & R. Haber (Eds.), *Please help me with this family: Using consultants as resources in family therapy.* New York: Brunner/Mazel.

Kadushin, A. (1985). *Supervision in social work* (2nd ed.). New York: Columbia University Press.

Kantor, D., & Kupferman, W. (1985). The client's interview of the therapist. *Journal of Marital and Family Therapy, 11*, 225–244.

Kaslow, F. (1986). Supervisor, consultation, and staff training: Creative teaching/learning in the mental health profession. *Clinical Supervisor, 4*, 1–16.

Keith, D.V. (1987). Intuition in family therapy: A short manual on post-modern witchcraft. *Contemporary Family Therapy, 9*, 11–22.

Keith, D.V. (1994). The family of origin as therapeutic consultant. In M. Andolfi & R. Haber (Eds.), *Please help me with this family: Using consultants as resources in family therapy.* New York: Brunner/Mazel.

Kennard, B., Stewart, S., & Gluck, M. (1987). Who is the ideal supervisor? *Professional Psychology: Research and Practice, 18,* 172–175.

Kiersey, K., & Bates, M. (1984). *Please understand me: Character & temperament types.* Del Mar, CA: Promtheus Nemesis.

Kitchener, K.S. (1984). Intuition, critical evaluation and ethical principles: The foundation for ethical decisions in counseling psychology. *Counseling Psychologist, 12,* 43–55.

Kitchener, K.S. (1985). Ethical principles and ethical decisions in student affairs. In H.J. Cannon & R.D. Brown (Eds.), *Applied ethics in student services.* San Francisco: Jossey-Bass.

Kitchener, K.S. (1986). Teaching applied ethics in counselor education: An integration of philosophical processes and philosophical analysis. *Journal of Counseling Development, 64,* 306–310.

Kivlighan, D.M., Angelone, E.O., & Swafford, K.G. (1991). Live supervision in individual psychotherapy: Effects on therapist's intention and client's evaluation of session effect and working alliance. *Professional Psychology: Research and Practice, 22,* 489–495.

Koestler, A. (1978). *Janus: A summing up.* New York: Random House.

Kramer, J. (1985). *Family interfaces: Transgenerational patterns.* New York: Brunner/Mazel.

Lankton, S., & Lankton, C. (1983). *The answer within: A clinical framework of Ericksonian hypnotherapy.* New York: Brunner/Mazel.

Lao Tzu. (1954). *Tao Te Ching, The book of the way and its virtue* (translated from Chinese and annotated by J.J.L. Duyvendak). London: Murray.

Lebow, J. (1984). On the value of integrating approaches to family therapy. *Journal of Marital and Family Therapy, 10,* 127–138.

Liddle, H.A. (1982). On the problems of eclecticism: A call for epistemologic clarification and human scale theories. *Family Process, 4,* 81–97.

Liddle, H.A. (1988). Systemic supervision: Conceptual overlays and pragmatic guidelines. In H.A. Liddle, D.C. Breunlin, & R.C. Schwartz (Eds.), *Handbook of family therapy training and supervision.* New York: Guilford.

Liddle, H.A., Davidson, G., & Barrett, M. (1988). Outcomes of live supervision: Trainee perspectives. In H.A. Liddle, D.C. Breunlin, & R.C. Schwartz (Eds.), *Handbook of family therapy training and supervision.* New York: Guilford.

Liddle, H.A., & Schwartz, R.C. (1983). Live supervision/consultation: Conceptual and pragmatic guidelines for family therapy trainers. *Family Process, 22,* 477–490.

Loganbill, C., Hardy, E., & Delworth, U. (1982). Supervision: A conceptual model. *Counseling Psychologist, 10,* 3–42.

Luepnitz, D. (1988). *Family therapy revisited.* New York: Basic.

Margolin, G. (1982). Ethical and legal considerations in marriage and family therapy. *American Psychologist, 7,* 789–801.

Mazza, J. (1988). Training strategic therapists: The use of indirect techniques. In H.A. Liddle, D.C. Breunlin, & R.C. Schwartz (Eds.), *Handbook of family therapy training and supervision.* New York: Guilford.

McCollum, E.E., & Wetchler, J.L. (1995). In defense of case consultation: Maybe "dead" supervision isn't dead after all. *Journal of Marital and Family Therapy, 21,* 155–166.

Mckenzie, P.N., Atkinson, B.J., Quinn, W.H., & Heath, A.W. (1986). Training and supervision in marriage and family therapy. *American Journal of Family Therapy, 14*, 293–303.

Mead, D.E. (1990). *Effective supervision: A task-oriented model for the mental health professions.* New York: Brunner/Mazel.

Minuchin, S. (1974). *Families and family therapy.* Cambridge, MA: Harvard University Press.

Minuchin, S. (1986). Foreword. In L.C. Wynne, S.H. McDaniel, & T.T. Weber (Eds.), *Systems consultation: A new perspective for family therapy.* New York: Guilford.

Minuchin, S. (1989). My voices: An historical perspective. *Journal of Family Therapy, 11*, 69–80.

Minuchin, S., & Fishman, C.H. (1981). *Family therapy techniques.* Cambridge, MA: Harvard University Press.

Montalvo, B., & Gutierrez, M. (1988). The emphasis on cultural identity: A developmental-ecological constraint. In C.J. Falicov (Ed.), *Family transitions: Continuity and change over the life cycle.* New York: Guilford.

Myers, I.B. (1962). *The Myers-Briggs type indicator manual.* Princeton, NJ: Educational Testing Service.

Myers, I.B. (1980). *Gifts differing.* Palo Alto, CA: Consulting Psychologists Press.

Najavits, L.M., & Strupp, H.H. (1994). Differences in the effectiveness of psychodynamic therapists: A process-outcome study. *Psychotherapy, 31*, 114–123.

Napier, A.Y., & Whitaker, C. (1973). Problems of the beginning family therapist. *Seminars in Psychiatry, 5*, 229–241.

National Association of Social Workers. (1993). *Code of ethics.* Washington, DC: NASW Distribution Center.

Nelson, T.S., & Figley, C.R. (1990). Basic family therapy skills, III: Brief and strategic schools of family therapy. *Journal of Family Psychology, 4*, 49–62.

Pedersen, P. (Ed.). (1991). Multiculturalism as a fourth force in counseling. *Journal of Counseling and Development, 70.*

Perls, F.S. (1969). *Gestalt therapy verbatim.* Lafayette, CA: Real People Press.

Perls, F.S., Hefferlein, R., & Goodman, P. (1951). *Gestalt therapy.* New York: Dell.

Pesso, A. (1973). *Experience in action: A psychomotor psychology.* New York: New York University Press.

Pesso, A. & Wassenaar, H. (1991). The relationship between Pesso system/psychomotor and a neurobiological mode. In A. Pesso & J. Crandell (Eds.), *Moving psychotherapy: Theory and application of Pesso system/psychomotor therapy.* Cambridge, MA: Brookline.

Piercy, F.P., Sprenkle, D.H., & Constantine, J.A. (1986). Family members' perceptions of live observation/supervision: An exploratory study. *Contemporary Family Therapy: An International Journal, 8*, 171–187.

Pirrotta, S. & Cecchin, G. (1988). The Milan training program. In H.A. Liddle, D.C. Breunlin, & R.C. Schwartz (Eds.), *Handbook of family therapy training and supervision.* New York: Guilford.

Pluut, R. (1989). *Resources in family therapy.* Workshop presentation, Columbia, SC: South Carolina Institute for Systemic Experiential Therapy.

Powell, D.J. with Brodsky, A. (1993). *Clinical supervision in alcohol and drug abuse counseling: Principles, models, methods.* New York: Lexington.

Rabinowitz, F., Heppner, P., & Roehlke, H. (1986). A descriptive study of process and outcome studies of supervision over time. *Journal of Counseling Psychology,* 22, 292–300.

Ridgely, E. (1994a). The self of the consultant: "In" or "out"? In M. Andolfi & R. Haber (Eds.), *Please help me with this family: Using consultants as resources in family therapy.* New York: Brunner/Mazel.

Ridgely, E. (1994b). *Couple therapy: Gender and generation.* Paper presentation, Toronto, Ontario: George Hull Centre for Children and Families.

Ridgely, E. (1995). *Gender and generation.* Workshop presentation at International Conference on Couples Therapy, Charleston, SC. South Carolina Institute for Systemic Experiential Therapy.

Roberto, L.G. (1992). *Transgenerational family therapies.* New York: Guilford.

Rogers, C.R. (1951). *Client-centered therapy.* Cambridge, MA: Houghton Mifflin.

Roller, B., & Nelson, V. (1991). *The art of cotherapy.* New York: Guilford.

Romans, J.S.C., Boswell, D.L., Carlozzi, A.F., & Ferguson, D.B. (1995). Training and supervision practices in clinical, counseling, and school psychology programs. *Professional Psychology: Research and Practice, 26,* 407–412.

Rubinstein-Nebarro, N. (1994). Sequential preventive meta-consultation (SPMC): A model of collegial consultation in systems therapy. In. M. Andolfi & R. Haber (Eds.), *Please help me with this family: Using consultants as resources in family therapy.* New York: Brunner/Mazel.

Ryder, R., & Hepworth, J. (1990). AAMFT ethical code: "Dual relationships." (1990). *Journal of Marital and Family Therapy, 16,* 127–132.

Samples, B. (1976). *The metaphoric mind.* Reading, MA: Addison-Wessley.

Satir, V. (1988). *The new peoplemaking.* Palo Alto, CA: Science and Behavior.

Satir, V., Banmen, J., Gerber, J., & Gomori, M. (1991). *The Satir model: Family therapy and beyond.* Palo Alto, CA: Science and Behavior.

Schwartz, R.C., Liddle, H.A., & Breunlin, D.C. (1988). Muddles in live supervision. In H.A. Liddle, D.C. Breunlin, & R.C. Schwartz (Eds.), *Handbook of family therapy training and supervision.* New York: Guilford.

Searles, H. (1965). The informational value of the supervisor's emotional experiences, In H. Searles (Ed.), *Collected papers on schizophrenia and related subjects.* New York: International Universities Press.

Simon, R.M. (1989). Family life cycle issues in the therapy system. In B. Carter & M. McGoldrick (Eds.), *The changing family life cycle.* New York: Allyn & Bacon.

Simon, R.M. (1993). Revising the notion of hierarchy. *Family Process, 32,* 147–155.

Simons, J., Liggett, P.D., & Purvis, M. (1994). Consultation in the training moment. In M. Andolfi & R. Haber (Eds.), *Please help me with this family: Using consultants as resources in family therapy.* New York: Brunner/Mazel.

Singer, J. (1973). *Boundaries of the soul: The practice of Jung's psychology.* New York: Anchor.

Skoveholt, T.M., & Ronnestad, M.H. (1992). *The evolving professional self: Stages in themes in therapist and counselor development.* New York: Wiley.

Slovenko, R. (1980). Legal issues in psychotherapy supervision. In A.K. Hess (Ed.), *Psychotherapy supervision.* New York: Wiley.

Sluzki, C. (1979). Migration and family conflict. *Family Process, 18,* 379–390.

Snyders, R. (1986). Emancipatory supervision in family therapy. *The Clinical Supervisor, 4,* 3–25.

Stoltenberg, C.D., & Delworth, U. (1987). *Supervising counselors and therapists: A developmental approach.* San Francisco: Jossey-Bass.

Sue, D. (1994). Incorporating cultural diversity in family therapy. *The Family Psychologist, 10*, 19–21.

Sue, D.W. & Sue, D. (1990). *Counseling the culturally different client* (2nd ed.). New York: John Wiley.

Szapocznik, J., & Kurtines, W.M. (1993). Family psychology and cultural diversity. *American Psychologist, 48*, 400–407.

Tannen, D. (1990). *You just don't understand: Men and women in conversation.* New York: William Morrow.

Tarasoff v. Regents of the University of California (1974). 529 P. 2d 553 (Cal. 1974); 551 p. 2d 334, 331 (Cal. 1976).

Tennyson, W.W., & Strom, S.M. (1986). Beyond professional standards: Developing responsibilities. *Journal of Counseling Development, 64*, 298–302.

Tomm, K. (1992). The ethics of dual relationships. *The Calgary Participator, 1*, 11–15.

Tomm, K.M., & Wright, L.M. (1979). Training in family therapy: Perceptual, conceptual, and executive skills. *Family Process, 18*, 227–250.

Upchurch, D.W. (1985). Ethical standards and the supervisory process. *Counselor Education and Supervision, 30*, 90–98.

Von Bertalanffy, L. (1968). *General systems theory.* New York: George Braziller.

Waldegrave, C. (1990). Just therapy: Social justice and family therapy. *Dulwich Centre Newsletter, 1*, 2–4.

Watzlawick, P., Bavelas, J.B., & Jackson, D.D. (1967). *Pragmatics of human communication.* New York: Norton.

Watzlawick, P., Weakland, J. & Fisch, R. (1974). *Change: Principles of problem formation and problem resolution.* New York: Norton.

Webster's unabridged dictionary of the English language. (1989). New York: Portland.

Wendorf, D.J., & Wendorf, R.J. (1985). A systemic view of family therapy ethics. *Family Process, 24*, 443–460.

Wetchler, J.L., Piercy, F.P., & Sprenkle, D. H. (1989). Supervisors' and supervisees' perceptions of the effectiveness of family therapy supervisory techniques. *American Journal of Family Therapy, 17*, 35–47.

Wheeler, D., Myers, A.J., Miller, L., & Chaney, S. (1989). Rethinking family therapy training and supervision: A feminist model. In M. McGoldrick, C. Anderson, & F. Walsh (Eds.), *Women in families: A framework for family therapy.* New York: Norton.

Wheelwright, J.B., Wheelwright, J.H., & Buehler, J.A. (1964). *Jungian type survey: The Gray-Wheelwright test manual.* San Francisco, CA: Society of Jungian Analysts of Northern California.

Whiffen, R. (1982). The use of videotape in supervision. In R. Whiffen & J. Byng-Hall (Eds.), *Family therapy supervision: Recent developments in practice.* New York: Academic.

Whitaker, C.A. (1976). The hindrance of theory in clinical work. In P.J. Guerin (Ed.), *Family therapy: Theory and practice.* New York: Gardner.

Whitaker, C.A. (1982a). Gatherings. In J.R. Neill & D.P. Kniskern (Eds.), *From psyche to system: The evolving therapy of Carl Whitaker.* New York: Guilford.

Whitaker, C.A. (1982b). Guest editorial: The impasse. In J.R. Neill & D.P. Kniskern (Eds.), *From psyche to system: The evolving therapy of Carl Whitaker.* New York: Guilford.

Whitaker, C.A. (1986). Family therapy consultation as invasion. In L.C. Wynne,

S.H. McDaniel, & T.T. Weber (Eds.), *Systems consultation: A new perspective for family therapy*. New York: Guilford.

Whitaker, C.A. (1989). *Midnight musings of a family therapist*. New York: Norton.

Whitaker, C.A., & Miller, M.H. (1969). A re-evaluation of psychiatric help when divorce impends. *American Journal of Psychiatry, 126*, 57–64.

White, M., & Epston, D. (1990). *Narrative means to therapeutic ends*. New York: Norton.

White, M.B., & Russell, C.S. (1995). The essential elements of supervisory systems: A modified delphi study. *Journal of Marriage and Family Therapy, 21*, 33–53.

Williams, A. (1995). *Visual and active supervision: Roles, focus, technique*. New York: Norton.

Williamson, D.S. (1992). *The intimacy paradox: Personal authority in the family system*. New York: Guilford.

Worthington, E.L. (1987). Changes in supervision as counselors and supervisors gain experience: A review. *Professional Psychology: Research and Practice, 18*, 189–208.

Wright, L.M. (1986). An analysis of live supervision "phone-ins" in family therapy. *Journal of Marital and Family Therapy, 12*, 187–190.

Wynne, L.C., McDaniel, S.H., & Weber, T.T. (Eds.) (1986). *Systems consultation: A new perspective for family therapy*. New York: Guilford.

Zygmond, M.J., & Boorhem, H. (1989). Ethical decision making in family therapy. *Family Process, 28*, 269–280.

Index

AAMFT 1991 code
  dual relationships, ethical supervision, 121
abuse, *see* children; marital therapy
acculturation, 60–61
Adler, Alfred
  Jungian psychology and, 82
advanced supervisors, characteristics, 57
Agassi, Andre, 63–64
ageism, 69–70
Allen, G.
  methodology, Jungian typology, 93
American Psychological Association, 110, 186
ancestors, influence of, 25
Anderson, Malcolm, 10
Andolfi, Maurizio
  beneficence, on, 116
  case note form, case management supervision, 144
  children's role in family, 26
  client's house metaphor, 25–30
  cultural considerations, 34
  family systems, 34
  generational differences, on, 25
  influence of, 9–10

live supervision
  intervention methods, 174–75, 175
  session phase, 170
  metaphorical objects, case management supervision, 160
Angelo, C.
  metaphorical objects, case management supervision, 159
anorexic, treatment of, 206
Aponte, H. J.
  choices of therapist, 36
Appelbaum, P. S.
  responsibility, ethical supervision, 125
apprentice cotherapy, 202–16
  anorexic, treatment of, 206
  cautions regarding, 207–8
  described, 137
  expectations of, 203
  gender alignment
    cross, 209–210
    meta-position alignment, 211, 214
    parallel, 209
    unbalanced alignment, 210–11
  gossip positions, 212–13
  grandstanding and, 207
  lessons learned in, 204–7

227

apprentice cotherapy (*Continued*)
 map of, 203–4
 meta-position alignment, 211, 214
 mirror/model position, 212
 mutual vulnerability, 208
 positions, 208–9
 therapeutic debate, 213–14
 therapist as patient, 211–12
art
 intuition, development of, 102
associations
 intuition, development of, 101
Atkinson, B. J.
 hierarchy in supervision, 44
attacks on therapist by client, 150–52
attention-deficit disorder, 178
autonomy
 Kitchener's model of ethical justification
  (meta-ethics), 115, 117, 119–120
Avanta Network (Satir), 85

Bates, M.
 intuition, Jungian typology, 86
Bateson, G.
 parallel processes, 41
Beauchamp, T. G.
 Kitchener's model of ethical justification
  (meta-ethics), 115–16
beginning supervisors, characteristics,
  57
beneficence
 Kitchener's model of ethical justification
  (meta-ethics), 116, 119–120
Berger, M.
 live supervision, 164
Bernard, J. M.
 cultural considerations, 60
Beutler, L.
 methodology, Jungian typology, 93
body experiences
 intuition, development of, 102
body language, 6–7
Boorhem, H.
 feminist values, place in therapy, 111
 Kitchener's model of ethical justification
  (meta-ethics), 112, 117–18
Boszormenyi-Nagy, I.
 Kitchener's model of ethical justification
  (meta-ethics), 112–13
boundaries, communication and, 49–52
Bowen, M.
 family of origin, therapist's, 78
 internal consistency, 79
 methodology, 93
 system's theories, 84–85
Bowersock, Roger, 10

Breunlin, D. C.
 robotization of supervisee, 149–150
 videotape supervision, 149–150, 152
Brodsky, A.
 counselor development, 54
Brofenbrenner, U.
 comprehensive model of supervision, 80
Brok, Lars
 acculturation, 60–61
 influence of, 10–11
 metaphorical objects, case management supervision, 160

case management form, *see* weekly case management form
case management supervision, 140–62
 breadth and depth dilemma, 142–49
 case note form, 144, *145*
 described, 136
 empty chair, 156–58
 experiential interventions, 136, 154–56
 intervention, consultation as, 193
 metaphorical objects, 159–61
  experiential work with, 154–56
 role play, 158–59
 videotape supervision, 136, 141, 149–53
 weekly case management form, *143*, 144–
  49, *148*
case note form, 144, *145*
Center for Application of Psychological
  Type, 81
Charney, I. W.
 responsibility, on, 47
children
 abuse of, ethical supervision and, 111,
  117
 adult bias, perception of, 31–32
 inference, 26
 intuition, development of, 101
 role in family, client's house metaphor,
  26–27
Childress, J. F.
 Kitchener's model of ethical justification
  (meta-ethics), 115–16
Cleghorn, J. M.
 comprehensive model of supervision,
  80
clients' house metaphor, 25–30
 children, role of, 26–27
 gendered supervision and, 70–72
 grandparents, role in family, 28–29
 parallel processes, professional house, 40–
  44
 parents, role in family, 27–28, 49
 traditions, family, 29–30
communication, boundaries and, 49–52

competencies of supervisor, 78
competition in supervisory relationship, 23–24
complexity
  phone intervention, supervisor to therapist, 176–77
comprehensive model of supervision, 78, 79–81
conceptual process, Jungian typology, 88
confidentiality, ethical supervision, 123–24, 130–31
Connell, G. M.
  consultant's role in therapeutic impasse, 187
consultation, 32–33, 39
  arrival of consultant, 190
  beginning of therapy, 197
  case management supervision and, 193
  centrality of consultant, 190–91
  described, 136–37
  evaluation, as, 199–200
  expansion of client system, 197–98
  flexibility of consultant, 191–92
  focus of therapy, shifting of, 193–97
  gender issues, 198–99
  hierarchy, reversal of, 200
  intervention, as, 183–201
  malpractice prevention and, 125
  overbounded impasse, 187, 188–90
  phases of encounter, 188–93
  preventive check-up, as, 199–200
  progression of consultative process, 189
  therapeutic impasse, role of consultant, 186–88
Cook, D. A.
  cultural considerations, 58–59
Cooper-Haber, Karen, 11
  apprentice cotherapy, 203–4, 209
    therapeutic debate, 213
  consultation, gender issues, 199
  Jungian typology, 81
  marital therapy, 137
cotherapy, development of intuition, 101
Counseling and Human Development Center, 10
couples therapy
  consultants, use of, 32–33
  lesbian relationship, 158–59
  personality characteristics of therapist and, 66–67
  previous therapist and, 107
  sexual harassment, 23
  see also marital therapy
critical-evaluation level
  Kitchener's model of ethical justification (meta-ethics), 114–18

cultural considerations, 56–63
  acculturation, 60–61
  culture as patient, 58
  gender, effect of culture on, 73–74
  popular culture, changing roles and, 24
  sexual orientation, 62–63
Dammann, C.
  live supervision, 164
debate
  apprentice cotherapy, 213–14
Delworth, U.
  comprehensive model of supervision, 80
  counselor development, 55
  supervisors, professional development, 55
dialectic thinking
  intuition, development of, 102
dialogic process, 109
differences, working with, 48–49
dimensions of supervision, 77–103
diversity in supervisor relationship, 46–76
divorce, therapy causing, 111–12
documentation, malpractice prevention and, 125
Dodson, Laura, 8
Doehrman, M.
  trainee-client triads, investigation, 41
Douce, L. A.
  supervisors, professional development, 56
Drane, J. F.
  Kitchener's model of ethical justification (meta-ethics), 115
dual-career families, 25
dual relationships, ethical supervision, 121–23

ecosystems of supervisor and supervisee (professional house metaphor), 19–24
  relational position of therapist, 35
  role of supervisor, 33–40
Elizur, Yoel
  influence of, 11
  isomorphism, live supervision, 166
  sexual orientation, on, 63
Ellis, M. V.
  supervisors, professional development, 56
emigration and immigration processes, 61
empty chair, 156–58
enuretic client, 169
Epston, D.
  externalization, 43
Ericksonian hypnosis, 87
Esalen, 7

ethical supervision, 104–32
    child abuse issues, 111, 117
    confidentiality, 123–24, 130–31
    divorce issues and, 111
    dual relationships, 121–23
    evaluation, 125–29
    everyday dilemmas, 106–8
    feminist values, place in therapy, 109–11
    grievance procedure, 131
    guidelines, 121–32
    individuals in the system, conflicting needs
        of, 111–12
    Kitchener's model of ethical justification
        (meta-ethics), 106, 112–21, 113
        critical-evaluation level, 114–18
        intuitive level, 114
        reporting vs. not reporting, 118–19
        therapeutic contract and, 119–121
    record keeping, 125
    reporting vs. not reporting, 105, 118–19
    responsibility, 124–25
    service requirements, 130
    supervision contract, 122, 129
    supervision requirements, 130
    therapeutic contract, 105–6, 119–21
    values and ethics, 108–9
evaluation, ethical supervision, 125–29
experiential interventions, see case manage-
        ment supervision
experiential learning
    intuition, development of, 102
externalization, 42
extroversion, Jungian typology, 82
eye contact, 108–9

Falicov, C. J.
    choices of therapist, 36
family of origin, therapist's, 78
family systems
    client's house metaphor, 25–30
    rigidity of, 33
    role of supervisor, 33–40
family therapy
    at-risk adolescent behavior, 194–97
    attention-deficit disorder, 178
    deleterious outcomes of, 112
    gendered supervision, 71–72
    isomorphism, live supervision, 167
    pre-delinquent behavior, 107
    structural therapists, live supervision,
        180
feeling, Jungian typology, 84–85
feminist values, place in therapy, 109–11
fidelity
    Kitchener's model of ethical justification
        (meta-ethics), 117, 119–20

Figley, C. R.
    comprehensive model of supervision, 80–
        81
Fishman, C. H.
    live supervision, structural therapy, 180
    methodology, Jungian typology, 94
Foulds, Mel
    ideology, Jungian typology, 91
    influence of, 3–4
Fox-Hines, Ruthann, 10
Freud, Sigmund
    Jungian psychology and, 82
Friedlander, M. L.
    interactional events in therapy, 41
Friedman, E.
    family of origin, therapist's, 78
friendships, development of, 28

gendered supervision, 70–76
    world view and gender, 72–74
gender issues
    apprentice cotherapy
        cross gender alignment, 209–10
        meta-position alignment, 211, 214
        parallel gender alignment, 209
        unbalanced gender alignment, 210–
            11
    consultation and, 198–99
    culture, effect of, 73–74
    financial arrangements in family, 75–76
    generational differences, 25, 30
    popular culture and, 24
    stereotypes, 110
    see also sex differences
generational differences, client's house meta-
        phor, 25–30
generational position of therapist, 30–33
"Generation and Gender" (Goldner), 51
genogram, professional, 3–5
George Hull Centre for Children and Fami-
        lies, 70, 74
gestalt
    ideology, Jungian typology, 91
    intuition, Jungian typology, 85
Gestalt-Marathon Group, 3
Gilbert, Brad, 63–64
Gilligan, C.
    sex differences, 51
Glazer, Bob, 6
goals of supervision, 35
Goldberg, P.
    intuition, Jungian typology, 98–99
Goldner, V.
    choices of therapist, 36
    gender, on, 72, 76
    generational differences, on, 25

"Generation and Gender," 51
hierarchy in supervision, 44
race differences, 51
sex differences, 51
good mother, therapist as, 39
gossip positions, apprentice cotherapy, 212–13
grandparents
grandchildren, relationship with, 2
role in family, client's house metaphor, 28–29
Gray, J.
gendered supervision, 71
Gray-Wheelwright Jungian Type Survey, 81
grievance procedure, ethical supervision, 131
Guest, P.
methodology, Jungian typology, 93
Guidelines for Therapy With Women (American Psychological Association), 110
Guinan, Jim, 49–50
consultation, reversal of hierarchy and, 200
influence of, 4, 8
intuition, Jungian typology, 100
Gurman, A. S.
marital relationship, effect of therapy on, 112
Gutheil, T. G.
responsibility, ethical supervision, 125
Gutierrez, M., 60
Guze, Vivian, 6

Haley, Jay
family of origin, therapist's, 78
goals of supervision, 35–36
influence of, 5, 10
methodology, Jungian typology, 94
Rogerian therapy, 89
sensation, Jungian typology, 87
hands, Jungian typology, see methodology
Hare-Mustin, R. T.
family therapy, on, 112
feminist values, place in therapy, 110
head, Jungian typology, see ideology
heart, Jungian typology, see self
Henderson, Hal
influence of, 5
Hepworth, J.
dual relationships, ethical supervision, 121
here and now, 6, 47
hierarchy in supervision, 43–44
Ho, M. K.
cultural considerations, 58
Hoffman, Lynn
live supervision, 163–64

Hogan, R. A.
counselor development, 54
Holloway, E. L.
apprentice cotherapy, 207
comprehensive model of supervision, 80
homosexuality, see sexual orientation
honesty, supervisor-supervisee, 48
Horney, Karen, 9
humor
intuition, development of, 101
hypnosis
sensation, Jungian typology and, 87

identity
professional, development of, 36–37
sex roles, 72
ideology
apprentice cotherapy, 208–9
Jungian typology, 89, 90–92
supervisee, of, 22–24
weekly case management form and, 147
indirect supervision, see case management supervision
individuals in the system, conflicting needs of, 111–12
inference
children and, 26
metaphorical objects, 154
"Ingredients of an Interaction, The" (Satir, et al.), 50
inspired process, Jungian typology, 88
integrative model of supervision, 79
internalized professional family, 12–13
interpersonal communications
metaphor, use of, 155
intervention
consultation as, 183–201
arrival of consultant, 190
beginning of therapy, 197
case management supervision and, 193
centrality of consultant, 190–91
evaluation, as, 199–200
expansion of client system, 197–98
flexibility of consultant, 191–92
focus of therapy, shifting of, 193–97
gender issues, 198–99
hierarchy, reversal of, 200
overbounded impasse, 187, 188–90
phases of encounter, 188–93
preventive check-up, as, 199–200
progression of consultative process, 189
therapeutic impasse, role of consultant, 186–88
unique aspects of, 193–200

intervention (*Continued*)
  live supervision, 174–82
    client joins supervisor, 180–81
    phone calls, supervisor to members of
      client system, 177–78
    phone calls, supervisor to therapist,
      175–77
    therapist joins supervisor, 179–80
    walk-ins (supervisor joins therapeutic
      system), 181–82
interventions, live supervision, 171–72
intrapsychic experience
  metaphor, use of, 155
introversion, Jungian typology, 82
intrusiveness
  phone intervention, supervisor to thera-
    pist, 176
intuition
  apprentice cotherapy, 208–9
  Jungian typology, 85–86, 89, 98–102
    development of intuition, 101–2
  Kitchener's model of ethical justification
    (meta-ethics), 114
  weekly case management form and, 147
"I" position, 99–100, 138
isomorphic model of supervision, 78–80
  case management supervision, 136
  live supervision, 166–68
"I-thou" relationship, 138

Jaynes, J.
  metaphorical objects, 154
Jung, C. G., *see* Jungian typology
Jungian typology, 81–102
  extroversion, 82
  feeling, 84–85
  four psychological functions, 83, 88–102,
    89
  Gray-Wheelwright Jungian Type Survey,
    81
  inferior functions, 83–84
  introversion, 82
  intuition, 85–86
  left- or right-handedness, 83
  Myers-Briggs Typology Inventory, 81
  sensation, 86–88
  supervision and, 88–102
    conceptual process, 88
    dimensions, 89
    ideology, 89, 90–92
    inspired process, 88
    intuition, 89, 98–102
    methodology, 89, 92–95
    personal process, 88
    pragmatic process, 88
    self, 89, 95–98
  thinking, 84–85

justice
  Kitchener's model of ethical justification
    (meta-ethics), 117, 119–20
Jutoran, S. B.
  consultation as evaluation, 199
  influence of, 10

Kadushin, A.
  comprehensive model of supervision, 80
Kantor, D.
  choices of therapist, 36
  personality characteristics of therapist, 67
Kaslow, F.
  professional roles, on, 22
Keith, D. V.
  grandparents' role in family, 28
  intuition, Jungian typology, 100
Kennard, B.
  methodology, Jungian typology, 93
Kibbutz Clinic (Israel), 11
Kiersy K.
  intuition, Jungian typology, 86
Kirby, Shirley
  apprentice cotherapy, 16, 202–16
  influence of, 11
Kitchener, Karen, *see* Kitchener's model of
    ethical justification (meta-ethics)
Kitchener's model of ethical justification
    (meta-ethics), 106, 112–21, *113*
  autonomy, 115, 117, 119–20
  balancing principle, 118
  beneficence, 116, 119–20
  critical-evaluation level, 114–18
    ethical principles, 115–17
    ethical rules, 114–15
    ethical theory, 117–18
  fidelity, 117, 119–20
  intuitive level, 114
  justice, 117, 119–20
  nonmaleficence, 116, 120
  reporting vs. not reporting, 118–19
  therapeutic contract and, 119–21
  universalizability, 117
Kivlighan, D. M.
  live supervision, 163
Kniskern, D. P.
  marital relationship, effect of therapy on,
    112
Koestler, A., 5
Kramer, J.
  choices of therapist, 36
Krasner, B.
  Kitchener's model of ethical justification
    (meta-ethics), 112–13
Kupferman, W.
  choices of therapist, 36
  personality characteristics of therapist, 67

Kurtines, W. M.
cultural considerations, 58

Lankton, C.
Kitchener's model of ethical justification (meta-ethics), 114
Lankton, S.
Kitchener's model of ethical justification (meta-ethics), 114
Lao Tsu
multimodal approach to supervision, 135
Lashley, Richard, 10
Lebow, J.
internal consistency, 79
left- or right-handedness, Jungian typology, 83
lesbianism, see sexual orientation
Levin, S.
comprehensive model of supervision, 80
Liddle, H. A.
ideology, Jungian typology, 91
isomorphism, 78, 80
live supervision, 163
methodology, Jungian typology, 93
parallel processes, 41
robotization of supervisee, 166
session phase, live supervision, 170–71
live supervision, 163–82
described, 136–37
form, post-session phase, 173
intervention, 174–82
client joins supervisor, 180–81
phone calls, supervisor to members of client system, 177–78
phone calls, supervisor to therapist, 175–77
therapist joins supervisor, 179–80
walk-ins (supervisor joins therapeutic system), 181–82
interventions, 171–72
isomorphism, 166–68
phases of process, 168–74
post-session phase, 172–74
pre-session phase, 168–70
session phase, 170–72
therapeutic and supervisory systems, 165
Loganbill, C.
counselor development, 54
lookism, 70
Luepnitz, D.
feminist values, place in therapy, 110

McCollum, E. E.
weekly case management form, 146

Mckenzie, P. N.
live supervision, 163
malpractice prevention, 125
Margolin, G.
feminist values, place in therapy, 110
marital therapy
apprentice cotherapy, 205–6, 214, 216
divorce caused by, 111–12
spousal abuse, therapeutic contract and, 105–6
Kitchener's model of ethical justification (meta-ethics), 119–21
see also couples therapy
Mazza, J.
self, Jungian typology, 95
Mead, D. E.
session phase, live supervision, 171
memory of supervisee, videotape supervision, 150–52
Menghi, P.
family systems, 34
live supervision
intervention methods, 175
session phase, 170
meta-ethics, see Kitchener's model of ethical justification (meta-ethics)
metaphorical objects
case management supervision, 159–61
experiential work, 154–56
intuition, development of, 101
metaphors
intuition, development of, 102
methodology
apprentice cotherapy, 208–9
Jungian typology, 89, 92–95
weekly case management form and, 147
middle floor of client's house (metaphor), see parents
Milan school, 94
Miller, M. H.
divorce, therapy causing, 111
Minuchin, Salvador
consultation as intervention, 184–85
influence of, 9–10
internalized professional family, 13
live supervision, structural therapy, 180
methodology, Jungian typology, 94
sibling relationships, 41
mirror/model position, apprentice cotherapy, 212
mirrors, one-way, see live supervision
Montalvo, B., 60
multimodal approach to supervision, 135–39
Myers, I. B., 81
Jungian typology, 83
Myers-Briggs Typology Inventory, 81

Najavits, L. M.
   apprentice cotherapy, 207
Napier, A. Y.
   apprentice cotherapy, 208
Nelson, Sue, 10
Nelson, T. S.
   comprehensive model of supervision, 80–81
Nelson, V.
   apprentice cotherapy, 202, 215
Neufeldt, S. A.
   apprentice cotherapy, 207
   comprehensive model of supervision, 80
nodal parts
   metaphor, use of, 155
nonmaleficence
   Kitchener's model of ethical justification (meta-ethics), 116, 120
nose, Jungian typology, see intuition
novice therapists
   apprentice cotherapy, 203–4
   breadth of caseload, 142

out-of-office client or referral contracts, ethical supervision, 130
overbounded impasse, 187, 188–90

paradoxical thinking
   intuition, development of, 102
parallel processes, 40–44
parents
   early childhood of, role in parenting, 2
   role in family, client's house metaphor, 27–28, 49
"Parts Party" (Satir), 65
PBPT, see Pesso-Boyden Psychomotor Therapy (PBPT)
Pedersen, P.
   cultural considerations, 58
Perls, Fritz
   empty chair, 156–58
   ideology, Jungian typology, 91
   influence of, 6
personal encounter, 138
personality characteristics, 65–67
personal qualities, supervisor relationship and, 63–70
   life cycle attributes, 67–70
   personality characteristics, 65–67
   physical attributes, 67–70
Pesso, A., 6–7
   children, needs of, 26
   influence of, 11
   synthetic memory, 152
Pesso-Boyden Psychomotor Therapy (PBPT), 6–7

Piercy, F. P.
   live supervision, 163
   videotape supervision, 149
Pirrotta, S.
   live supervision, collaboration of supervisor and therapist, 179
play
   intuition, development of, 101
Pluut, R.
   difference, on, 45
   influence of, 10–11
popular culture, changing roles and, 24
positive reinforcement
   phone intervention, supervisor to therapist, 176
post-session phase, live supervision, 172–74
Powell, D. J.
   counselor development, 54
   evaluation, ethical supervision, 127
   supervisors, professional development, 56
pragmatic process, Jungian typology, 88
pre-session phase, live supervision, 168–70
professional development, 1–16
   identity, development of, 36–37
   stages of, 53–56
   supervisors, of, 55–56
   therapists, of, 53–55
professional house metaphor, supervisory relationship, 19–24
   culture, archetypical issues and changes evidenced in, 24
   evaluation, ethical supervision, 127
   expectations of supervisee and agency, 22
   gendered supervision and, 70–72
   ideology of supervisee and treatment agency, 22–24
   parallel processes, clients' house, 40–44
   relational position of therapist, 35
   role configuration and environment of work context, 21–22
   self of professional, role vs., 20–21
   workplace, culture of, 22
Purvis, Marsha
   consultation, on, 201
   influence of, 11

Rabinowitz, F.
   methodology, Jungian typology, 93
race differences
   cultural considerations, 58–60
   minority client, 108, 116
   minority therapists, 62
   resistance and, 51
   working with, 49
reality check, 47
record keeping, ethical supervision, 125

Reich, Wilhelm, 6
reporting vs. not reporting, ethical supervision, 105
    Kitchener's model of ethical justification (meta-ethics), applicability to, 118–19
resistance
    boundaries and, 49
    race differences and, 51
respect, 138
response-ability, 47–48
responsibility
    consultant's role in therapeutic impasse, 187
    ethical supervision, 124–25
Ridgely, Elizabeth
    apprentice cotherapy, 202
    children's role in family, 26
    consultation, gender issues, 198
    gendered supervision, 14, 70
    grandparents' role in family, 28
    hierarchy in supervision, 44
    influence of, 10
    phone intervention, supervisor to members of client system, 178
robotization of supervisee, 166
Rogerian therapy, 89
Rogers, Carl
    reality check, 47
role
    changes, development of intuition, 101
    family, 26–27
    professional vs. self, 20–21
role play
    case management supervision, 158–59
Roller, B.
    apprentice cotherapy, 202, 215
Romans, J. S. C.
    videotape supervision, 149
Ronnestad, M. H.
    apprentice cotherapy, 207
Rubinstein-Nebarro, N.
    consultation as preventive check-up, 199
Russell, C. S.
    comprehensive model of supervision, 79
Ryder, R.
    dual relationships, ethical supervision, 121

Samples, B.
    metaphorical objects, 154
Satir, Virginia
    apprentice cotherapy, 216
    differences, working with, 49
    family therapy, 7–8
    feeling (Jungian typology), 85
    influence of, 5, 7–9

"Ingredients of an Interaction, The," 50
Kitchener's model of ethical justification (meta-ethics), beneficence, 116
"Parts Party," 65
traditions, family, 30
"With Whom Am I Having the Pleasure" exercise, 46–47
Schwartz, R. C.
    robotization of supervisee, 166
    session phase, live supervision, 170–71
Searles, H.
    generational position of therapist, 31
    hierarchy in supervision, 44
    parallel processes, 40–41
second cybernetic process, videotape supervision, 149–53
self
    apprentice cotherapy, 208–9
    Jungian typology, 89, 95–98
    professional, of
        differences, working with, 49
        parallel processes and, 41
        role vs. self, 20–21
    weekly case management form and, 147
self-reflection, 48
self-supervision, 153
sensation, Jungian typology, 86–88
service requirements, ethical supervision, 130
session phase, live supervision, 170–72
sex differences
    boundaries and, 51
    see also gender issues
sex roles, gendered supervision and, 72
sexual attraction, supervisor-supervisee, 47–48
sexual harassment
    couples therapy, 23
    gay males, of, 63
sexual orientation, therapeutic relationship and, 62–63
sexual relationship between therapist and client
    ethical supervision and, 105, 118
sibling relationships, parental subsystems and, 41
Simons, J.
    consultation, on, 201
Singer, J.
    Jungian typology, 82
Skoveholt, T. M.
    apprentice cotherapy, 207
Slovenko, R.
    consultation as intervention, 186
Sluzki, C.
    emigration and immigration processes, 61

Small, Judy, 10–11
Snyders, R.
 session phase, live supervision, 170
Spencer, Leon, 10
Stevens, Barry, 6
Stoltenberg, C. D.
 comprehensive model of supervision, 80
 counselor development, 55
 supervisors, professional development, 55
Strom, S. M.
 dialogic process, 109
Strupp, H. H.
 apprentice cotherapy, 207
Sue, D.
 cultural considerations, 58
Sue, D. W.
 cultural considerations, 58
super-vision, 34
supervision contract, ethical supervision, 122, 129
supervisory relationship, generally, 19–45
 client's house metaphor, 25–30
 competition within, 23–24
 culture, archetypical issues and changes evidenced in, 24
 expectations of supervisee and agency, 22
 ideology of supervisee and treatment agency, 22–24
 professional house metaphor, 19–24
 role configuration and environment of work context, 21–22
 self of professional, role vs., 20–21
 workplace, culture of, 22
 see also specific topics
symbolic language, 154
synthetic memory, 152
systems theory, 41
Szapocznik, J.
 cultural considerations, 58

Tannen, D.
 gendered supervision, 71
 sex differences, 51
Tarasoff v. Regents of the University of California, 115–16, 124
Tennyson, W. W.
 dialogic process, 109
therapeutic contract, ethical supervision and, 105–6
 Kitchener's model of ethical justification (meta-ethics), 119–21
therapeutic debate, apprentice cotherapy, 213–14
therapeutic impasse, role of consultant, 186–88

therapeutic teams, live supervision, 165
there and then associations, 46–47
thinking
 experiencing and, 6
 Jungian typology, 84–85
Tomm, K. M.
 comprehensive model of supervision, 80
 dual relationships, ethical supervision, 121
 methodology, Jungian typology, 94
tourism, 71
traditions, family
 client's house metaphor, 29–30
trainee-client triads, investigation, 41
transference and countertransference, 67–68
treatment agency, ideology of, 22–24

underbounded impasse, 187, 188
universalizability
 Kitchener's model of ethical justification (meta-ethics), 117
Upchurch, D. W.
 ethical supervision, 121

values, ethics vs., 108–9
veto power
 phone intervention, supervisor to therapist, 177
videotape supervision, see case management supervision
Von Bertanlaffy, L.
 systems theory, 41
Von Franz, M. L.
 sensation, Jungian typology, 87

Waldgrave, C.
 gender, on, 73
Walker, Gillian
 race differences, 51–52
Warkentin, J.
 influence of, 4
Wassenaar, H.
 synthetic memory, 152
Watzlawick, P.
 metaphorical objects, 154
 session phase, live supervision, 170
weekly case management form, 143, 144–49, 148
Wendorf, D. J.
 feminist values, place in therapy, 110
Wendorf, R. J.
 feminist values, place in therapy, 110
Wetchler, J. L.
 videotape supervision, 149
 weekly case management form, 146
Wheeler, D.
 gendered supervision, 72

Wheelwright, J. B.
  Gray-Wheelwright Jungian Type Survey,
    81
Whiffen, R.
  videotape supervision, 153
Whitaker, Carl
  apprentice cotherapy, 204, 208, 216
  consultation, on
    expansion of client system, 197
    role in therapeutic impasse, 186–87,
      191
  divorce, therapy causing, 111
  grandparents' role in family, 28
  ideology, Jungian typology, 91
  inference, on, 26, 154
  influence of, 4, 8–10
  intuition, Jungian typology, 99–100
  "I" position, 99–100
  Kitchener's model of ethical justification
    (meta-ethics), beneficence, 116
  metaphorical objects, case management su-
    pervision, 160
  methodology, Jungian typology, 94
  person of therapist, 138
  "process not progress" credo, 86
White, M.
  comprehensive model of supervision, 79
  externalization, 43
Williams, Antony
  comprehensive model of supervision, 81

  metaphorical objects, 43
    case management supervision, 160
  methodology, Jungian typology, 93
  parallel processes, 41
  supervision contract, 129
Williamson, D. S.
  parents, role in family, 27
withdrawal
  intuition, development of, 102
"With Whom Am I Having the Pleasure" exercise (Satir), 46–47
workplace, culture of
  supervisory relationship and, 22
world view and gender, 72–74
Worthington, E. L.
  counselor development, 54
Wright, L. M.
  comprehensive model of supervision,
    80
  methodology, Jungian typology, 94
  phone intervention, supervisor to thera-
    pist, 176
Wynne, L. C.
  consultation as intervention, 183

Zygmond, M. J.
  feminist values, place in therapy, 111
  Kitchener's model of ethical justification
    (meta-ethics), 112, 117–18